Routledge Revivals

Narrative Exchanges

First published in 1992, *Narrative Exchanges* shows how a general model of communicative exchanges can be refined to deal with the complexities of narrative fiction. Going beyond the two-way structure of reciprocity, it gives particular attention to the processes of framing, substitution and dispossession by which written texts generate meaning. The title provides an innovative way of combining narrative and exchange theory, bringing the two areas of thought into a mutually critical relationship. Using a wide variety of narrative texts, literary and non-literary, canonical and non-canonical, authors discussed include Flaubert, Achebe, Mansfield, Boccaccio, Duras, Daudet, Moorhouse, DeLillo and Wordsworth.

Drawing on perspectives from anthropology, linguistics and education, and combining accessible readings with theoretical debate, Ian Reid makes a significant contribution to the debate about narrative theory.

Narrative Exchanges

Ian Reid

First published in 1992
by Routledge

This edition first published in 2014 by Routledge
2 Park Square, Milton Park, Abingdon, Oxon, OX14 4RN
and by Routledge
711 Third Avenue, New York, NY 10017

Routledge is an imprint of the Taylor & Francis Group, an informa business

© 1992 Ian Reid

The right of Ian Reid to be identified as author of this work has been asserted by him in accordance with sections 77 and 78 of the Copyright, Designs and Patents Act 1988.

All rights reserved. No part of this book may be reprinted or reproduced or utilised in any form or by any electronic, mechanical, or other means, now known or hereafter invented, including photocopying and recording, or in any information storage or retrieval system, without permission in writing from the publishers.

Publisher's Note
The publisher has gone to great lengths to ensure the quality of this reprint but points out that some imperfections in the original copies may be apparent.

Disclaimer
The publisher has made every effort to trace copyright holders and welcomes correspondence from those they have been unable to contact.

A Library of Congress record exists under LC control number: 93104769

ISBN 13: 978-1-138-80094-6 (hbk)
ISBN 13: 978-1-315-75518-2 (ebk)
ISBN 13: 978-1-138-80102-8 (pbk)

NARRATIVE EXCHANGES

Ian Reid

London and New York

First published 1992
by Routledge
11 New Fetter Lane, London EC4P 4EE

Simultaneously published in the USA and Canada
by Routledge
a division of Routledge, Chapman and Hall, Inc.
29 West 35th Street, New York, NY 10001

© 1992 Ian Reid

Typeset in 10/12pt Baskerville by
Ponting–Green Publishing Services, London
Printed in Great Britain by
TJ Press (Padstow) Ltd, Padstow, Cornwall

All rights reserved. No part of this book may be reprinted or reproduced or utilized in any form or by any electronic, mechanical, or other means, now known or hereafter invented, including photocopying and recording, or in any storage or information retrieval system, without permission in writing from the publishers.

British Library Cataloguing in Publication Data

A catalogue record for this book is available from the British Library.

Library of Congress Cataloging in Publication Data

also available

ISBN 0 415 07234 4

CONTENTS

	Preface	v
	INTRODUCTION	1
1	BEYOND NARRATOLOGY?	19
2	FRAMING THE TEXT	40
3	CUTTING A LONG STORY SHORT	59
4	VOICE, SEQUENCE AND CONTROL	76
5	FICTIONS OF CHALLENGE AND RIPOSTE	103
6	'ALWAYS A SACRIFICE': EXECUTING UNITIES	124
7	THE CHARACTERS OF DANGER AND DESIRE	143
8	WAITING TO BE TOLD	166
9	'DOWN A STRANGE STREET': EMERGENT EXCHANGES	188
	Appendix A: Extract from Edda	207
	Appendix B: Extract from The Prelude	216
	Appendix C: 'The Hind of the Further'	222
	Notes	236
	References	248
	Index	261

PREFACE

A full account of this book's development would be no short story, and I will not tell it here; but there are important acknowledgements to be made. The Australian Research Council and Deakin University's Research Committee both gave financial support, and periods of release from teaching were granted by the School of Humanities and the Leave Committee of Deakin University. Having benefited substantially from those forms of assistance, I record here my appreciation. To journals in which earlier versions of some sections have appeared, I am also glad to extend my thanks: *Aumla, The Australian Journal of French Studies, Cahiers de la Nouvelle, Southern Review,* and *Textual Practice;* also to the editors and publishers of the following books: *Short Story Theory at a Crossroads* (1989), edited by Susan Lohafer and Jo Ellyn Clarey (Louisiana State University Press); *Semiotics, Language, Ideology* (1986), edited by Terry Threadgold *et al.* (Sydney Association for Studies in Society and Culture); and *Mapped but not Known* (1986), edited by F.H. Mares and Robin Eaden (Wakefield Press). All this material has now been considerably revised.

For several other kinds of valuable exchanges I am more grateful than I can say. Former colleagues and students in Literary Studies at Deakin University, where this book was written, have provided over many years the stimulus of collaborative work on narrative topics; particularly helpful at various stages of my own project have been David Carter, Brenton Doecke, Brian Edwards, Anna Gibbs, Garry Gillard, Sneja Gunew, Jacqui Howard, Jenna Mead and Wenche Ommundsen. From different quarters, Malcolm Crick and Patrick Hutchings also offered useful criticism. Alert audiences who heard and discussed draft portions of this book at a number of other universities (Angers, Cornell, East

PREFACE

Anglia, London, Macquarie, Melbourne, Michigan, Monash, Murdoch, Ohio State, Queensland, Sydney, Western Australia and Western Michigan) have made it seem worthwhile. Above all, my warm and affectionate thanks to several patient friends outside my own institution: John Dixon, Anne Freadman, John Frow, Barry Hill, Marie Maclean, Michael O'Toole, Reeve Parker and Robert Wilson all made thoughtful comments on earlier drafts of some of this material, encouraging me to proceed and helping me in the nicest way to think harder. I'm also glad to acknowledge the help of Robyn Gardner and Wendy Waring in the final preparation of this manuscript. My deepest personal indebtedness is to two people: without Ross Chambers's generosity I would hardly have known how to begin it all, and without Gale MacLachlan's faith and reason I would probably not have finished it.

NOTE ON TRANSLATIONS

In quoting from any text first published in a foreign language, I have used a standard English-language version when possible, having checked it against the original. In other cases, as indicated in the notes, the translation is my own.

INTRODUCTION

THEORIES FOR CRAVINGS

We crave narrative, and we crave exchanges. Both compulsions seem inherent in human culture: to interpret our experience as story-shaped and to interpret it as reciprocally transactional. In recognition of this, two conceptual models have emerged during recent decades to become remarkably influential in the study of a broad range of cultural practices. One model, associated with narrative, has spread throughout the humanities field and beyond; the other, associated with exchange, has enjoyed popular acceptance in the social sciences. Yet neither has proved itself comprehensive or precise enough to achieve its potential – perhaps because they have not yet been brought together into a close relationship.

So readily are storytelling structures now discernible in diverse kinds of human activity that we can contemplate without surprise large claims for narrative as 'an explicit resource in all intellectual activity' (Rosen 1984: 15), even as 'the central function or instance of the human mind' (Jameson 1981: 13). We make our world go round by chasing our tales. In several domains, from anthropology to education, from psychoanalysis to historiography, and above all in literary theory and criticism, the typologies and tools of narrative analysis have been circulating widely. How should they be used? That is less clear. 'We still do not appreciate as fully as we ought', says Jonathan Culler (1981: 186), 'the importance of narrative schemes and models in all aspects of our lives.' Even specialists in 'narratology', the highly developed system of discourse analysis based on structural features of language, admit that theirs is 'a discipline in crisis' (Bal 1986: 555).

NARRATIVE EXCHANGES

Attempts to establish a precise model of exchange have similarly faltered. In part, this is because the basic notion itself tends to be invoked too loosely. When social scientists claim that 'exchange theory can account for almost all social phenomena' and 'provides an intelligibility that can cut across historical circumstance' (Gergen 1980: 280), they are relying on extremely abstract formulations. When cultural analysts in other fields appropriate transactional metaphors, they tend towards hyperbole. 'Exchange recuperates everything', declares Roland Barthes (1975: 24); 'money can be substituted for every relation', states Michel Serres (1982: 150); but such slogans have little explanatory force without the discriminations of a developed theory. It would seem useful at least to distinguish initially between many types of transaction that sometimes become blurred together under the general rubric of 'exchange'. (While in practice they may merge somewhat, the different tendencies remain to be specified conceptually.) Are there no significant structural distinctions between swapping and bartering, between loan and reimbursement, between revenge and sacrifice? How does buying a loaf of bread differ from buying a lottery ticket, or paying an insurance premium? What about a vendor's replacement of a defective or worn-out item of merchandise: is that kind of exchange just the same in theory as the original purchase? Might a seemingly unilateral act such as stealing be part of a transaction? Is the giving of a birthday present isomorphic with the donating of blood? Do all forms of restitution, from parking fines to workers' compensation, count as exchanges? What of a sequence of moves in a card game, or of shots in a tennis match? What of ritual participation (whether amongst a group in common – affirmations voiced through the singing of hymns and national anthems, the recital of a creed – or between a couple, as in a formal declaration of marriage vows)? Are all uses of language transactional, even when one isolated person writes down a story? These disparate instances are cited indicatively; I do not intend to take up each in a direct way, let alone to propose in this book a definitive macro-typology for exchange relations at large. My general point is that theoretical refinements are still needed; and my particular aim is to show how a model of exchange can be finetuned to deal more exactly with such phenomena as the arts of narration.

INTRODUCTION

WHY LINK NARRATIVE WITH EXCHANGE?

There should be no surprise at the proposition that storytelling involves an act of exchange, for in a broad sense almost any social process conforms to that basic structure. Humans habitually deal with one another through relations of giving and taking: since the 1950s this idea has become commonplace, following the observations of numerous social scientists. Intuition suggests that the same is true of narrative activity. If I tell you a story, I purport to offer 'interest' (such as useful knowledge or pleasurable edification) in return for your attention. But the very fact that narrative is so obviously amenable to a simple exchange model should lead one to doubt whether real insights can be gained from looking at it in that light unless the model is made much more precise. Since stories get told in a great variety of situations, the mere notion of textual exchange may be too pat, too banal, to explain what goes on across that range of diverse socio-historical circumstances. Does such a generalised idea even allow one to distinguish between 'live' face-to-face telling and the more intricate written forms of 'literary' narration? Do different sorts of exchange occur in different sorts of text? Indeed, could it be the case that a two-way structure of reciprocity (usually supposed to characterise exchange) is substantially at odds with the manner in which writing generates meaning?

There are strong reasons for pursuing an inquiry into narrative exchanges. Separately, as we have noted, both narrative theory and exchange theory are seen as possessing great explanatory potential for a wide band of cultural practices; yet neither has been able to clinch its promise to elucidate them cogently. Exchange theory has not so far proved itself very supple with regard to factors that exceed any rational gauging of rewards, and it needs to be applied with more exactness to verbal behaviour in particular, especially to written fictions. Narrative theory, for its part, needs now to proceed beyond the early narratological agenda, to investigate more fully not only the pragmatics of storytelling as a relationship between communicants but also the textual devices that work against any fixed framework of exchange. This book attempts to bring those two areas of theory into a mutually critical engagement.

The topic of exchange theory itself is far from ready to be closed, because by their own admission those social scientists who favour it 'have often laboured in ignorance or disregard of relevant departures in other disciplines' (Gergen 1980: x). Consequently little attention has yet been paid to the workings of exchange in those situations (from playing hopscotch to telling a joke or reading a novel) where motives plainly go beyond the scope of any simple, calculable benefit. In any case very few transactions can be satisfactorily explained in terms of such utilitarian criteria as 'payoff motives' or such generalised metaphors as 'homo reciprocus'.[1] Even at a rudimentary level, it takes two to have an exchange, and what is useful to one will seldom be of equal use to the other. Acts of giving and taking hardly ever fit a balanced pattern of intersubjective reciprocity. On the contrary, as Jean Baudrillard (1975: 75) puts it, 'exchange does not operate according to principles of equivalence'. In large part, it is the art of securing the upper hand; and some negotiation of power and desire is normally involved. But merely to note these things is not to go far enough. Exactly what kinds of power are at stake? What kinds of desire? Narrative is a particularly challenging field in which to further such an inquiry because it can engage power and desire in complex, subtle ways.

EXCHANGE AND INDIVIDUAL SELF-INTEREST

At the turn of the twentieth century, Georg Simmel attempted in his pioneering work *The Philosophy of Money* to give equal weight to 'the technical form of economic transactions' and to their 'subjective-personal substructure' (1978: 79), but ultimately favoured the view that analysts should 'reduce the economic process to what really happens in the mind of each economic subject' (83–4). Most subsequent sociological and anthropological accounts incline either towards individually based models of exchange ('Here's what I need for my personal ends, and it can mesh with what you need') or towards institutionally based models ('Social structures shape all needs and ways of needing').[2] In the former, interactive processes are seen largely in terms of reasoned choice and enlightened self-interest. According to George Homans (1961), individuals learn to seek satisfaction by estimating directly the cost and reward of exchanges of activity with other individuals. In the same tradition Peter Blau (1964), while recognising that any such process is 'a mixed game in which there are some competing and some compatible interests' (315),

INTRODUCTION

still posits a framework of assumed rationality even when it touches on the role of desire.[3] This emphasis persists in the title of Anthony Heath's 1976 book, *Rational Choice and Social Exchange*, which reviews a range of exchange theories, from those oriented towards economics in their emphasis on motives of material gain to those oriented towards sociology or cultural anthropology in their emphasis on values and institutions. Heath concludes firmly that the most satisfactory theories take rational choice to be the main motive for human behaviour; and yet the book's final sentence undermines this altogether with a throwaway admission that people 'may also be driven by unconscious desires' (184) and obey structured social rules as they engage in symbolic forms of interaction in order to interpret their world.

In any case, a preoccupation with merely personal factors is distracting if one wishes to understand how exchange can operate (and be undone) through a particular linguistic medium. While an individual reader's choices and desires may contribute, as we shall see, to the semantic framing of a narrative text, there are also other forces at work; and these pull against any intended structure of investments and returns. Instead of the neat closure implicit in a two-way transactional model, textual exchanges often involve substitutive relays and dispossessive stratagems whose effect is indefinite. These factors will be explained soon.

EXCHANGE AND SOCIAL STRUCTURES

That structures of social exchange dominate what people do is a view associated most famously with the work of Marcel Mauss, in his classic study of gift-giving (1950), and with that of Claude Lévi-Strauss (1949), who argues for example that kinship systems should be seen as *producing* personal interactions, not as being produced by them – and as doing so in accordance with a pervasive symbolic code that underwrites certain concepts of nature and culture. Such systems depend primarily, according to this idea, on relations between families rather than within families; and thus exogamy, the bridal exchange of women by different clans, guarantees reciprocal obligations that serve the interest of the amalgamated social whole. While there is wide acceptance of Lévi-Strauss's insistence on the basic symbolic importance of kinship rules, the terms of his model continue to be debated. Luce Irigaray (1985), for instance, has questioned the gendered assumptions in what she sees as a complicit way of theorising the commodification of female value, whereby women as homogenised objects of an exchange relation have no power to participate in it actively as differentiated subjects.

In connection with kinship analysis, some general findings by Marshall Sahlins (1972: 196–209) may be pertinent for an inquiry into narrative exchanges. He establishes that different social 'distances', particularly degrees of proximity between kin, determine the nature of different exchange relationships. The closer their kinship positions, the less individuals try to maximise their own rewards at each other's expense; theft from a stranger is less outrageous in this perspective than theft from one's sibling. Sahlins's view does not reject the framework proposed by Blau, Homans and others, but rather places it within a range of possibilities that are structurally constituted. There is a simple principle here that suggests a rough analogy with different degrees of narratorial detachment in storytelling. One factor influencing the nature of a textual exchange will be the distance or closeness that the narrator's voice establishes as the measure of a narratee's participation. For instance, a quasi-avuncular or paternal tone ('tenor', in linguistic parlance) puts the kin-reader, *relatively*, in a position of subordination-within-intimacy. (Complicated examples from Flaubert's *contes* are examined in chapter 4.) A sister-to-sister tone seems to indicate another sort of contract (as with some of Mansfield's stories, which figure in chapter 6). A close child-to-parent dependence (as discussed in chapter 9) is importantly different again. Of course the kinship analogy for reading relations will not take us very far, because in all but the simplest narrative texts the communicative positions are multiple and shifty. (Even Achebe's novel *Things Fall Apart*, seemingly straightforward in its tenor, blends two distinguishable narratorial voices, as we shall see below in chapter 3; several other chapters of the present book deal with more intricate examples.) However, at least a broad parallel between kinship and textual transactions places salutary emphasis on general structural features that govern the tenor of a text's figurative economy, whereas that other tendency in some anthropological studies, towards seeing exchange merely as a negotiation of individual needs, corresponds to a penchant for the simplicities of either author-centred or reader-centred criticism in literary studies.

INTRODUCTION
EXCHANGE, TEMPO AND BALANCE

Another perspective has emerged more recently within the general field of exchange theory, one that has further implications for narrative analysis. Pierre Bourdieu (1977), while accepting the value of structuralist insights such as those of Lévi-Strauss, regards them as limited by their preoccupation with synchronic models and paradigmatic relations. As a corrective he draws attention to the important function of temporal sequences in the structure of most sorts of exchange, from giving presents to taking revenge:

> Even the most strictly ritualised exchanges, in which all the moments of the action, and their unfolding, are rigorously foreseen, have room for strategies: the agents remain in command of the *interval* between the obligatory moments and can therefore act on their opponents by playing with the *tempo* of the exchange.
> (15)

This point is directly relevant to narrative situations, which are characterised, as we shall see, by dispossessive manoeuvres. Bourdieu's emphasis, valuably, falls on conflictual aspects of language: he argues that 'every exchange contains a more or less dissimulated challenge, and the logic of challenge and riposte is but the limit towards which every act of communication tends' (14). Chapter 5 will look at a group of texts which play out elaborately this logic of what he calls 'symbolic violence' (237), and which also show the pertinence of his remarks about imbalance and ideology. All exchange structures, Bourdieu observes, function ideologically 'whenever the *de facto* state of affairs which they tend to legitimate by transforming a contingent social relationship into a recognised relationship is an unequal balance of power' (195).

LANGUAGE: AN EXCHANGE OF MEANINGS?

Hallidayan systemic linguistics makes available a useful theory of verbal exchange, as later discussions in this book will show. Its special strength is in its classification of enunciative features of language, particularly with regard to the situational variables of field, tenor and mode. But it has yet to develop a fully adequate analysis of the discursive forces that converge on a highly crafted textual artefact, especially a written fiction, and striate it in subtle ways. There is a need to go beyond the general point, which Halliday (1978: 140) makes in passing, that a text 'is perhaps the most highly coded form of the gift' and to clarify the point of different gift exchanges (or any other sort) as they manifest themselves verbally, in the very texture of fictional language as well as in the enunciative situations that generate it. Textual relations are by no means invariably gift-like, even in an ample sense that covers contestation; for instance while they may take at times the shape of (say) an exogamous ritual, they may also be fundamentally transgressive, like rape or theft. (Chapters 5 and 8 will look at examples.)

Despite its valuable insistence that a text is not an object but an interactive process, the systemic-functionalist school of linguistics tends to formulate its concept of 'an exchange of meanings' in a way that has attracted criticism for being indiscriminate (Freadman 1987). In this respect there has still not been a substantial advance on the work of the pioneer semiotician Ferdinand de Saussure (1983), which did much to inspire the structuralist movement in literary criticism and other fields. Saussure saw language, like money, as a system of signs regulated by conventions of equivalence and difference in such a way that a certain word can signify (stand for, be substituted for) a certain idea by virtue of its comparative relationship with other words – just as a certain amount of coinage can be swapped for a certain commodity. One of the ways in which Halliday attempts to develop these insights towards a more fully function-based social semiotic is by deriving from Bronislaw Malinowski, via J.R. Firth, a supplementary notion of 'contexts' (Halliday and Hasan 1985: 5–14, 46, 55–6) – contexts both of 'situation' (the text's immediate environment, e.g. a classroom lesson) and of 'culture' (the text's larger background of community practices, e.g. the schooling system generally).

The notion of a 'contextual configuration', a specific set of social processes and values that realises a text's field, tenor and mode, is potentially important, but has yet to prove its adaptability for the study of written fictions. Relations between text and context have not been subtly articulated in Hallidayan theory, mainly because of two procedural shortcomings. First, systemic linguistics does not sufficiently acknowledge how arbitrary is the circumference it often imposes on what it is inspecting. An excerpted passage, for instance, can be treated unreflectively as a 'coherent whole'.[4] This

INTRODUCTION

problem needs the corrective of a theory of framing, as we shall see later. Second, systemic linguistics narrows its scope unduly in taking speech as the basic and exemplary mode: 'It is natural to conceive of text first and foremost as conversation: as the spontaneous interchange of meanings in ordinary, everyday interaction' (Halliday 1978: 140).[5] Although Halliday carefully notes that one should 'draw a rather clear line between this [spoken dialogue] and other, less immediately contextualisable acts of meaning such as a poem or prose narrative' (140), he still regards the latter kind as exceptional, 'untypical of texts as a whole' (137), and takes the former for analytic purposes as the norm of textual practice. Thus in a later summary of his position Halliday states quite baldly that 'the fundamental form of a text is that of a dialogue, of interaction between speakers', and that 'every kind of text... is meaningful because it can be related... to ordinary everyday spontaneous conversation' (Halliday and Hasan 1985: 11).

These may be problems of injudicious emphasis rather than inherent confusion. But two criticisms remain pertinent here. One is that when systemic linguists do turn their attention in any detail to a literary text, which happens seldom, the resultant commentary tends to treat the text as little more than an illustration of the elaborate taxonomic system previously developed to analyse spoken language. This is the gist of Stanley Fish's trenchant assessment of an early study by Halliday describing how language works in Golding's *The Inheritors*, a novel that distinguishes between two prehistoric tribes according to their language processes. Fish insists that the interpretation Halliday offers is merely measuring the supposed deficiencies of the neanderthal tribe 'by the inability of their language to fill out the categories of his grammar' (1980: 83). Rather than being derived, as is claimed, from the stylistic data, that interpretation precedes and frames the way Halliday reads the data. While the syntactic patterns that he reveals are indeed meaningful, the source of their meaning is 'not the capacity of a syntax to express it, but the ability of a reader to confer it' (83). That is to say, applying the term that the present study will use, in Halliday's reading of this novel (as in all readings of all texts) perceptions of coherence depend on acts of *framing*. Ironically, in overlooking this fundamental factor Halliday is missing the implications of his own maxim that a text is a semantic exchange; for he is proceeding, Fish points out, 'as if meanings arose independently of human transactions' (84).

The second criticism to be made of the way systemic linguistics applies itself to literary texts is this: Although the emphasis on conversational 'dialogue' may not be intended to refer only to situations that literally involve no more than two interlocutors, its effect is nevertheless to establish a dual relationship as normative. And yet when framed as fictional, narrative exchanges do not confine themselves simply to two parties, writer and reader. Refracted through intermediary figures of the narration, literary fictions may permit and often encourage a plurality of positions so that the ostensible 'message' directed to a narratee is distinguishable from the fuller one understood by an implied reader, which is further modifiable by an actual reader's interpretive framing. That Halliday's schematisation cannot deal satisfactorily with these complexities is plain from his attempt to analyse the 'tenor' (discursive role positioning) of a well-known fable by James Thurber, 'The Lover and his Lass'. As fictions go, it is a fairly slight text – short and didactic; but even so, when Halliday tries to deal with it in terms of just two 'levels', those of content and narration, he falls at once into rudimentary imprecision. The tenor, in his view, has a double aspect in this fable: it comprises (1) the relationship between the characters, as shown in their dialogue, and (2) the relationship between 'narrator' and narratee. Confusedly, the latter level is described as encompassing 'writer and readers; writer adopting role as recounter: specifically as humorist (partly projected through subsidiary role as moralist), and assigning complementary role to audience' (1978: 146). This conflation of author with narrator, and reader with narratee, will not account for the semantic potential of even the little Thurber text, much less for that of the considerably more intricate narratives to be discussed in the present book. Take for example the final Thurber sentence: 'MORAL: *Laugh and world laughs with you, love and you love alone.*' At face value, this sums up for a narratee the significance of the characters' behaviour, doing so in a way that lumps together the two couples (parrots and hippos) as double illustrations of a single and simple theme. But, as A.J. Greimas (1985: 361–2)) remarks in discussing the same tale, a more subtle moral is implied, for what appears 'on the surface of the text as two equal parts is a false symmetry – false because the hippos are right and the parrots wrong'; and to read in these terms is to recognise that the final sentence, purporting to frame the meaning circumtextually, is too platitudinous a summary to

INTRODUCTION

deserve the authority it seems to claim. Indeed further readings are always possible, further departures from any simple dialogic relation or fixed frame that appears to be proffered by the text. Suppose for instance that a reader sees in the explicit terminal moral a meta-application, a reflexively ironic comment on the humorous narratorial tone itself and on the generic limitations of fables; surely such an interpretation cannot be located analytically at the same 'level' as a straight acceptance of the moral by the narratee? It depends not on that 'complementary role' assigned by the narrator to the narratee but on a reader's independent activity of (re)framing.

Mikhail Bakhtin conceives of dialogue in an ampler sense than Halliday; for him, the very nature of signification, written as well as spoken, is dialogic in the sense that every textual utterance situates itself in a mutually responsive relation to other utterances, whether preceding it or anticipated. His project shifts linguistic analysis away from the Saussurean emphasis on the primacy of a closed system (*langue*) towards an interest in the modification of rules within particular discursive settings. 'All verbal interaction', he declares, 'takes place in the form of an *exchange of utterances*, that is, in the form of a *dialogue*.' But unlike Halliday, Bakhtin is at pains to insist on the inadequacy of a dual model of communicative exchange:

> The author (the speaker) may have inalienable rights upon the discourse, but so does the listener, *as do those whose voices resonate in the words found by the author* (since there are no words that do not belong to someone). Discourse is a three-role drama (*it is not a duet but a trio*). It is played outside of the author, and it is inadmissible to inject it within the author.
>
> (quoted in Todorov 1984: 52; italics added)

When one reads with this awareness foremost, one is framing the exchange of utterances intertextually. Bakhtin's emphasis on this is salutary, though other elements may also enter the 'contextual configuration' through which texts are framed, as we shall see later.

THEORIES OF EXCHANGE IN LITERARY TEXTS

Sometimes a lexicon starts to come together before the full advent of the theory towards which it is gesturing, and terms that allude in a general way to exchange have recently become fairly familiar in literary criticism and cultural studies. A few words semi-naturalised in an earlier lingo are undergoing revaluation for less innocent usage, including the Leavisite shibboleth 'revaluation' itself, and others are being added: texts not only 'circulate' now, they are likely to do so within an 'economy of desire', for instance. A phraseology of 'currency', 'investment', 'interest' and 'negotiation' tends to be employed with more deliberate emphasis than before on its metaphorical import. The increase in this kind of vocabulary, of course, is partly attributable to a growing partiality for describing literary interpretation in broadly transactional terms (though in fact so-called 'reader-response criticism' covers diverse theoretical positions, some of them inexactly formulated);[6] more specifically it often borrows its appeal, though not always a systematic conceptual underpinning, from topical French theorists such as Baudrillard (e.g. 1988: 57–63, 119–48).

It remains true, however, that surprisingly few literary critics have tried to utilise concepts of exchange in more than a casual way, and very little of their work has extensive theoretical scope, or covers textual varieties.[7] Of writings that deal mainly with single texts or groups of texts, those by medievalists happen to predominate, and are not well known to many outside that special field.[8] The most extended studies of literary aspects of exchange are by Jean-Joseph Goux (1973, 1984) and Marc Shell (1978, 1982), both of whom focus mainly on ideas about monetary equivalence. Goux develops a general account of symbolic production as an economy, looking specifically at homologies between the modern departure from gold-standard currency and the decline of realism in fiction. His books, available only in French, pursue a specialised thesis and have not yet proved influential on critical theory in English.[9] Shell, in two elaborately argued and stimulating studies, *The Economy of Literature* and *Money, Language and Thought*, discusses a range of texts from several periods that show how ideas may be commodified into a kind of 'money of the mind', as for instance in *The Merchant of Venice*, with its 'series of bonds in which individuals and properties are exchanged for each other' – or how, sometimes, ideas may be endowed with a transcendent, supra-commercial quality, as in Christianised Arthurian romance stories of 'a cornucopian grail, an extraordinary gift both infinitely large and free, which was said to be able to lift men out of the ordinary world of exchange'. Incisive though Shell's work is, it

INTRODUCTION

has been seen as limited by its apparent adherence to a residual base/superstructure model of cultural production, supposing too direct a correspondence between economic and artistic modes and making the invention of coinage 'a kind of originator of all forms of semiosis' (Reiss 1981: 185). Exactly how texts 'interiorise aspects of the political economy' (Shell 1978: 8) is not explained.

Apart from sections of these books and a handful of miscellaneous articles, very little published criticism brings any concept of exchange to bear on the written fictions that represent imaginary relationships (not only through 'characters' but also through narrator and narratee, interposed between author and reader). Closest to elements of my own approach is Marie Maclean's chapter on contracts in her *Narrative as Performance* (1988). Like the work of Ross Chambers, to which it acknowledges a particular debt, Maclean's study moves beyond the constraining dyadic categories of structuralist narratology towards an analysis of ways in which texts are reflexively inscribed with the conditions of their tellability. Instead of viewing narrative in orthodox neo-Aristotelian fashion as the mimesis of an action, she regards it primarily as 'the site of an interaction' (ix). In this perspective, a story-text is not a fixed object but a performed and therefore variable occurrence which depends for its efficacy on the active participation of listeners or readers.

FRAMING EXCHANGES AND SUBVERTING FRAMES

Anyone who exchanges things is thereby deeming them to be valuable. But what value, exactly, gets attributed to the content of an exchange will depend on how it is framed. Participants in a textual exchange always need to negotiate its terms with regard to framing factors. These factors comprise several kinds of semantic evaluation, different ways of enclosing and controlling signs so as to confer a certain sense on them.

In a pragmatic perspective, framing is something that a reader does to a text; it is the application of an interpretive procedure. Conversely the text has already provided various elements (title, chapter divisions, and so forth) that solicit particular framings, thus tending to curtail what the text can be made to mean. Yet while any framing has the intent of fixing an exchange rate, there are other factors that counteract it in the case of written narrative: the textual features that I shall call substitution and dispossession. These disturb what framing would regulate; and to understand how they work is to grasp the structural specificity of written narrative.

Narratology has tied itself to an event-based concept of story structure. Although no-one would simply dismiss that way of thinking about narrative texts as 'wrong', it is patently limited, for reasons to be discussed at length in chapter 1. Instead of persisting with a story/discourse dichotomy (or its variants), narrative theory today is beginning to turn its attention to the means by which texts engage readers in semantic exchanges. But such an engagement, I will argue, is much more intricate than the figure of 'exchange' would usually be taken to indicate, for reader-text relations cannot be properly explained in terms of a reciprocal deal between a pair of communicants. Complicating and even subverting this apparently basic two-way transaction are certain processes that involve very different forms of exchange: a substitutive movement within the told tale and a dispossessive movement within the telling situation. That is, the structure of a written narrative utterance can be seen more productively as a matter of rhetorical successivity (a substitutive shuffle of signifiers) than as a chain of actions, and correspondingly its enunciative aspect is better understood as a struggle to possess the meanings of what is told than as the mere capacity to impart a tale.

It is fairly obvious in most settings that there can be no 'pure' exchange. In a commercial venture or even in an amorous encounter, some context of values is always applied, albeit only implicitly in some cases. But how does this principle apply to the contemplation of a work of art? The example of a picture gallery provides a simple analogy (though an incomplete one, as we shall see): a viewer 'pays' attention to a displayed artefact with the aim of receiving an experience of cultural worth in return, and perceives the meaning of that exchange by framing it with reference to 'currency rates' (whatever are seen as criteria of its equivalence). These framings are of several sorts.

In the most literal and primary sense, the set of material borders that shape and surround a painted surface, separating it from the rest of the plane on which it hangs, constitute a frame. This itself is not semiotically neutral; a large, ornate gilt perimeter makes one sort of statement about how to regard the pictorial object, while a non-rectilinear frame (being markedly unusual) designates its content in a very different fashion. But whatever form it takes, that proximate boundary is not the only physical one to be placed around the given painting. Any adjacent caption or commentary can inform one's response; also pertinent are more dispersed features of the surrounding space, notably other pictures, which may in turn be part of the context of a featured exhibition or special collection; and then there is the nature of the particular gallery itself, which contributes to the perceptual positioning of any single item within it. All such elements are able to frame the visual object 'circumtextually'.

It is likely to be framed in other ways as well. For instance, sometimes a gallery spectator will interpret a picture partly in terms of internal subdivisions. Perhaps this 'intratextual' framing may have regard to segmented panels, as in a Bosch triptych or in Dali's painting *The Night and Day of the Body*. Or in some cases it may recognise lines of disjuncture between incongruous components, as in several of Max Ernst's collage works. It may respond to overtly reflexive elements, as in van Eyck's *The Arnolfini Wedding* ; or to the insertion of verbal matter within the painted space, as in Altdorfer's *Battle of Alexander* and Magritte's *Ceci n'est pas une pipe*.

Further, in some cases one's hermeneutic response to the painting will be 'intertextually' framed by a recognition that it is visually quoting other paintings, alluding to certain pictorial traditions, parodying stock motifs, and so on. Thus an informed viewer will set certain works by Picasso within a perceptual frame through which they are seen as transforming into cubist terms the contours of works by Velasquez or Cézanne. Sometimes intertextual framing is directly reinforced by circumtextual framing, as Turner emphasised when he bequeathed one of his productions to his country's National Gallery on the condition that it be hung next to some by Claude Lorrain; sometimes it is reinforced by intratextual framing, as when Colin McCahon inscribes upon one of his canvases the words *Here I give thanks to Mondrian*.

And then there are the various interests, expectations, knowledges and tastes that an individual brings into the gallery in order to frame a picture 'extratextually'. Of course these would normally include at least some awareness of what a gallery has to offer and what people do there; in addition, extratextual factors could range from an intense curiosity about conventions of Renaissance portraiture or a general liking for expressionist uses of colour to a stock of mythological lore used to decipher the action represented in a particular painting.

NARRATIVE EXCHANGES

The broad analogy between reading a literary text and viewing a picture in an art gallery is plainly imperfect. In some respects, the exchange that occurs when one peruses a novel may more closely resemble the constructive and reconstructive kind of work that goes on in an atelier. For reading, too, is a craft of composition, a practice of frame-making that overlaps with the artist's creative labour. By bringing interpretive frames to bear on a text, its reader actively draws its elements into a significant configuration. But there is little profit in fussing over analogical nuances. For beyond any simplified parallel with a painting, written storytelling typically involves textual processes that belong in a distinctive way to its own medium. When these processes – substitution and dispossession – come into play, they can allow a narrative exchange to elude to some extent the fixture of any frame.

NOW READ ON

This present book undertakes to show how literary texts can complicate the kind of transaction posited in usual models of exchange. In doing so it will also advance a new view of the workings of written narrative, a view which parenthesises the commonsensical axiom that a story definitively represents a succession of events. This does not mean ignoring such traditional concepts as 'plot' and 'character'; the following chapters (especially 1 and 7) will suggest ways of rethinking them in relation to devices of textual exchange, while also taking a further look at certain stock structuralist notions such as the metaphor/metonymy doublet (especially in chapter 6). There will be an attempt to enlarge the application of post-structuralist theory, which as Edward Said remarks has been surprisingly neglectful of narrative texts (Said 1983: 192–3), and in doing so to enlarge also the range of what counts as literary narrative, since too many critics (including Said himself) virtually identify it with the novel. Summarily, the argument developed in the following chapters involves these propositions.

(1) Every case of exchange depends on perceptual acts of framing in order to delimit a semantic field, not just initially but through continual reframing.

(2) In the case of textual exchanges, a pragmatic typology of

INTRODUCTION

different framing potentialities can help one to avoid false text/reader dichotomies. In cursory terms (definitions must wait until chapter 2), it can be said that extratextual framing serves to establish the broad terms of an exchange, being adduced by individual readers but ultimately regulated by social institutions, while the other sorts of framing are also activated by certain exchange practices (such as the way a text may be 'packaged' – circumtextually framed – as, perhaps, Realist Novel or Women's Writing not only by authorial labelling but by publishers, editors, booksellers, librarians, teachers, through the adjunctive apparatuses of catalogues, cover designs, shelf classifications, syllabuses; or the way it may make a rhetorical bid for the reader's attention – through devices apt for intratextual and intertextual framing – as to the kind of use it solicits).

(3) In the case of written narrative fictions, the operations of exchange and framing tend to be complicated by two subversive textual activities: substitution and dispossession. In brief, 'substitution' refers to a process within the utterance (*énoncé*: what is told) whereby narrative momentum occurs through a serial shuffling of scenes or takes or rhetorical figures, and 'dispossession' refers to a process within the enunciation (*énonciation*: the story-producing activity, which may in turn be figured within the *énoncé*) whereby the balance of narratorial power is revealed as shifty.

(4) Each narrative text will achieve its own particular metabolic ratio between substitution and dispossession, and its own particular strategy for trying to frame the ways in which readers frame it.

The desires that various texts purport to satisfy through imaginary relationships differ considerably, not least because the social formations within which a fictional give-and-take occurs will always tend to shape it in terms of particular constraints: those of available discourses. My aim here can only be to show in an assortment of exemplary texts how certain patterns of substitution and dispossession work to inflect, and reveal tension in, the amalgamated discursive norms that allow them to be framed. Each stage of the argument develops through a detailed reading of some fictional narrative. There are a dozen or so in all, drawn from a range of periods, generic affiliations and cultural situations. Because the generic specificity of narrative is a matter of degree, not of essential category, there is little profit for present purposes in attempting to contradistinguish narrative from (say) poetry. In so far as some lyric or epic poem may work in substitutive or dispossessive ways, to that extent it partakes of narrative.

I begin in chapter 1 with a conspectus of the most salient issues in current narrative theory, such as the nature of (ostensible) textual unity and the locus of (would-be) textual authority, eliciting these issues from an appraisal of two samples of narrative studies from the mid-1980s, and one sample of an earlier study. The first chapter also introduces the concepts of substitution and dispossession through a short commentary on a well known *Decameron* tale. Further implications of the line of argument sketched there are traced in subsequent chapters. Chapter 2 expounds a typology of framing with reference to different versions of a story by Alphonse Daudet. Chapter 3, which includes analyses of work by Don DeLillo, Snorri Sturluson and Chinua Achebe, develops the exposition of framing *vis-à-vis* the processes of substitution and dispossession. Chapter 4 links those processes with the problematic concept of an 'implied author', testing its applicability to three tales by Gustave Flaubert and a novel by Marguerite Duras. Chapter 5 considers gendered exchanges among a cluster of closely interrelated texts by Frank Moorhouse, Michael Wilding, Amy Witting and Louise Dow. Chapter 6 pursues the issues of a 'female voice' and of narrative as a means of exclusion, through a reading of stories by Katherine Mansfield. Chapter 7 shows how William Wordsworth's narrative poem *The Prelude* tries to occlude the personal and political tensions that shape it, fabricating a unified persona and an ideal of reciprocity which it cannot sustain. Chapter 8 considers general arguments about the place of narrative in modern and postmodern culture, with reference to a novel by Patrick White and a collage text by Jaimy Gordon. Chapter 9, using as evidence a text produced by a 5-year-old, mounts a critique of theories by linguists and educators about the early development of one's sense of a 'story world', and concludes with summary remarks about the primary constitutive elements of narrative.

1

BEYOND NARRATOLOGY?

> The *histoire* is the what
> and the *discours* is the how
> but what I want to know, Brigham,
> is *le pourquoi* . . .
> Why are we sitting here around the campfire?
>
> (Le Guin 1980: 192)

I

Most studies of narrative, whatever their theoretical persuasion, have adopted uncritically the commonsensical assumption that narrative is to be defined as representing a succession of events. Repeated so often that it hardly seems open to question, this routine formulation is nevertheless misleading; for it not only implies (against all logic) that successiveness and eventfulness can be prior to representation, but also elides the problem that a concept such as 'succession-of-events', rather than being inherent in a form of representation, depends on some unifying or framing act of perception. Accordingly a more accurate definition – and the difference here is no mere quibble – might state that (1) narrative *represents events as successive*; and (2) the 'events' should be understood as ontologically problematic, *existing only as gestures in language*. Moreover any perception of these gestures as constituting a chain of action or story or plot (such terms vary) should itself be a matter for narrative theory to explain.

The continuing tenacity of an unsatisfactory notion about what narrative itself comprises would be more surprising if versions of it had not become so familiar – apparently 'natural' – not only in specialised academic discussion but also in many a popular handbook over the years. To glance through publications such as Mildred P. Forbes's quaint *Good Citizenship Through Storytelling: A Textbook for Teachers, Social Workers and Homemakers* (1923) is to see how widely disseminated were those precepts about interlinked events, completeness, and so on, which then became reinforced in the 1960s and 1970s by the seeming rigour of structuralist methods of analysis.[1] Produced under the banner of 'narratology', the linguistically oriented work which flourished most confidently during that period can now be recognised as – for all its air of novelty – sharing some doubtful assumptions with a much older critical tradition, broadly Aristotelian.

Despite its notable successes, there is increasing disappointment with mainstream narratology. The feeling even among its adherents that it has not quite managed to deliver the goods stems largely, so this chapter will suggest, from the limitations of a basic structuralist (and pre-structuralist) axiom: that it is important to distinguish between 'a sequence of actions' and their 'manifestation in discourse' (Culler 1981: 169–70), between 'the organisation of events' and 'the organisation of their telling' (Cohan and Shires 1988: 53). Variously formulated (e.g. *histoire* or *story* versus *discours* or *discourse* (Chatman 1978: 19) and variously modified (e.g. by tripartite refinements such as *fabula/story/text* (Bal 1985: 5) and *histoire/récit/narration* (Genette 1972: 71–6), any such procedural dichotomy or trichotomy is still suspect in so far as it hypostatises an eventful content. As narratological analysis burgeoned through the 1960s and 1970s, most theorists took it for granted that a text's structure is operationally separable from its linguistic 'surface' (Hendricks 1980: 36). Folklorists, semioticians, discourse grammarians – virtually all have been inclined to base their work on the notion that an 'underlying' series of states and events is the primary constituent of narrative. Although it has been challenged (notably by Smith 1980), this implicit dualism continues to generate studies as substantial as Shlomith Rimmon-Kenan's *Narrative Fiction: Contemporary Poetics* (1983), which will be examined below. But another orientation has emerged, one that turns more attentively towards the ways in which pragmatic features of a narrative occasion may inscribe themselves textually; this is a major emphasis in Ross Chambers's *Story and Situation: Narrative Seduction and the Power of Fiction* (1984), also to be discussed soon.

BEYOND NARRATOLOGY?

Together, these two books can fairly be taken to represent the main directions of recent work in narrative studies. Rimmon-Kenan's serves primarily as a neat digest of received ideas within the narratological tradition established in the late 1960s, on the foundation of early Russian formalism, by theorists such as Tzvetan Todorov (whose classic *Grammaire du Décaméron* (1969) will be revisited later in this chapter). While offering some very useful insights of her own, Rimmon-Kenan acknowledges that these are incidental; her *Narrative Fiction* organises itself according to the orthodox structuralist categories of event, focalisation, and so forth, whereas Chambers pursues a more original line of argument. Both critics recognise that we have reached a point in the growth of narrative studies where a general appraisal is needed of the gains and losses of the narratological program. Rimmon-Kenan's epilogue asserts that structuralist poetics is 'still alive and kicking, although (or perhaps because) it no longer enjoys the privilege of the latest fashion' (130); Chambers, in contrast, begins by indicating a deficiency in that body of narratological lore with its elaborate 'grammar' of stories:

> What is lacking is recognition of the significance of situational phenomena – of the social fact that narrative mediates human relationships and derives its 'meaning' from them; that, consequently, it depends on social agreements, implicit pacts or contracts, in order to produce exchanges that themselves are a function of desires, purposes, and constraints.
> (4)

He contends that literary fictions, at least in the form of the canonical nineteenth-century short story, indicate self-referentially the particular stipulations desired for their readability. His *Story and Situation* argues convincingly not only the need for a development beyond narratology but also the basis on which it is possible: a more careful scrutiny of the enunciative 'situation'. First, however, let us consider the nature of Rimmon-Kenan's emphasis on 'story'.

II

The chief virtue of *Narrative Fiction* is in providing a clear retrospect of the ground over which narratologists have trod, have trod, have trod, rather than in opening up any new terrain. It takes

21

its place as one of several lucid and sensible surveys of the major topics in orthodox narrative poetics.[2] Among those 'algebraists of Paris' (as Poe's Dupin, in an unwitting prolepsis, characterised structuralism's leading exponents) on whose work she draws, Rimmon-Kenan's closest affinity is with Gérard Genette, the least mathematical of them and the one who, in contrast to the likes of Bremond, is particularly alert to the modal qualities of narrative discourse itself and seldom dwells on the so-called contents of an *histoire*. Rimmon-Kenan describes her own theoretical formulations as 'post-Genettian' (85), but this indicates only a measure of independence from his work, not a different direction. Their relatively minor disagreements are stated with courtesy on both sides; thus, in a book first published in the same year as hers and later translated as *Narrative Discourse Revisited* (1988), Genette devotes several pages to a respectful consideration of previous criticisms respectfully made by Rimmon-Kenan. What they share, apart from a gift for crisp exposition, is a preference for investigating the organisational principles of a text (*récit*) and the process of enunciating it (*narration*) over any abstraction of story-grammar (*histoire*). Genette (1988: 16) declares that 'the sole specificity of narrative lies in its mode and not in its content'. Rimmon-Kenan is less forthright: occasionally she registers passing doubts about reductive schemata such as Bremond's division of all sequences into either those of amelioration or those of deterioration (27), but for the most part her Genettian alignment emerges implicitly in a contrast between the perfunctory tone of her opening chapters on 'story' elements and the more engaged, vigorous writing of subsequent chapters on such matters as time, focalisation and voice. She retains a fondness for multiple typologies; for instance, the variety of possible narrative techniques is neatly ordered according to level (extra-, intra-, and hypodiegetic), degree of participation (hetero- and homodiegetic), and degree of perceptibility (with a list of six signs of overtness). For the most part this method produces very serviceable distinctions. Those on different 'participants in the narrative communication situation' (86–9), are especially precise, improving on Chatman's definitions of 'implied author', 'narrator', and so on.

Only on two counts does Rimmon-Kenan's manual fall short, in balance and cogency, of achieving the intended 'synthesis' (5) of contemporary approaches to narrative fiction: it neglects to deal with narration as a bid for discursive power, and it remains unduly attached to the structuralist notion that narrative axiomatically 'represents a *succession of events*' (2; Rimmon-Kenan's emphasis). Regarding the first point: narratorial authority is *always at stake* in a storytelling situation, whatever the tactical variations. When discussing characterisation, Rimmon-Kenan attempts (60-1) to distinguish neatly between, on the one hand, instances of 'direct definition' of a character's traits by 'an authoritative narrator' and, on the other hand, 'indirect presentation' through what a character says or does or is associated with. In a note, she adds: 'However, there are texts, like Lawrence's *Sons and Lovers*, where such [direct, authoritative] definitions clash with indirect characterisations, and the result is perplexing' (138). This remark is not wrong, but it does seem to miss the point, for the engendering of perplexity in such cases is one of the regular ploys by which the balance of power between participants in a narrative situation can tip in the teller's favour – all the more effectively for not being overtly seized. So Chambers's book demonstrates, as we shall see.

A critical perspective on narratological dogma about the fundamental status of action is the other lack in Rimmon-Kenan's work. True, she does remark that, since language cannot imitate anything other than language, the Aristotelian concept of 'an imitation of an action' cannot be transposed unproblematically from drama to narrative (107–8); and she does try to resist 'the subordination of character to action' in formalist poetics (34). But the issues are not followed through. Genette has argued, in response to her criticism that he pays too little attention to character, that it is only one textual effect among many, and therefore does not demand separate analysis:

> In my view it is decidedly, although relatively, preferable (more 'narratological') to decompose the study of 'characterisation' into the study of its constituting devices (which are not all specific to it): denomination, description, focalisation, narrative of words or thoughts or both, relation to the narrating situation, etc.
>
> (1988: 136)

Should not the same line of argument apply with equal force to action as to character? Rimmon-Kenan appears not to have confronted this question. 'Structural descriptions', she asserts, 'show how *events* combine to create *micro-sequences* which in turn combine to form *macro-sequences* which jointly create the complete story' (16; cf. 23). One problem with this view is that it presupposes either a single cohesive storyline (restricted to one set of characters and actions), which is often quite obviously not the case,[3] or at least the possibility of determining that one line is predominant – and, as she admits without pursuing the implications of this point, 'there are no clear-cut criteria for predominance'. Another problem is that principles of 'combination' are not self-evident; whereas some narratologists such as Prince think causality is necessary, Rimmon-Kenan argues that temporal succession suffices (18). But what remains dubious in any case is the underlying assumption that narrative consists definitively of combined events. And there is a third problem lurking in Rimmon-Kenan's statement: exactly how can mere combination, in itself, guarantee a story's completeness, since the number of events per sequence, or of sequences per story, is variable? The point must be stressed that a sense of narrative completeness cannot be a property of any action sequence; it is a function of reading, an interpretive fiction, a confidence trick that the text entices readers to play on themselves, no matter how 'naturally' unified a given sequence or set of sequences may purport to be. Rimmon-Kenan comes near to recognising this in some exact local observations (e.g. 93–4, on *Tristram Shandy*), but cannot bring herself to question radically the theoretical framework itself.

Dissatisfaction with this kind of actionist orthodoxy has been registered by some writers on narrative theory, notably Ruthrof (1981: 110), who contends that 'the ardent attention structuralists have given to action sequences tends to support ... a one-sided view of narrative structure' by neglecting the 'presentational process' as realised within the reading process. Ruthrof's argument, which depends on phenomenological premises, may be complemented from another perspective by the following proposition, which the present book will develop: 'action sequences' (when indeed they can be constructed by the reader, which is not invariably so) are largely a sediment of transformations taking place at the rhetorical level, for narrative may be more comprehensively defined as *the discursive mode that imparts an illusion of eventful serial movement to its constituent figures.*

BEYOND NARRATOLOGY?

III

The broad hypothesis just proposed, though it merely foreshadows what will have to be expounded carefully in the ensuing chapters, cannot go altogether unexercised at this point. Before turning to Chambers's book, let us pause to see how vindicable (at least in a preliminary way) is the concept of narrative as rhetorical momentum, through analysis of an apparently resistant text: a tale from the *Decameron*. Such a choice should be fairly challenging for two reasons. First, this kind of fiction is reputedly so infatuated with 'action for action's sake' (Alberto Moravia's remark on 'the mechanism with which Boccaccio's world operates'; 1976: 102–7) that a contrary case cannot be glibly made. Second, it has in fact been taken as an exemplary instance of event-based fiction by Todorov in that narratological landmark *Grammaire du Décaméron*, to which we shall turn our attention later in this chapter.

Our selected tale will be the second of the fourth day, well known in the critical canon because of the discussion of it in Erich Auerbach's *Mimesis* (1953). Here is a summary of IV, 2 in the words of the text's own synoptic preamble:

> Brother Alberto convinces a lady that the angel Gabriel is in love with her; then, he, disguised as the angel, sleeps with her many times; fearing her relatives, he flees from her house and seeks refuge in the home of a poor man, who, on the following day, leads him into the piazza dressed as a wild man of the forest, and there he is recognised by his brother monks and is put into prison.[4]

Now some would see a simple and sufficient demonstration of the basic structuralist postulate in the very fact that this kind of synopsis, comprising an action sequence, carries the authority of the text itself: surely a convincing testimony to the centrality of an *histoire* as the *sine qua non* of narrative? Not so. A précis, especially when merely prefacing a story (and in this case it is only one prefatory element among several, as we shall see later), is not the essence of the story but just a conventional trailer ('Did you hear the one about ...?'), an attention-getting device whose efficacy depends on a reader's sense that it is too drastically reductive and partial to have narrative shape or force in its own right. The pith of the full telling should no more be confused with this simple lure than the 'point' should be equated with the moralistic final judgement, in which Alberto is deemed to have been punished 'as he deserved' (precisely the sort of reduction practised by Todorov, as we shall see, in his book on the *Decameron*, which classifies plot sequences into limited variations on a small group of actions, mainly 'transgression' and 'punishment'). To take this at face value is to shrink the text into a banal exemplum on the theme that crime doesn't pay. One problem with such a reading would be its failure to fit the outcome neatly; crime (financial trickery and abuse of trust) does pay for the treacherous Venetian who leads Alberto into the public trap.

If it is appropriate to castigate so severely Brother Alberto, 'wicked and thought to be good', what of the fact that his helper, 'the good man' who betrays him after extracting fifty ducats, gets away with it? In so far as Alberto's misfortune seems 'deserved', the reason is not consequential in the sense of arising directly from a chain of events *per se*; rather it involves, in a kind of *poetic* justice, further figurative twists to the process whereby the ingenious villain had initially turned Lisetta's folly to his advantage. For what we have is less a series of entailed actions than a protracted comic play on linked transformations, and these are generated not from the underlying action-stratum that Todorov posits but from within the linguistic medium itself.

Through that medium, the most strongly marked connective principle progressively revealed to the reader is a series of conceits associated with the verbal figure 'fly', these being particular developments of a transfigurative rhetoric that permeates the story. Pampinea, the narrator, uses from beginning to end the lexicon of metamorphosis: Alberto 'turned himself into a minor friar ... he changed from a wolf into a shepherd' – and so on, through the main part of the story ('he went in disguise ... having changed himself into an angel') right into the closing paragraph: 'Thus a man who... dared to turn himself into the angel Gabriel ... instead was converted into a wild man ... ' Prominent in the text, words such as *trasformato* and *trasfiguro* provide a rhetorical context for the main trope: having armed himself – that is, winged himself – in order to exploit the credulous literalism of Lisetta's conceit and gain access to her bed, where he 'flew many times ... without his wings', Alberto finds his imposture made parodically literal in the dénouement: after her brothers resolve 'to find this angel and to see if he knew how to fly', he must leap through the window; and having 'flown away, leaving his wings behind him', he must later be tormented by gadflies and humiliated in the feathers not of an angelic figure but of a savage.

This trope is transformational; more precisely, it operates as a *device of substitutive propulsion*. Alberto's series of shams – friar, angel, savage – articulates the moves by which the successful rogue changes into the abject prisoner, and the rhetorical embellishments of these successive states (wolf or shepherd, flying high or lying low) similarly impel the story along as they rapidly replace one another. While there is certainly a temporal element to Alberto's trajectory, the narrative momentum that ends with his diminishment comes mainly from a dynamic of troping (in the most specific sense of that word – 'turning'): not so much any succession of abstractable events or any logic of entailment as a veritable flight of fancies in which figure follows figure as if from a repertoire of disguise.

Before examining another important aspect of this tale we should gather up some implications for an understanding of narrative exchanges in general. A text is, axiomatically, a negotiated framing of sign-values – but this occurs in an interpersonal context and therefore cannot be perfectly stable.[5] One potentially destabilising factor in a narrative text is its capacity to shuffle its deck of tropes in order to extend options as to how and where the story will move and stop; witness the mobile figure of Brother Alberto, now up, now down, now soaring, now fleeing: with each turn of the rhetorical screw, his trajectory acquires a different significance. Another factor that can contribute to the renegotiation of semantic control is evident in this same *Decameron* tale: a textual strategy for pre-empting or usurping interest as to whose side of the story will be heard. For convenient reference, the structural effects of these two factors need names: the former, *substitution*; the latter, *dispossession*. That is: whereas 'exchange' normally (and too simply) indicates a mutual giving-and-taking of signs by two or more parties, 'substitution' will refer to an altering of the value of the signs and 'dispossession' will refer to a wresting or arresting of control over the relative positions of the parties. The former has been illustrated: what makes Alberto's story move along as it does and arrive where it does is the figurative mutation that his 'flying' undergoes. Dispossession, which in an oral storytelling situation would take such simple forms as the interjection of subversive comments by a listener, can enter written narrative in more subtle ways, often projecting itself into enunciative acts represented within the utterance. In Boccaccio's story its effects are on display in the means by which narratorial initiative shifts from one position to another: as Alberto, the initial agent, becomes the acted-upon, the power to tell is revealed as perturbable and even reversible. To begin with, Alberto's amorous scheme develops from one narrative relation (in which he, as pseudo-confessor, receives the inept story of Lisetta's vanity from her own lips and finds it 'lacking in force' – *fastidio ad udire*) and is then put into action by means of another (his more compelling fiction about what Gabriel had told him). The subsequent reversal stems from Lisetta's wish to share the news in a kind of secular confession with her confidante, who relates what is teasingly called 'the whole story' further until it spreads through this city of gossips and makes Alberto the object of pursuit. After escaping, he invents a tale to explain his bedraggled condition; but this, while gaining initial credence, is soon overpowered by the one that has circulated more widely. Alberto's host then tells *him* a false story to gain his trust and bring him to the public place where the story can be arrested along with the character, since nothing remains undivulged to anyone – the secret is fully out. Thus the balance of power alters in each shift from receiving to retelling: confessor becomes fabricator, confidante becomes gossip, protector becomes proclaimer, and so the seducer becomes the se-duced, himself led astray and away. Alberto is punished not because he fails to be a 'good man' but because he loses narrative control.

There are, after all, other clerical rogues elsewhere in the *Decameron* whose final fortunes are less grim – because in the long run they show greater command of enunciative dexterity. Cross-reference to these involves reframing the 'circumtext' more extensively, but in a way that Pampinea's story licenses. For she herself draws attention to the question of alternative storytelling strategies by her own decision at the outset to introduce a subversive shift of tone: in lieu of the kind of tale requested by her king-for-the-day, she offers something her female companions will prefer. Then she proceeds to deliver a diatribe on hypocrisy in the Church, and this irresistibly calls to a reader's mind other *Decameron* stories, from the very first (in which the villainous Ser Cepparello hoodwinks a friar with a false confession, so eloquent that eventually he is worshipped as a saint) to VI, 10 (in which the

BEYOND NARRATOLOGY?

virtuoso fictioneer Fra Cipolla plans, like Alberto, to profit from a fraud concerning the angel Gabriel – in this case by touting as a sacred relic a feather allegedly from the angelic pinion – but has to improvise ingeniously when his conjuror's bag turns out to contain the wrong prop). Such instances, as in IV, 2 but with better ultimate success for the chief fibber, highlight narrative agility as a means of turning tables, shifting positions, reallocating discursive power. (Indeed, Day VI is explicitly devoted to tales of narratorial cunning and power reversal, including notably some in which women use verbal skills to extricate themselves from positions of discursive and social disadvantage.)

Through the processes of embedding, this power to shift the balance of relation extends from the tale Pampinea tells to her own situation in telling it, and beyond that in turn to the master-narrator's frame. For Boccaccio – or, rather, 'Boccaccio', an extradiegetic narrator impersonating an author – has himself effected an enunciative shift by entering the frame of Day IV with an introductory story that is incorporated into an apologia addressed directly to his audience of 'dearest ladies' and indirectly to his audience of carping critics. And in telling this story he makes explicit the question of narrative unity:

> I should like to recount not an entire tale (for in doing so it might appear that I wished to mix my own tales with those of such a worthy company as I have described to you) but merely a portion of a tale, so that its very incompleteness will separate it from any others in my book.

This tongue-in-cheek disclaimer is followed by an anecdote that is indeed brief, but no less self-evidently whole than others. While not articulating an elaborate plot, it does put into play a set of rhetorical figures that, in the context of the apologia and address, links narrative acts with 'the pleasures or the power of natural affection' (specifically, appetites for food and sex) and with the social exchange of gratifications.

At this point our demonstration may be allowed to rest temporarily, for it has brought us to the issue of self-situational storytelling, which is Chambers's main concern.

IV

Chambers's achievement is to have brought formalist and contextualist approaches into a distinctive convergence. Instead of regarding narrative as just a relation *of* happenings, Chambers regards it primarily as a relation *between* communicants – one that, for each party, 'rests on the assumption of exchanging a gain for a loss' (51): attention for information, and vice versa. Within the texts chosen for analysis Chambers discerns 'indices of contractual and transactional understandings' (10), but the form they take is not generalised as a universal narrative quintessence; they are seen as registering the particular historical situation of these exchanges. Following Walter Benjamin (1969), who observed a decline in the authority of the storyteller and in the informational or use-value of narration, Chambers traces the implications of this phenomenon: the less utilitarian a commodity becomes, the more seductive it must become (commercial advertising bristles with examples, as Judith Williamson (1978) has shown), and thus the literary text under capitalism, materially alienated from its potential readership, enters a system of exchange value 'in which its significance, or worth, is a function of its interpretability as a complex sign for which other discursive signs can be substituted' (12). Accordingly, in the group of nineteenth-century French and English short stories that he examines in detail, Chambers finds embedded figural acknowledgements of the necessity for fiction to 'trade in the manipulation of desire (that is, the desire to narrate must seek to arouse some corresponding desire for narration)' (11).

The most distinctive form of this embedding is the self-referential reduplicative textual effect to which Gide first gave the name *mise-en-abyme* and which Dällenbach has codified systematically in *The Mirror in the Text* (1989). Whereas Rimmon-Kenan gives it only passing mention (1983: 93) with an apology for not treating it properly, *mise-en-abyme* is at the heart of Chambers's discussion. What is it? Three sorts of specularity are involved: (1) a direct synecdochic reflection (e.g. the parable of the doorkeeper in Kafka's *The Trial*, or the Pyramus and Thisbe tapestry in Maupassant's *Une Vie*); (2) an infinite series of identical analogies (e.g. the receding images arranged by De Selby's parallel mirrors in Flann O'Brien's *The Third Policeman*); (3) an *aporia* in which the reflexive relation is paradoxical (e.g. Escher's drawing of an autographic pair of hands). These various hypodiegetic reflections may function as models, or ironic anti-models, of some aspect of the text within which they sit. In one kind of case, *mise-en-abyme de l'énoncé*, some figure (episode, character, image) serves to repeat in miniature the text's thematic statement; thus, as Chambers remarks, the song that Michael Furey is reported as having sung in Joyce's 'The Dead' confirms the sense of exclusion from intimacy that pervades the enclosing tale. In another case, *mise-en-abyme de l'énonciation*, it is the act of narration rather than its content that gets internally replicated; thus, in Balzac's 'Sarrasine', the narrator's own intimate storytelling relationship with Mme de Rochefide, shaped by desire and circumstance, corresponds to the story's account of motives that govern the unconsummated affair of the young artist and his beloved. There are further sorts of mise-en-abyme but they are generally variants on this mirroring of an enunciatory situation, which is the sort most relevant to Chambers's investigations because it highlights the mixture of freedom and constraint in one's dealings with 'readerly' (*lisible*) texts: it 'allows for relatively intense interpretive involvement on the part of the reader' and yet, on the other hand, 'limits the reader's options in approaching the text, and does so in a way that is more precise and explicit, more directive of a specific reading, than, say dialogic interplay between segments of the text' (35).

Through several intricate analyses of individual stories, Chambers gives nuance to Paul de Man's bold generalisation that 'any narrative is primarily the allegory of its own reading' (1979: 76). He begins with a chapter on Poe's 'The Purloined Letter', where the previous sportive acts of Lacan (1970) and Derrida (1975) prove none too hard for Chambers to follow, and then a chapter on Balzac's 'Sarrasine' that rivals in its finesse even the outstanding commentaries by Roland Barthes (1974) and Barbara Johnson (1980). To indicate a rivalrous element in the way each interpretation proceeds is only to note something of which Chambers is well aware. Indeed, with a fitting sense of irony, his text in its turn embeds a shrewdly self-situating component, which reflects not only on nineteenth-century fictional practice but also on current critical practice and on its own place within that practice. Rivalry itself, as one of the lineaments of a critical 'Will to Power', is thus confronted, confessed, contextualised. This occurs most explicitly in the chapter on Henry James's 'The Figure in the Carpet', a story that concerns a closed world ... of professionalism in which the text–reader relationship is at the centre of a network of rivalries and ambitions, and critical 'mastery' of a text is seen (in the event, rather falsely) as the key to reputation and authority – in short, a career.

(152)

Chambers notes that 'the struggle for power among James's characters is still pursued in the discourse of their descendants', and in this connection he cites a debate on 'The Figure in the Carpet' between Rimmon-Kenan and J. Hillis Miller. The former, in her 1977 book on James, 'set out with exemplary clarity and exhaustiveness the conflicting evidence that makes the traditional questions (What is the secret? Is there a secret?) undecidable' (Chambers 1984: 167) but, in presuming to adopt a position of authoritatively neutral adjudication, did not manage to escape the trap into which most critics of this story (like its narratee Drayton Deane) have fallen: allowing their own focus on the text 'to be determined by the narrator's obsession with Vereker's "secret"' (165). Chambers's leaning is evidently towards Hillis Miller's side of the debate in *Poetics Today*; Miller argues that what Rimmon-Kenan regards as 'a relatively closed phenomenon' of logically incompatible interpretations is in fact an incessantly oscillating recognition that each reading inheres in the other.[6] And yet Chambers, seeing Miller's polemic, too, as caught within the narrow hermeneutic circle imposed by the narrator, goes beyond it to indicate the more varied social relations inscribed in the story through its embeddings of different readerships and listeners.

He concludes his book by emphasising that the reflexive communicational models included within his chosen texts function paradoxically: '*without* them the story could not "work", but *with* them it cannot work since they reveal the conditions under which it works and thus defuse its action.' While noting the deconstructive affiliations of this view, Chambers gently dissociates it from that of the Yale critics such as Hillis Miller; for he sees this self-undoing power of narrative 'less as a universal quality of texts than as a situational necessity, tied to the current position of literature in our culture' (221).

Although Chambers's work puts us well on the road towards an ample theory of narrative exchanges, it cannot take us all the way. Its drawbacks for our purposes here are twofold. First – as he himself points out – it does not establish whether his method is applicable beyond the range of writings that so canonically represent the alienated status of literary art in industrial society. (His more recent book *Mélancolie et opposition* (1987), fine though it is, still confines its scope to the period when modernist fiction was emergent.) What of narrative in other times and places: do medieval and postmodern texts alike, and African and Australian and Icelandic, also 'trade in the manipulation of desire' (or in anything else), and if so how are their different discursive contexts registered and framed? What of genres other than the novel and short story – say a mythic tale, or an autobiographical poem? What of fictions that have not been institutionalised as 'literature' – say an avant-garde collage of words and pictures, or the kind of text that a child invents, dictates to an adult scribe, and conjoins with graphics? Our inquiry in this book will gather in examples of each of these.

A second impediment is that Chambers consistently attributes quasi-personified and seemingly autonomous agency to a text, with scant regard to the actual variety of operations that may be performed on it by its differently situated readers. Literary texts have 'the power of producing meanings', they are 'seductive', they 'take the initiative', they 'exert authority' (13–14, *et passim*). Without a complementary theory of framing, his analyses seem lopsided, and considerably less 'pragmatic' than they aspire to be. In this respect, *Story and Situation* appears after all to remain nostalgically attached to the structuralist notion that texts are treatable as self-contained semiotic systems. Have we been too hasty, then, in crediting Chambers with an advance on those early quasi-linguistic approaches to story structure? In order to assess what remains at stake in the search for a post-narratological theory, it will be convenient for us to go back now to the tale of Brother Alberto and to see how fully it yields to the kind of scrutiny methodised in Tzvetan Todorov's *Grammaire du Décaméron* (1969a), which was hailed as 'the most important step forward in basic narratology' since the one taken by the pioneer Vladimir Propp and which can be regarded as representing the heyday of structuralist confidence.[7] While it may seem late in the day to be offering a critique of something that others have already appraised thoroughly, this will serve as an economical way of reviewing important issues – not all of which are salient in previous commentaries. There is special interest for us in the fact that *Grammaire du Décaméron* partly surpasses the limitations of its rigid analytical schema to produce an astute, though flawed, account of exchange in the social context of Boccaccio's stories.

V

Todorov's general argument is that the structure of narrative discourse can be represented in quasi-grammatical terms. This does not mean literally examining grammar as such. The linguistic organisation of an individual text in no way enters into his analysis. Instead he distils only the most basic formulaic ingredients, considering these without reference to their rhetorical medium of actual words and sentences as constituting an abstract schema, a summary of a putative ur-syntax 'at the level of the deep structure' (1969a: 19).[8] In effect, this amounts to a substructure of plot or interlinked actions which the linguistic patterns supposedly manifest and decorate.

Thus he begins by indicating three general features of any *récit*: semantic (the content evoked), syntactic (the combination of parts) and rhetorical or verbal (diction, figurative qualities and so forth). Declaring that the third of these is irrelevant to his inquiries, Todorov ignores it, concentrating mainly on 'syntactic' elements of plot with some passing attention to semantic aspects. This neglect of verbal features is a damaging flaw in his system; for, as our earlier discussion of the tale of Alberto showed, far from lying outside the structure of narration, they can do much to shape it.

More specifically, Todorov's procedure is to dismantle any single *Decameron* story into 'sequences', themselves consisting of 'propositions', which in turn consist of 'categories'. His breakdown of units does not stop there, but those are the three main subsystems. Now a sequence is a series of propositions that we recognise to be complete, *achevée*, and may therefore constitute a whole story in itself. (Here, surely, the question of textual unity is obviously begged; but for the moment let us pass on to other items in Todorov's list.) A proposition is, so to speak, an independent clause – 'the basic syntactic unit' (19) – within a plot synopsis. A category is a narrative part-of-speech, and there are three sorts: proper nouns (which denominate characters – these, then, are the subjects of propositions), adjectives (which describe the attributes of characters) and verbs (which designate the action).

BEYOND NARRATOLOGY?

It is unnecessary to follow Todorov's triadic compulsion into his refinements of the adjectival category, but the classification of verbs is worth noticing here. What he does is to compress Propp's thirty-one plot 'functions' into three types: (1) to modify a situation, (2) to commit a misdeed, (3) to punish. Any action in the *Decameron*, he asserts, can be boiled down to one of these or its negative or opposite. This looks very tidy indeed, compared with Propp's straggling list. But it is either too reductive or not reductive enough. On the one hand, precision is lost by making 'modify' (verb 1) cover such very different plot developments as the seduction of A by B and the moral reform of Y by Z. On the other hand, reduction could just as logically proceed even further, because verb 1 is broad enough to include the other two; yet when that is recognised, Todorov's elaborate system of posited categories subsides into the very routine observation that a plot normally involves a change of situation.

Todorov would not deny that differential qualities disappear in his reductive operation, but he would regard them as merely aesthetic and thus irrelevant to the business of structural analysis. Quite forthrightly he states (1969b) that 'the individual specificity of each work' does not come within his project. Hence his unapologetic disregard of what he calls 'the verbal aspect', the range of rhetorical features in Boccaccio's stories, since it is at that material level of signifiers that the individual specificity of a work is most evident. His contention is not that stylistic qualities are trivial. Admitting that 'the verbal aspect can often be the most important in the text' (1969a: 18), he mentions such examples as the witty inventiveness of dialogue that extends one *Decameron* story (VII, 9) far beyond the demands of its narrative syntax. Yet his conviction is that 'we are obliged to choose a single aspect of the story and to examine it in its totality'. Again the major question is begged in this last phrase. Where does the completeness of a given tale lie, and how does it incorporate any subtotal, any self-contained 'aspect', any 'basic unity'?

Todorov's procedure is faulty on another count as well, which has more often been noticed: it is innocent of the reading process. What he says about a narrative grammar, with elements analogous to those which constitute our real language, omits to explain or even ask how a reader comes to perceive such an analogy. By what specific tokens are plots recognisable as plots? What is it at the 'surface' level that leads us to detect the subterranean formula?

What exactly is the relation between the actual verbs that occur in a text and our awareness of those basic verbal types (transgress, punish, modify) that are said to underlie them? In our ordinary reading experience, is plot indeed virtually identical with structure, as Todorov apparently assumes, or do we derive our sense of the latter from elements that he excludes?[9]

Holloway (1979) pinpoints a major defect in Todorov's concentration on event-items: that it fails to consider the importance of suppositions in linking what happens with what might happen. This line of argument is valuable in its demonstration that 'the totality of a narrative is greatly more than the totality of its events' (50), and there is considerable subtlety in Holloway's discussion of the process whereby various suppositions are progressively advanced or altered. But he neglects in turn to consider exactly what constitutes narrative totality. One may well say that 'the structure of the whole is ... represented by the entire *series* of ... relational propositions' (9) – yet when is a series entire? By implication Holloway suggests that a series is entire, a story unified, when the reader meets a 'terminating event': one that, while it need not be 'what comes in the very last place ... is indeed what resolves the narrative and finally determines its conclusion'. Thus in *Decameron* stories the terminating event achieves a 'dexterous resumption and modulation of earlier events' (13).

Though apt enough as a broad generalisation, this is not a great advance over Todorov's own analysis, according to which a story may comprise one or more 'sequences', a sequence being 'a series of propositions that one perceives as complete, as being able to constitute an independent story' (1969a: 20); as we noted in passing earlier, since 'a novella can contain several sequences', the kind of unity that Todorov attributes to a sequence is unable to determine that of the text *in toto*. All Todorov can suggest later in his book by way of clarification is that 'the syntactic structure of the novella' can be divided into two: 'the first part reveals a certain state of affairs, while the second provides a transformation of it' (76). Again: 'the second part takes up again the story of the first, while making it undergo diverse transformations' (77). This, he says, is like a question-and-response dyad, which forms 'a unity both logical and spatial'.

If this is in some sense true, it is also a little facile, remaining too distant from textual particulars to reveal just what makes a given story seem to cohere. How much can it say about the tale of Alberto? As it happens, Todorov barely mentions this particular story, though a few passing references do confirm what one would expect his method of drastic précis to produce: it is a case of transgression followed eventually by punishment. But even in Todorov's terms this summary is not adequate, for as he himself notes briefly (69) the story of Alberto juxtaposes two sequences end-to-end; and while he wants to cite this as an example of linkage through entailment (*enchaînement*), he seems uneasily aware that an inconvenient question still lingers: 'How is a combination of sequences achieved?' (70). Our own earlier discussion has shown that the text's seriality is much more complicated than any linking of action sequences, and that any construction of it 'as a whole' (or a seeming whole) needs to recognise (1) the unfolding of several figurative elements and positional moves not accounted for in Todorov's schema, and (2) the fact that unity can only be a semantic concept, indicating an investment of meaning within a framed textual field.

Nevertheless, it did not escape Todorov's notice that exchange has an important bearing on the *Decameron* tales. Indeed, he sees it as a theme that unifies the work as a whole. His observations on this matter come right near the end of his book, are the most incisive part of it, and step surprisingly outside the ambit of his previous analysis. They seem almost an afterthought, an attempt to counter the excessive attention to syntactic elements by giving final emphasis to the semantic. He argues otherwise, contending that the exchange pattern he discerns is isomorphic with the story-grammar already delineated: 'the formal structure of question and response and the semantic structure of exchange are in fact one and the same' (82). But it is from Todorov's interpretive activity as a meaning-maker, not from any independent evidence locatable empirically in a story-grammar, that he draws his recognition of ways in which Boccaccio's work enacts multiple exchanges.

Only in the final pages of his book does Todorov leave aside his elaboration of a 'syntactic' schema and pass 'to the semantic side of the tales', where he finds this pervasive theme of exchange. The social world represented in the *Decameron* is one in which a certain system of exchange relations dominates everything; but this, he observes, is violated in story after story. Sometimes characters blatantly disregard the rules supposed to govern their dealings, sometimes circumstances prevent them from complying, sometimes they cheat while pretending to comply, sometimes they try to alter the terms of exchange, sometimes they are powerful enough simply to take what they want rather than interacting reciprocally – and so on. Todorov sees in this transgressive pattern a championing by Boccaccio of 'free enterprise': there is supposedly a macro-structural homology between action sequences in the *Decameron* and nascent capitalist impulses in the society it represents. He asserts that the contesting of exchange norms by the new bourgeoisie is 'the moral of the *Decameron* tales. Free and non-coded action (which we called modifying action *a*) is the most valued in that system.' This comment lacks cogency, for two reasons. The first is that if 'modification', as we have noted, is broadly applicable to the structure of almost any story in any place and time, it cannot also be in itself a specific index to the political economy of fourteenth-century Italy. The second is that (as Fish points out in his critique of Halliday[10]) one cannot infer evaluative meanings from formal structures alone: there is nothing in the mere repetition of exchange relations or plot devices that makes a free enterprise ideology seem commendable rather than the contrary. Although Brother Alberto is a spectacular rule-breaker, infringing for his own ends the established exchange structures of ecclesiastical confession and marital contract, one can hardly say that his transgressions are appreciatively endorsed by this story's 'syntactical aspect'. On the face of it the subsequent outcome might seem to support Todorov's view, since the crafty Venetian in whose hands Alberto places himself does act with proto-capitalist opportunism in duplicitously extracting fifty ducats from the friar before handing him over to the authorities. But this false bargain, capping the previous false bargain that Alberto had struck with Lisetta, is not itself a 'rupture of the old system'. After all, the finale reconfirms that system by exposing Alberto to public chastisement and then handing him over to his religious order for incarceration.

Besides, the major problem is that Todorov confines his discussion to the represented content of these stories, to exchange as a theme of their utterance (*énoncé*), without considering at all how power-relations are enunciated negotiably within their narrative structure, which is itself constituted by substitutive rhetoric. Due attention to those factors would have revealed that the *Decameron* stories engage not just with one system of economic exchange but with a discursive amalgam in which values of an utterance can quickly replace one another and positions of enunciation can shift accordingly. Several registers mix in the tale of Brother Alberto, and that mix greatly complicates the transaction it offers to a reader. They include folk wisdom (the specious introductory proverb, according to which a reputation for goodness can be an aid to wickedness), diatribe against clerical hypocrisy ('their voices humble and soft whenever they want to extract your money'), derision of the garrulous local citizenry ('telling him a lot of things about herself, like the true Venetian she was – nitwits, all of them'), legal parlance ('no will was drawn up but he was named trustee and executor'), religious pontification ('began admonishing her, saying she was guilty of the sin of vainglory, and many another thing besides'), mercantile bargaining ('if he didn't want to be turned over to Lisetta's kin, he had better see to it that he secured fifty ducats') and moral invective ('called him the vilest names and told him the worst things that were ever said to any living scoundrel'). This mixture of registers makes possible various rhetorical analogies, as in the frequent play on religious images linked with the pervasive trope of transfiguration: the visit of the 'angel' to Lisetta parodies the Annunciation, the vocabulary of paradisial transport is wittily appropriated in the bedroom scenes, and that of salvation is punningly hinted at in the description of Alberto's final plight as *uom salvatico convertito* (turned into a savage). It is out of all those assorted linguistic transactions that the second tale of the fourth day fashions its own narrative exchanges; and that tale in turn is situated, as we have already seen, within a number of enunciative ploys that show how discursive power may reinflect itself.

In retrospect it is clear that his 1969 study of the *Decameron* shows narratology at a crossroads that Todorov could not yet fully recognise. Before long he would come to see that 'narrative is a discourse, not a series of events' (1977: 55). But as Rimmon-Kenan's book shows, narratology has not altogether relinquished the classic structuralist premise that unity is inherent in a syntax of events. The following chapters will show in more detail how the unitary patterns on which interpretation depends stem from acts of framing, which are always susceptible to reframing in terms of the rhetorically substitutive movement of figures (whether tropes, characters or situations) and by the power-charged interplay between narrator and narratee.

2

FRAMING THE TEXT

> Framing occurs, but there is no frame.
> (Derrida 1978: 83)[1]

I

In my Introduction, through a loose analogy with factors that impinge on the contemplation of a painting, I indicated broadly how a reader is able to 'frame' a textual exchange and how the text conversely frames the reader's act of framing. It is time to pursue these points more fully, but in order to do so I need first to sketch in some detail a particular scene of reading and to defer for a moment the analysis of its implications.

Suppose that you pick up a book, open it at random, and find this:

> The bugles of England were blowing o'er the sea,
> As they had called a thousand years, calling now to me;
> They woke me from dreaming in the dawning of the day,
> The bugles of England – and how could I stay?. . .

Just below those lines, your eye falls next on an untitled, unattributed couplet, alluding to an ancient battle between Greeks and Persians:

> Beneath our scarlet fields Thermopylae's secret ran,
> The speech of Freedom is one, and one is the Soul of Man.

Overleaf, a poem entitled 'Bell-birds' has an unmistakably Australian provenance. But turning the pages now in the opposite direction, you find that the bugles-of-England verses are preceded by an account of 'The Homecoming of Ulysses'; and before that comes this:

FRAMING THE TEXT

> They whisper that you are dying,
> Mother of mine and me:
> Like a sick old eagle crying
> Out of the northern sea.
>
> But we answer, Mother, O Mother,
> Back to thy breast we come,
> We of thy breed, and seed, and none other
> From the beat of an alien drum.

Reference in later stanzas to 'the new world' confirms that this is a declaration of colonial dependence on the mother country. Preceding it in turn is another episode from Homer's *Odyssey*, in which Ulysses survives the deadly temptations of the Sirens' song. Before that is James Hogg's 'The Skylark', plainly Scottish in setting and language, and before that an Australian story by Mary Grant Bruce in which a thoughtless little lad from the bush has a remedial dream that admonishes him not to keep domestic animals tethered. And so on in either direction through the book: a strange miscellany – but not without a pattern.

If you open it now at another spot and browse a bit more, this same pattern soon emerges again: not just Australian settings and themes side by side with British (as Clancy of the Overflow rubs shoulders with Robin of Sherwood, and a paragraph on harvest season in the Mallee comes next to an ode to Boadicea), but also a tendency to conflate British and Australian patriotism indistinguishably, along with a dash of ancient classical heroism, and a preoccupation with images of voyaging at a distance from one's homeland. Further examples are plentiful. Straight after a passage about travels in the north Australian outback there is a poem by the Irish Romantic Thomas Moore called 'The Journey Onwards', its imagery suggesting an analogue to the colonial condition:

> As travellers oft look back at eve
> When eastward darkly going,
> To gaze upon that light they leave
> Still faint behind them glowing –
> So, when the close of pleasure's day
> To gloom hath near consigned us,
> We turn to catch one fading ray
> Of joy that's left behind us.

NARRATIVE EXCHANGES

A few pages later, this motif is reinforced in a poem by Arthur Hugh Clough that begins:

> Where lies the land to which the ship would go?
> Far, far ahead is all her seamen know.
> And where the land she travels from? Away,
> Far, far behind, is all that they can say.

And soon after that, these explicitly antipodean lines from Adam Lindsay Gordon:

> Hark! The bells on distant cattle
> Waft across the range,
> Through the golden-tufted wattle,
> Music low and strange;
> Like the marriage peal of fairies
> Comes the tinkling sound,
> Or like chimes of sweet St. Mary's
> On far English ground.

What is this quaint collection, and why the quick trot here through some of its contents? Our concern is with framing; but before coming to detailed explanations, let us look now at just one story within the book. It is called 'The White Goat', and its opening paragraph goes like this:

> When the white goat reached the mountain, there was general delight. Never had the old fir-trees seen anything so pretty. They received her like a princess. The chestnut-trees bent to the ground to kiss her with the tips of their branches. The golden gorse opened wide to let her pass, and smelt just as sweet as it could. In fact the whole mountain welcomed her.

There follows a description of this small goat's pleasure in her new-found freedom. Blanchette, as she is called, has wilfully slipped her tether and left the security of home. Now read on.

> Once, coming to the edge of a slope with a bit of laurel in her teeth, she saw below, far below in the plain, the house of her master with the meadow behind it; and she laughed till she cried. 'How small it is!' she said. 'How could I ever have lived there?' Poor little thing! Being perched so high, she fancied she was as tall as the world.

> Suddenly the wind freshened. The mountain grew violet; it was dusk.... She shuddered. There came a howl on the mountain: 'Hoo, hoo!'
> She thought of the wolf. All day that silly young thing had never once thought of it. At the same moment, a horn sounded far, far down the valley. It was that kind master of hers, making a last effort. 'Hoo, hoo!' howled the wolf. 'Come back! Come back!' cried the horn.
> Blanchette felt a wish to return; but, remembering the stake, the rope, the hedge around the field, she thought that she never could endure that life again, and it was better to remain where she was. The horn ceased to sound. The goat heard behind her the rustling of leaves. She turned, and saw in the shadow two short ears erect and two eyes shining. It was the wolf.

Then we are given a description of this menacing beast, and told that Blanchette, though without hope, resolves to defend herself as long as she can. And so to the last couple of paragraphs:

> More than ten times she made the wolf draw back to get breath. During each of these truces, the dainty little thing nibbled one more blade of her dearly loved grass; then, with her mouth full, she returned to the combat. It lasted all through the night. From time to time, the little white goat looked up at the stars as they danced on the cloudless sky, and said to herself, 'Oh, if only I can hold out till dawn!'
> One after another, the stars went out. Blanchette redoubled the blows of her horns, and the wolf the snap of his teeth. A pale gleam showed on the horizon. The hoarse crowing of a cock arose from a barnyard. 'At last!' said the poor little goat, who had only awaited the dawn to die; and she stretched herself out on the ground in her pretty white coat all spotted with gore. Then the wolf fell upon her, and ate her up.

Now the meanings derived from this story will depend substantially on the ways in which it is framed in the course of reading. The term 'frame' has been variously used in literary criticism and related fields with no systematic analysis of the different senses involved, which extend from that which is current in cognitive linguistics (a mental schema for organising information)[2] to that which is current in narratology (an embedded structure of tales within tales).[3] There is a need to sort out, clarify and amend these usages. In what follows, four distinguishable but interrelated kinds of 'framing' will be labelled, schematised and cursorily illustrated, with increasing attention to ways in which they are intricated with the narrative processes of substitution and dispossession. The general basis for regarding acts of reading as acts of framing is quite simple: when a text is made to mean something, it is always by being both separated from and joined with a variety of references. The metaphor of framing aptly indicates that in order to perceive and understand anything (say, a poem) one must provisionally distinguish it from other things while also relating it to them – as one distinguishes figure from ground, picture from wall, words from page, foreground from background, here from there. Framing is the process of demarcating phenomena in a double-edged way that is simultaneously inclusive and exclusive.

II

The most tangible basis for framing consists of a text's immediate, material environment. One looks at the surrounding items that situate, label and sign it, constituting one's perception of its outside and inside. As a convenient if inelegant shorthand, the reading operation that draws on such adjunctive elements will be called *circumtextual framing*. It may include aspects of the physical format through which a text is presented, any cover or prefatory information, general titles, authorial ascriptions, blurbs, dedications, epigraphs, marginalia, footnotes, opening and closing markers (such as the 'moral' of a fable) and – if the particular text under consideration does not reach fully to those palpable borderlines – any other texts incorporated into the same physical unit, which in the present case is a book.[4] This is not to say that such items simply provide a rigid boundary fence around the text, or that a reader can always be sure where a text stops and its surroundings start. Nor indeed is 'the text' an unproblematically given entity; only through a reader's interpretive act can any items be *perceived* as delineating a space occupied by the text, a space within which that assemblage of verbal signs (itself also a merely perceptual unit) can acquire coherent sense. Jacques

FRAMING THE TEXT

Derrida's aphorism is very much to the point: 'Framing occurs, but there is no frame' (1978: 83).

Although deprived so far of full information, you already know something about the framing (in this circumtextual sense) of the story of Blanchette because you have glanced at a selection of the textual segments that surround it. Even from those brief samples it is easy to recall one or two recurrent themes or motifs that could have a bearing on an interpretation of 'The White Goat': most obviously, the sadness or danger leaving one's home behind, and the rhetorical link between sacrifice and freedom. Closer comparative analysis might show that the values attached to sacrifice and freedom differ importantly from one piece to another according to the values attached to home. At any rate, it is high time to reveal more about the larger circumtextual frame of this book itself.

'The White Goat' appears in the middle of a school anthology called *The Victorian Readers: Sixth Book*, published by the Government Printer, Melbourne, in 1929. A whole generation of Australian students was nurtured on the series to which it belongs, and no doubt class sets can still be found in some school storerooms and libraries. The Ministry of Education for the state of Victoria has now reprinted the series of eight readers, neatly and nostalgically boxed, for the general 'gift' market: a wonderful time capsule, not least in its blithe mixture of miscellaneous representations of Australian life with numerous tributes to British flora, fauna and pluck. Several bits of prose and verse already mentioned exemplify those juxtapositions, but even the visual components reinforce them: a portrait of Charles Dickens faces a drawing of a little lad wandering past gumtrees, a sketch of Henry Lawson's 'Loaded Dog' is soon followed by a Wordsworthian scene of daffodils, and so on. The predominance of those sorts of mingled elements, when considered as framing circumtextually the story about Blanchette and the wolf, seems to imply that an Australian/British conjunction is ideologically normative; and any occasional item fetched from a different cultural source, such as the Homeric extracts or this tale of 'The White Goat' (translated and adapted from a book by Alphonse Daudet, set in provincial France), will probably tend to be interpreted less in terms of that particular source than as a general parable. Thus Blanchette's story becomes a cautionary tale about the dire results of undervaluing one's protective home, mistaking wilful independence for freedom – and even more specifically, within this *Sixth Book* of the *Victorian Readers*, a little allegory for restive colonial Australians of that period, with the 'Come back' appeal of the kind master's horn seeming to echo those 'bugles of England' that were calling in the first poem quoted.

And now to another kind of framing. Just as the meanings of a text will be shaped in part, as we have seen, by the various physical adjuncts that can seem to enclose it circumtextually, so in a broader sense the text also gets framed by any kind of information, expectation or preoccupation that a reader may bring to bear as material for interpreting it.[5] To call this *extratextual* is not, of course, to ignore the poststructuralist axiom that there can be no *hors-texte*, for while nothing may evade textuality it is certainly the case that many things do fall outside the verbal matter that is pragmatically taken to comprise a particular text, outside whatever is regarded as conjoined circumtextually with it, and outside whatever it is held to cite or refer to explicitly (e.g. other texts).

Some kind of extratextual framing always occurs; one cannot read without it. Thus in the case of 'The White Goat', at a very simple level, all readers will make sense of the story's movement towards its finale partly in terms of what they know about the ways of real goats and wolves and about the attributes of animals in certain kinds of texts (for instance their ability to talk and think and feel like humans). It may also happen that some readers adduce other considerations for extratextual framing, according to what they know and what interests them. Someone well informed about the private life of the author, Alphonse Daudet, might look at 'The White Goat' as an autobiographical fable. Or a feminist reader might analyse the way gender roles are represented in this text.

Inevitably there is some arbitrariness about the extratextual framing of a particular reader's engagement with a particular text, since it depends largely on his or her stock of things known and assumed. It is responsible for most disagreements between readers because it can encompass a multitude of variable preconceptions as well as different degrees and sorts of cultural learning. But such differences are not capriciously personal; they stem from institutionalised reading practices. For instance, extratextual framing may sometimes include rigid notions about literary genres, derived mostly from certain educational formations: a set of assumptions, let us say, concerning 'the' short story, linked perhaps with a tenacious attachment to protocols of realism for characters and plots. Or it may be a prejudice, whether fully conscious or not, about what counts as literary value, or a habit of trying to extract a summarisable theme or authorial intention from whatever is read.

In any case, however, what makes any particular frame of extratextual reference more or less apt is the scope it gives a reader to draw meaning from other framing elements in and around the given text – from circumtextual elements, of the sort already looked at, and from two more framing elements yet to be discussed. This latter pair is often elusive, and sometimes hardly evident at all. No salient examples of them can be found in the 'The White Goat', and their inconspicuousness in that case is the result of editorial curtailment. The difference that this makes will be clear when we turn to another white goat.

III

Suppose you are now holding a different book instead. Above a brightly depicted harvest scene, its front cover announces that this one is the 'Penguin Classics' (1978) version of Daudet's *Letters from my Windmill*. The back cover tells you a few things about the author, and about this edition. (There are also incidental trade details, such as the recommended retail price, explicitly marking it as an item for commercial exchange; but exhaustive description is unnecessary here.) Part of the cover material, you find, is repeated inside on the preliminary pages. The contents list adds certain information, notably that the book comprises a sequence of parts, most of them numbered and individually titled.[6] Then come various prefatory materials from author and translator, then three of the 'Letters' themselves – whereupon you reach, as the fourth numbered item, 'Monsieur Seguin's Goat', which is a fuller version of the piece encountered in the *Victorian Reader*. Beyond 'Monsieur Seguin's Goat' lie a score of other 'Letters', and the book is rounded off by a few pages of advertisements for other 'Penguin Classics' translated from the French, such as Victor Hugo's *Notre Dame de Paris*. And so to the back cover again.

What you have just been contemplating is a particular set of circumtextual materials for framing this different version of the story. 'Monsieur Seguin's Goat' is surrounded by concentric rings, and marked off from them by certain aspects of layout: it has a separate set of pages to itself, a new section number and its own title; and what might be thought of as 'the story itself' or the 'inner text' is introduced by an epistolary formula, a quasi-postal address ('To Monsieur Pierre Gringoire,/Lyrical Poet,/Paris'). Yet on closer inspection the dividing lines are not at all clear-cut. Meanings are partly dispersed among those outer casings that seem to enclose the 'inner text' so neatly, and correspondingly its internal structure also comes to seem more and more onion-like. To recognise this is to differ, at least in emphasis, from Genette (1987), whose general discussion of what are here called circumtextual elements assumes that their status is quite distinct from that of any text they accompany, and also from Maclean (1988: 24–7, 31), who designates them as first-order illocutionary acts on the part of an author or editor, in contrast to an enclosed fictive world of second-order speech acts.

'Monsieur Seguin's Goat' is less compartmentalised than that. As a brief example of the spread of signification through its circumtextual membrane, take a passage from Daudet's preface in which he recounts how he would dream away the hours in his hillside windmill until sunset, when, 'at the call of a marine conch, the horn of Monsieur Seguin calling home his goat, I used to return for the evening meal' – return, that is, to the farmhouse where he would spend the evening listening to a hospitable old dame as she reminisced about such things as having once danced a farandole with a handsome officer who 'made her skip like a goat... all night long'. Available here, passingly and partially, is a proleptic framing of the yet-to-come story about the goat's non-return and night-long tussle: a reader is already being encouraged to place the experiences of Blanquette (as this version calls her, faithful to the French) in relation to either of these possible but different terms of reference that concern the old lady or the narrator himself. Such suggestions are undeveloped and by no means definitive; the signifier 'goat' cannot be tied to either the narrator or the old lady, for all three are later associated with other signifiers as well. Nevertheless they make the relation between text and circumtext rather complicated, working against any simple detachment of 'Monsieur Seguin's Goat' from the rest of the book.

But not only do circumtextual limit-markers shift somewhat, there is also a converse shiftiness of junctures *within* the 'text itself'. Now this is a matter of *intratextual framing*, so called because it takes shape directly from the pages themselves, in particular from whatever subdivisional signs interrupt or modulate the flow of words. The most obvious of these are spatially emphatic paragraph breaks (or line breaks in verse), section numbers and typographically marked transitions; but any component that can suddenly alter a reader's mode of apprehending the text may count as material for intratextual framing. This includes the insertion of non-verbal graphic items, from the startling blank spaces left in Faulkner's *As I Lay Dying* and Sterne's *Tristram Shandy* to the more usual ingredients of 'illustrated' books. It also includes any abrupt stylistic change (often indicating an ironic dimension), or a significant shift in focalisation. A heightened form of intratextual framing is the tale-within-a-tale, or embedded narrative, which will often have the reflexive function of commenting implicitly on the text that encloses it. And indeed any part of a text that seems to be set off in some way from the rest, a descriptive passage for instance, has the potential to work like that: to serve as an inset model or *mise-en-abyme* of the whole. Even a significant phrase that is repeated prominently during the story may have a similar framing effect, very much like the refrain in a song.

Consider the wording used right at the end of 'Monsieur Seguin's Goat': 'Hear well these words, Gringoire: "... then in the morning the wolf ate her".' This concludes the brief epilogue, which links up with the preamble to form a layer of direct admonition to the addressee or narratee, supposedly a contemporary Parisian poet for whose benefit the enclosed cautionary tale from Provence about a wilful white goat is being told. Yet epilogue merges back into tale, through a repetitive intratextual device of embedding. That formula, 'then in the morning the wolf ate her', occurs three times to signal something of structural importance about the text, something omitted from the abridged *Victorian Reader* version. For not only is the last line a variant of the sentence that concludes the account of Blanquette's demise, it has also appeared earlier with reference to one of her predecessors. Just as Blanquette's misadventure is narrated to Gringoire, so too within this account there is embedded a further misadventure story narrated to Blanquette. The concluding formula repeats almost exactly the words used earlier about one of Monsieur Seguin's previous escapees, Renaude, whose sad fate had been recounted to Blanquette as a would-be deterrent. That 'story of old Renaude' comes belatedly to the latest victim's mind when she herself eventually meets the wolf, and it is as a conscious reenactment of Renaude's night-long struggle and subsequent capitulation that Blanquette completes her own plot. In a sense, then, the story of 'Monsieur Seguin's Goat' figures as an episode from a larger implied tale. It suggests a series of reiterations, with Blanquette substituted in this instance for Renaude – who in turn was just another in a long line of lost goats. Regarded thus, Blanquette is not so much an individual delinquent as a creature whose emblematic sacrifice the narration itself requires. When the narrator uses the formula *To cut a long story short*, Monsieur Seguin's goat spent a wonderful day' (emphasis added), a reader's attention is drawn intratextually to the paradox that this text must curtail the substitutive pattern by which it proceeds: the replacement of one figure by another and then another, serially, is itself an instance of and a figure for the ongoing narrative impulse that pulls against the generic ('short' story) halter-rope.[7]

Because signs are endlessly substitutable, textual meaning is always apt to slip its tether; and because a narrator's role may in principle be taken over by another narrator, there is further potential for instability, which may also be generically troublesome. According to its preamble, the story of Blanquette's compulsion to seek out a dangerous freedom is supposed to be specifically relevant to the situation of a writer, Gringoire, in pointing a moral about the self-destructiveness of bohemian life. But though ostensibly a simple little epistolary fable as far as Gringoire the narratee is concerned, this becomes a rather different sort of text for a reader who goes beyond the purported simplicity of tone and reference to consider allegorising the anxieties of narratorial dispossession along the following lines. An explicit parallel is drawn, certainly, between Gringoire and the goat; but in that case, what might the other characters, Monsieur Seguin and the wolf, stand for? In some respects the former resembles the narrator, whose warnings to Gringoire are like Seguin's to Blanquette. To accept that equivalence is of course to regard the narrator's tale as either ironic or misconceived (at least in terms of its apparent cautionary purpose), since Seguin is said to be ignorant of goatishness and his warnings do no good at all. For all Seguin's didactic injunctions, and those of the narrator likewise, goats will be goats – and writers, writers. In a further ironic twist, this may even be taken to imply that, failing to recognise the incorrigible nature of the artist's self-destructive impulses, the narrator is no true writer himself. The overt moral can hardly be taken at face value, then; accordingly this is hardly a straightforward Aesopic fable after all, but rather a display of the need for alert self-possession in anticipating problems of narratorial control. The figure of the wolf is relevant in this regard. Given that Blanquette (the Gringoire-poet surrogate) repeats 'the story of old Renaude' as if acting out a scripted role, it follows analogically that the weaker writer is *textually* consumed while the wolf represents the irresistible force of the stronger narratorial strategy.

IV

Such intricate considerations are further complicated by another kind of framing, which is *intertextual*. This is not a matter of just casual allusions, or traces of 'influence'. Intertextuality works through devices by which a text signals how its very structure of signification depends on both similarity to and difference from certain other types of text, thus modifying a previous discursive system. When the narrator pauses in his description of Blanquette to say, 'She was nearly as charming as Esmerelda's little goat – you remember, Gringoire?', the specific reference is to Victor Hugo's *Notre-Dame de Paris* (known to English readers as *The Hunchback of Notre Dame*), in the course of which a gypsy girl called Esmerelda has problems with her small white goat and a poet called Gringoire rescues it. What larger significance does this passing mention have here? As a device for propelling the narrative movement, it works substitutively – not that Seguin's goat is expelled and Esmerelda's installed, or that one Gringoire effaces another; rather, it seems to be what Christian Metz calls 'the possibility of a substitution' that occurs here: in a Lacanian sense, 'the signifying chain reduplicates itself, a space of language opens up, one signifier is held suspended "behind" another' (Metz 1982: 210). These small shufflings have generic implications. For one thing, Hugo's poet-character had in turn been based on a well known actual writer of three centuries earlier; so Daudet's narrator, by conflating his supposedly contemporary addressee with an historical figure already fictionalised in a prior text, acknowledges that Gringoire is a type rather than a person and that the modern address-frame is just as fictive as the story it contains. At the same time the reader is implicitly invited to notice how different is the cheeky semi-conversational mode of 'Monsieur Seguin's Goat' from the massive nineteenth-century historical novel typified by *The Hunchback of Notre Dame*. Quite another kind of characterisation is at work, through quite another type of text, and intertextual framing can help a reader to recognise this.

More discreetly intertextual is an echo from Charles Perrault's 'Little Red Riding Hood'. Again, this should be understood not in terms of the empty notion of the 'influence' of one writer on another but semiotically, as the passage from one kind of sign system (or more than one) to another (Kristeva 1980: 15). A text type, such as a traditional French fairy story, can be thought of as a sign system in so far as it generates meanings in a particular set of ways – for instance through highly conventional sets of motifs (Propp 1968). The final sentence of Daudet's story (apart from a brief epilogic return to Gringoire) is this: 'Then the wolf hurled himself on the little goat and ate her.' The precise phrasing and rhythm of the original, 'Alors le loup se jeta sur la petite chèvre et la mangea', follow this particular fairytale's well-known concluding formula so closely that a French reader could hardly miss the link: ' ce méchant Loup se jeta sur le Petit Chaperon rouge, et la mangea.' A further kind of precursor text, less specifically invoked but obviously pertinent all the same, is the beast fable: and there is a particular link through La Fontaine's account of 'The Dog and the Wolf', which shares with 'Monsieur Seguin's Goat' an explicit comparison of the attractions of perilous freedom and those of safe tethering. Yet more is involved, for the wider intertextual field includes previous adaptations by Daudet himself of both Perrault's fairytale and La Fontaine's fable.[8] These were among the satirical fantasies published during his apprentice days, in the decade before *Letters from my Windmill*, and both of them anticipate 'Monsieur Seguin's Goat' in evoking the dangerous delights of bohemian freedom for a writer. But they do so in surprising ways. In Daudet's version of 'The Dog and the Wolf', it is the *latter* who is equated with the wilful freelance poet. And in his version of 'Little Red Riding Hood', which brings in additional characters drawn from Shakespearean and other sources, the closing moral about the sticky outcome of blithe hedonism is ironically qualified by being attributed to sententious old Polonius – whereas Little Red Riding Hood herself, cheerfully accepting her death as destined, advises everyone to seek pleasure without regret.

FRAMING THE TEXT

While on the one hand 'Monsieur Seguin's Goat' reworks some things written by Daudet before the *Letters*, on the other it figures as an insertion in one of his later texts. Produced in 1872 with music by Bizet, the play *L'Arlésienne* (*The Girl from Arles*), which is itself a dramatised expansion of a story from the *Letters*, incorporates virtually word for word the ending of 'Monsieur Seguin's Goat'. The play opens and closes with an account of Blanquette's surrender to the wolf, narrated by a shepherd; and just as the goat in the *Letters* had seemed to confront her death in conscious compliance with narrative exigencies, following the same pattern of night-long resistance and then death in the morning as in 'the story of old Renaude', so also in the playscript version of *The Girl from Arles* the lovesick youth, just before committing suicide, draws a direct parallel between his situation and the end of the goat's struggle (Daudet, n.d.: 334, 340–1, 429–30).

What then is to be made of these several possibilities for intertextual framing? At least they should make one cautious of any tendency to assign the text to a neat generic monotype. If a term such as 'short story' is retained, it must be with an awareness that, as Anne Freadman remarks (1987: 98), 'the rules of a genre and the formal properties of a single text will not correlate', since 'texts may, and frequently do, play several games – and thus, several partners – at once'. (By partners she means other texts.) 'Monsieur Seguin's Goat' presents itself less as a told *histoire*, stable in form, than as an adaptable *set of storytellings*, directly affiliated with a play, a novel, a fairy story, a fable – and more: for through other intertextual devices, too, the text signals its status as a meeting-place for various generic tendencies and discursive formations. While ostensibly aligning itself with homespun Provençal folktales ('If you ever come to Provence, our farmers will talk to you often about Monsieur Seguin's goat') in explicit contrast to the manner of Parisian journalists, it goes on to show that this opposition between metropolitan and provincial modes is not at all simple. For one thing, some oral features of the tale are recognisably derived from the Parisian news-sheet or *chronique*, which, as MacNamara (1972: 297) notes, often sought a style based on the personal voice; Daudet's stylistic choices here amount to 'a refusal to separate the anecdote from the actions of its telling and its hearing, from an identifiable narrator telling it in an identifiable situation'. For another thing, as Sachs (1965: 41) notes, the tone of ironic observation is characteristic of the 'Parisian boulevard wit'

– and of the things Daudet himself had been writing for years in city magazines, where indeed the *Windmill* letters themselves first appeared. Or, moving beyond contemporary affinities, one could attempt to trace the story's intertextual relations further back – only to find, once again, that 'origins' remain elusively deferred and that one is no closer to fixing the generic nature of Daudet's text. This was A.H. Krappe's (1925) discovery when he investigated the resemblance between 'Monsieur Seguin's Goat' and the tenth-century Latin poem *Ecbasis Captivi*, written in a Lorraine monastery; he could only hypothesise a common source for them in French folklore.

To return, finally, to *extratextual* framing: as pointed out earlier, this draws on the range of general knowledge and expectations that a reader needs in order to activate those other three sorts of framing; but there can be no guarantee of its adequacy to the latter in any particular instance.[9] While preconceptions are necessary to reading, they may also impede it. Among them, for example, is likely to be a set of notions based on the perceived status of the author and the supposed nature of his writings. In the present case, knowing that Daudet has long ago lost his place in the ranks of so-called 'major' writers, and is generally regarded as just a sentimental humorist specialising in bucolic vignettes, most readers will take it for granted, as if naturally, that 'Monsieur Seguin's Goat' is a lightweight piece needing none of the careful scrutiny one would expect to bring to a tale by (say) his contemporary and compatriot Flaubert. One critic notes that 'Daudet has for some time been considered too simple in his techniques, and too obvious in his meanings, to challenge an age which takes particular pride in penetrating the hermetic world of the "difficult" obscure artist' (Sachs 1965: vii).

To sharpen this point, one need only entertain the possibility of arguing that 'Monsieur Seguin's Goat' is a work of parody or pastiche; that its mixture of fable, folktale, letter and other forms accentuates the elusiveness of those generic types on which it teasingly touches. Would that seem an implausible reading of it? If so, only because of particular assumptions brought to bear on Daudet's *Letters*, for parody is not so much a quality inherent in a text as a latency made visible by extratextual framing through which a reader construes or subdues the other framing elements. Daudet does not have a reputation as a subtly self-reflexive parodist; in recent times, hardly any critic has taken him up at all, let alone in a spirit attentive to textual play; in short, there is little to dissuade anyone from *under*-reading 'Monsieur Seguin's Goat' as merely an artless, moralised piece of rustic nostalgia.

Indeed the 'almost umbilical attachment to Provence' that the Penguin Classics cover blurb attributes to the author, associated with the notion that these *Letters* are essentially reminiscences ('to invent, for him, was to remember'), is so unquestioned an orthodoxy that his work has become fixed in an ideological frame through which it seems both thematically and formally *organicist* in the sense that Terry Eagleton uses this term, 'to signify social and aesthetic formations with the supposedly spontaneous unity of natural life-forms' (1978: 103). What it involves here is a tacitly assumed link between these propositions: (1) the *Letters* are cohesive in subject matter, representing an integrated community's 'natural' way of life; and (2) accordingly (as it were) there is a 'natural' unity of form that shapes each piece individually and the book as a whole. A remark of my own, made some years ago in my monograph *The Short Story*, may seem to endorse that way of reading Daudet's text; I mentioned his *Letters* as one of the 'notable nineteenth-century prototypes' of modern 'short-story cycles... [which] locate their unity of place in some rural region' (Reid 1977: 49). In part I amended this by going on to observe that it is too much of a miscellany to fit that unificatory pattern neatly, since it 'seems casually conjoined, and comprises a heterogeneous assortment of narrative types – sketches, yarns, fables, "ballades en prose" – set into an informal frame' (51–2). But I should have gone further, to show that the organicist notion of a rustic 'unity of place' is itself ironically treated within the *Letters*. It would be a mistake to think that the tone of the first section, celebrating the harmony of the Provençal countryside and its pastoral routines in explicit contrast to 'noisy, dirty Paris', pervades uniformly the rest of the sections as well. After all, the narrator confesses on the book's last page that Paris haunts him in his rural retreat; he acknowledges that it is through 'the Paris newspapers' that he reaches his readership; and the 'memories' on which his final emphasis falls are not of the little regional community but of that beloved city, now distant: 'Oh Paris!... Paris!... Always Paris!'

Extratextual framing often involves pedagogic habits, regulated by educational systems and by various practices that support institutionalised learning, such as the production of school editions of texts. For instance, a widespread notion (whose earliest proponent was Edgar Allan Poe) that the chief formal property of a short prose tale is 'unity of impression' lends itself all too readily in classrooms and textbooks to a reductive preoccupation with eliciting a theme or message. Such an approach to 'Monsieur Seguin's Goat' would ignore latently ironic elements that run counter to its own overt moralising closure. To ask 'Quelle est la morale de l'histoire?' (as does the editor of the Classiques Larousse edition[10]) is to err by supposing that it *can* be considered unitarily as a single-story-with-single-pointed-message, rather than as an unstable area of textual play. The Classiques Larousse paperbacks, presenting an instructional apparatus of notes and questions, epitomise the superimposition of certain extratextual norms on circumtextual material in ways that can induce one to view 'Monsieur Seguin's Goat' in generically constricted terms.

Extratextual framing is unavoidable. No text can be understood apart from what readers bring to it. The important thing, especially in a pedagogic situation, is not to be locked preclusively into one or two kinds of extratextual framing. For example, instead of fixing on the idea that Daudet's tale is a moralised fable, a teacher could make the text more productively meaningful for students by foregrounding gender issues: what does it mean that Blanquette is a pretty and wayward female who disobeys her male custodian and therefore falls prey to the male wolf? This linking of the text with sex role socialisation would give significant recognition to intertextual elements, particularly *Little Red Riding Hood* and *The Girl from Arles*.[11] Similarly, instead of relying on the notion that narrative should be understood and taught primarily in terms of plot (conceived as a regular sequence of linked events) – thus framing this text in a narrow way that simply overlooks most of the interesting and distinctive things going on in it – students could be encouraged to compare in detail the relatively simple story of Blanchette (in the *Victorian Reader*) and the more elaborate story of Blanquette (in the *Penguin Classics*). Although identical in 'action sequence', those two versions are very different, as we we have seen, in all other narrative structures. One further example of the need for educational practices to dislodge customary forms of extratextual framing by attending to other framing factors: a question in the notes to the *Victorian Reader* version asks, 'Judging by the story, what kind of man was

Alphonse Daudet?' Looking to the author's character and intentions as the source of textual meaning or the goal of interpretation tends to be a circular and empty search; here, the same notes have just asserted that Daudet 'is a master of delicate wit and simple pathos', and so the answer is already assumed in a way that makes text and author seem simply extensions of one another. Given, however, that there is no point in 'forbidding' students to be curious about authorial dimensions of a text's production, at least the complexity of the matter could be usefully addressed by considering, again, the mediating role of that sub-author, the translator. In this regard, other renderings of Daudet's tale into English would be of interest; for instance, there is a little-known translation by Katherine Mansfield, which appeared in *The New Age* in 1917, and which the editors of her *Collected Letters* have recently linked to images she used in her correspondence to describe her own struggle against death by consumption.[12]

V

What, in summary, does this chapter's account of framing contribute to a theory of reading, and of narrative exchanges in particular? As we saw in the previous chapter, even highly sophisticated literary criticism often lapses into false dichotomies, investing stories with self-contained power over readers rather than recognising precisely the interactive quality of any reading process. A pragmatic typology of framing provides the corrective to that tendency, being based on the fact that no textual exchange can occur unless a semantic field is perceptually delimited and certain sign-values are brought into play.

As a way of trying to deal with the complexities of a reader's engagement with a text, several semioticians persist with the metaphor of *codes*. But as Umberto Eco (1984: 164) remarks, 'the meaning of this term seems to have become exaggeratedly generous, covering... linguistic competence, a language, a system of rules, world knowledge or encyclopedic competence, a set of pragmatic norms, and so on'. Although Eco proceeds to suggest that *code* is still a useful term, it should be clear that the typology of framing outlined above has several advantages over the best-known attempt to analyse so-called 'codes' in a narrative text: the analysis by Roland Barthes (1974) of Balzac's 'Sarrasine'. The five disparate Barthesian codes stem from a relatively formalistic view of textual properties, divorced from the contingencies of any situation where one takes a book in one's hand. In contrast, the concept of 'framing' attends more directly to the occasions and processes through which readings actually occur, allowing in a flexible way for the importance of various institutional and interpersonal factors (in classrooms, for instance) during reading, since these themselves may serve to frame what is read. Moreover, Barthes's codes virtually assume an intricate literary text and a ready-made subtle reader of high literary competence, whereas the account of framing indicates how all reading occurs and how the particular practices associated with 'literary' reading may be acquired and developed. Codes do not in themselves account for durational and retrospective factors in interpretation (particularly important in a narrative exchange), but the concept of framing can readily be extended to reframing – and indeed, since there are no fixed and separate frames, the perception of any one framing element may involve an adjusted perception of others, and so on indefinitely. Further, the relation of codes to genres is unclear; the very notion of framing, however, clearly has a close bearing on generic perceptions (cf. Reid 1988). And while the metaphor of 'code' suggests a set of fairly clearcut constituents, that of 'framing' draws attention directly to the problematic nature of heuristic distinctions between what is inside textuality, or inside interpretation, and what is outside them.

The next chapter will provide further exposition, *vis-à-vis* assorted text types, of the basic concepts adumbrated so far. Since two of them, substitution and dispossession, were linked earlier with the utterance/enunciation doublet (*énoncé* and *énonciation*), it will also be necessary to take a closer look at these; for if, as chapter 1 has argued and chapter 2 has implicitly reasserted, a dichotomy between story and discourse is unacceptable, on what grounds should this other pair of terms be retained?

3

CUTTING A LONG STORY SHORT

> The story of this man who had killed a messenger and hanged himself would make interesting reading. One could almost write a whole chapter on him. Perhaps not a whole chapter but a reasonable paragraph, at any rate. There was so much else to include, and one must be firm in cutting out details.
>
> (Achebe 1976: 148)

I

Something very startling occurs two-thirds of the way through Don DeLillo's novel *White Noise* (1985), something whose significance within the narrative structure could hardly be described in terms of plot.[1] It is in fact a classic instance of narratorial *dispossession*, with interesting consequences for the implied reader.

Told by unheroic well-meaning middle-aged small-time college professor Jack Gladney, the story of *White Noise* concerns his family's day-to-day dealings with one another amidst a welter of technological menace: a rogue cloud of toxic chemicals pursues them, their futurist supermarket intimidates them, all sorts of electronic phenomena infiltrate every corner of their lives. By the time we get to chapter 26, the bemusedly affectionate and almost ingenuously candid tone of Jack's narration has managed to give us not only a strong sense of the omnipresence of these environmental hazards but also a compensatory trust in the counter-efficacy of domestic love, embodied especially for him in the sturdy, nurturing vitality of his calm wife Babette. The cheerful warmth and wry wisdom he finds in her seem to quell Jack's anxieties, giving him the equanimity to contemplate his mortality and to savour the unspectacular, poignant pleasures of conjugal and parental routines.

Then comes the sudden moment of overturning. Jack has discovered that Babette, in an extremely furtive way, is taking mysterious tablets, labelled 'Dylar'; worried, he has had them chemically analysed, but their function remains unidentifiable; and when he now asks her for an explanation, she relates something which, given the novel's narrative strategy up to that point, is as devastating to a reader as to Jack. It turns out that, far from being the 'joyous person' that Jack's side of the story has insistently represented her as being, Babette is utterly phobic: though apparently the epitome of good health, she is obsessively afraid of dying. This deep morbidity, she now reveals, has led her to respond credulously to an advertisement seeking volunteers for a secret psychobiological experiment by 'Gray Research'; and such is the desperation of her desire for a cure from her fearful condition that she has allowed herself to be regularly bedded by 'Mr Gray' in return for a supply of 'Dylar' pills which could purportedly bring relief – though she has come to see that they have failed to do so.

As Babette's tale starts to unfold, Jack attempts to ward it off with nervously phatic interruptions and solicitous suggestions:

'Just let me tell it in my own way,' she said in a small voice.
'Would you like a liqueur?'
'No, thank you.'
'Take your time,' I said. 'We've got all night. If there's anything you want or need, just say so. You have only to ask. I'll be right here for as long as it takes.'
Another moment passed.
'I don't know exactly when it started. Maybe a year and a half ago. I thought I was going through a phase, some kind of watermark period in my life.'
'Landmark,' I said. 'Or watershed.'
'A kind of settling-in-period, I thought. Middle age. Something like that. The condition would go away and I'd forget all about it. But it didn't go away. I began to think it never would.'
'What condition?'

'Never mind that for now.'
'You've been depressed lately. I've never seen you like this. This is the whole point of Babette. She's a joyous person. She doesn't succumb to gloom or self-pity.'
'Let me tell it, Jack.'
(191)

But Jack finds it painfully hard to let her tell the story he has required of her, because his loss of narrative prerogative is also a loss of his delusively idealised view of his wife. By ceding to her the right to tell in her own way how she feels and what she has done, he is being dispossessed of storypower and therefore of his rhetorical control over the personal exchange rate between them. As Babette's confession proceeds, he keeps breaking in and referring to her in a third-person manner as if to keep her in place as a character subject to his knowledge:

'All this without my knowing. The whole point of Babette is that she speaks to me, she reveals and confides.'
'This is not a story about your disappointment at my silence. The theme of this story is my pain and my attempts to end it.'
'I'll make some hot chocolate. . . .'
(192)

Her disclosure that her 'condition' is a stark fear of death disturbs Jack more profoundly than her sexual infidelity. 'Don't tell me this', he pleads. But because she *has* told him, he makes the only counter-move left to him in order to regain the ascendancy. It is the middle of the night; she is exhausted after completing her sad story; and now Jack relates to her *his* secret. A computer analysis, carried out after he was exposed earlier to toxic gas, has revealed that death is already written on the wall of his body.

'So we are no longer talking about fear and floating terror,' I said. 'This is the hard and heavy thing, the fact itself.'
(202–3)

Her reaction to his repossession of narrative control is abject animal-like despair.
But to the implied reader, shocked as much as Jack is by Babette's story, there can be no restoration of the earlier terms of the narrative exchange that this text had seemed to offer. Because one's previous knowledge and attitude in reading *White Noise* has

been derived almost wholly from Jack's account of things, untroubled by any structural irony, one shares now his bafflement. Having given credence to his view of his wife, the reader must absorb the discovery that all parties have been gullible: Babette's narrative, in showing that she is the dupe of 'Mr Gray', shows simultaneously that Jack is a dupe and that those of us who have taken his narration at face value are dupes as well. The dispossession is repercussive: what occurs here between characters in the *énoncé* (text as utterance) destabilises the *énonciation* (text-producing situation) at the same stroke. And yet it does so in such a way that, by shaking our confidence in what is conveyed directly through the narrator-narratee relationship, the text ultimately secures its cunning grip on us, for we no longer know how to 'take' what Jack tells us or how to predict what will ensue. By forcibly reclaiming the dominant storytelling role at the end of chapter 26 he achieves only a Pyrrhic victory, since his uncertainties are now paramount. In his increasingly febrile imagination, the unknown 'Mr Gray' has come to embody the power that he himself has lost; Jack visualises him moving 'bedward, plotward', and sees Babette through the eyes of that 'hazy gray seducer' as 'emotionally captive. I felt his mastery and control. The dominance of his position' (241). Even when Jack tracks down his adversary and shoots him, this gruesome act just absurdly confirms his narratorial incompetence, for the proleptic 'story' of revenge that he keeps reciting beforehand turns out to backfire on him literally: having placed the gun in his (apparently) dying victim's hand to counterfeit suicide, Jack is then wounded by an answering shot. Once dispossessed, the narrator (a figure within the utterance) cannot wrest back decisively his authority; and by the same token, the enunciator or implied author asserts *his*.

Here we should pause in order to clarify the distinction between utterance and enunciation in general. Is it a return of the repressed in our argument, an unwitting demonstration that narrative theory still continues to be 'afflicted ... with a number of dualistic concepts and models' (Smith 1980: 213)? Why preserve this utterance/enunciation doublet if, as argued in an earlier chapter, binary pairs such as story/discourse are to be treated sceptically?

It is true of course, in a general deconstructive sense, that all such distinctions stem from the differential compulsions of reading. A reader produces inferentially an enunciative dimension as the 'other' of the tangible text, and this may seem the same process as that through which a sequence of events is read into a series of rhetorical substitutions. But it is not quite the same. Whereas 'story' (along with similar terms in orthodox narratological usage) is no more than a projection – often inappropriate, I have argued – from a discourse, the relation between utterance and enunciation is of another kind, and indeed logically necessary. Utterance being that which is said or written and regarded as a textual entity, enunciation covers the communicative capacities by virtue of which that utterance can circulate as such. The utterance always carries traces or markers of the enunciation.[2]

Enunciation, the domain in which semiotic competence turns into performance, includes not only the enunciator or implied author but also the enunciatee or implied reader – for the latter is no mere recipient of a transmitted message (as in unidirectional models of communication such as the one proposed by Roman Jakobson) but a *framer* of signification, one who makes textual meanings operative by construing their import.[3] Enunciative acts of framing are thus among the very conditions of possibility for a textual exchange. They draw on, and are correspondingly represented by, virtual frames inscribed in the utterance: a narrator–narratee relationship provides a simulacrum of a transaction, which a reader interprets with recourse to circumtextual, intertextual and intratextual framings.

II

In order to take further our inquiry into the framing of dispossession, it is instructive to turn to a story (let us regard it for the moment as self-contained) told in Snorri Sturluson's thirteenth-century Icelandic *Prose Edda* (Appendix A).[4] Before looking at the workings of dispossession within the text, we should consider briefly how substitution operates when actantial functions become either flexible or duplicitous. The concept of actant comes from A.J. Greimas, and is not equivalent to the traditional notion of character. Actants are abstract agencies defined by their interrelations, for example sender/receiver, and by their position in a narrative syntagm. They are distinguishable from actors, who occupy designated individual roles in a story (Greimas and Courtés 1982: 5–6). According to Greimas, several categories of 'dramatis personae' elicited by Vladimir Propp (1968) in his proto-structuralist analysis of folktale functions can be actantially compressed, for example by subsuming 'donor' and 'provider' into 'helper'. But this reduction of categories obscures the point that sometimes a distinction between them, by permitting substitution, may serve to mobilise part of the narrative. Thor's chariot-pulling goats exemplify this quite simply: after being consumed, they are revived to serve again as transport, so the story can proceed. Substitution also happens when an actantial role is dissolved ambiguously among several actors through character doubling. Thor's companion Loki confronts a near-duplicate Logi in the eating contest organised by his alter ego Utgard-Loki ('Loki of the outer regions'), who has previously appeared to them as Skrymir; moreover the latter's giant status (Skrymir means 'Whopper') reminds us that Loki himself is not one of the Æsir, though he inhabits Asgard with them, but is of giant origin, and indeed has fathered the Midgard serpent which Thor wrestles as part of his contest.[5] The substitutive doublings pose enigmas as to who is whose real opponent, and who belongs with whom – thus generating narrative momentum.[6]

To some extent these substitutive moves could be regarded as stemming from the nature of narrative semiosis in general, the ongoing production of storied signs, never static and therefore partly resistant to the controlling designs of any communicative transaction. But semiosis takes different forms in different texts.[7] The particular pattern of substitution in Snorri's tale serves to reveal and inflect the discursive mix that forms its social context, which is predominantly a syncretised one. Several traditions had gone into the making of thirteenth-century Icelandic culture, variously represented by competing stories. Snorri and his immediate readership were situated on an overlap between Christian-humanist and pagan systems. Snorri himself, an eminent politician, poet and historian, combined a strong attachment to his Norse heritage with a training in the dogma of Christianity and acquaintance with classical lore. Different mythologies converge intertextually on his *Prose Edda* through the syncretic structure of its circumtextual framing elements, most notably in the Prologue to the first of its three sections, *Gylfaginning*, which contains the story of Thor's visit to Utgard. To syncretise different systems of religious belief is to entail a substitutive narrative structure because the correspondences, being in apparent tension, need to be 'explained' syntagmatically.

Beginning with a summary of the Hebrew account of creation and human history up to the aftermath of Noah's flood, the Prologue goes on to relate that, as the postdiluvian population spread, people neglected the worship of God and eventually forgot even his name. The narrator then gives a geographical survey of the earth's three parts, Africa, Europe and Asia, and develops from this a history that starts with 'that building and dwelling which has been the most splendid ever' near 'the middle of the world': Troy. King Priam, according to Snorri's story, had a grandson 'called Tror – we call him Thor'. A man of great strength (not a deity), Thor travels far and wide, overcoming giants, and marrying 'a prophetess called Sibyl, whom we call Sif'. (This pattern of appropriation-through-conflation continues: several places and personal names are 'translated' into Norse equivalents.) Among Thor's descendants is Odin, 'an outstanding person for wisdom and all kinds of accomplishment'(4), who sets out with others from Asia on a northward journey. 'And whatever countries they passed through, great glory was spoken of them so that they seemed more like gods than men'(4). Having taken possession of many lands in Europe, and left his sons to rule them, Odin himself presses on into Scandinavia, where he settles. It is at this point that the general syncretic prologue moves to its conclusion by setting up a further narrative situation out of which will emerge the mythological tales that constitute *Gylfaginning* (the first section of the *Edda*). *Gylfaginning* means *The Deluding of Gylfi*, and Gylfi is a Swedish king who, 'when he learned of the arrival of the men of Asia, who were called ... Æsir, went to meet them and offered Odin as much power in his realm as he wished himself' (4).

This issue of authority is crucial in their subsequent narrative dealings, and through it the text foregrounds its own enunciative ploy. Once the Æsir have settled nearby, Gylfi, himself a wise man with magical powers, wanting to discover the secret of the Æsir's might, sets out in the guise of an old man called Gangleri on a visit to their stronghold, Asgard. But the Æsir, with foreknowledge of his identity and purpose, 'prepared deceptive appearances for him'(7). This involves illusions of scale: when Gylfi alias Gangleri arrives, it seems to him that their hall is so lofty 'that he [can] scarcely see over it' (7) (a phrase echoed in the embedded story when Thor arrives at Utgard-Loki's stronghold). Inside, Gylfi finds an enigmatic trio called High One, Just-as-High, and Third, whom he cross-examines about divine power. They reply with stories, but he is told that his life depends on proving himself wiser than his informants; challenge and riposte are salient in this narrative exchange. After several tales have been unfolded, Gylfi asks about the formidable Thor: was there ever an occasion when he encountered something so powerful that it was too much for him? The three respondents seem to hesitate, and, taking at face value their apparent disinclination to tell him about the limits of Thor's power, he insists on hearing what happened. The ensuing tale cunningly offers Gylfi/Gangleri an admonitory analogue to the relationship in which he is the narratee, thus framing intratextually through a *mise-en-abyme* effect the exchange which simultaneously frames it circumtextually.

In other words, the 'inner' tale of Thor, told at a subordinated or 'hypodiegetic' level of the utterance (Rimmon-Kenan 1983: 92), embeds a dispossessive model that thematises the circumstances of its own telling to Gylfi (at the diegetic level of enunciation-within-utterance). It indicates that when different sorts of cultural knowledge and discursive power are in tension, superior narrative guile may win the day. Because tales about Thor's strength have had such currency, the giants are forewarned and can plan to counter it with magical disguises, cutting big Thor down to size just as they out-Loki the trickster Loki. Correspondingly, Gylfi is subjected to narrative manipulation. And a reader of the text, at the level of the actual enunciation, is placed in a similarly deluded position, knowing only part of the story until it suits Utgard-Loki, and the enigmatic trio, and Snorri, to divulge the rest.

Power, then, as this text represents it, is not invested only in social roles or relations as such. The counterpoint between the preamble (Thor's dealings with the farmer) and the subsequent story (Thor's dealings with the conjuror-giant) illustrates this: although the farmer is host to Thor, it is Thor who dominates their encounter by force and magic; but in the main part of the story Thor is dominated by Utgard-Loki, whose superior dexterity in magic and disguise (rather than his hostly status) is what controls their exchanges. Thor becomes deprived of his power because the narrative (fictional) advantage has been seized by Utgard-Loki. Throughout the text, magic and disguise are figures for the substitutive and dispossessive capacities of narration. For instance, in addition to examples given already, aetiological stories become activated through Skrymir's illusionist feats: serrations in hills were caused by Thor's huge hammer blows, invisibly deflected; tidal fluctuations by Thor's prodigious draughts from a drinking horn while under the giant's spell. (Significantly, 'spell' has the basic sense of discourse as well as enchantment.) The importance of disguise, as a means of effecting narrative dispossession, has been emphasised in our earlier discussion (chapter 1) of Alberto's story in the *Decameron*.

Michel Serres, in his provocative book *The Parasite*, argues that 'a human group is organised with one-way relations, where one eats the other and the second cannot benefit at all from the first'. In particular, he denies that a host–guest relation is principally an exchange. 'The flow goes one way, never the other', Serres (1982: 5) contends; and he goes on: 'I call this ... relation without a reversal of direction, "parasitic".' Even allowing for the ironic play of metaphors in Serres's work, one can regard this quoted statement as a hyperbole. For while parasitic elements may disturb an exchange, they certainly cannot efface it. Nor is power attached unilaterally to one particular role. As Snorri's tale shows, dealings between host and guest can go either way, or both ways – depending on the strategems of discursive control.

Parallel motifs and formulaic phrasing alert the reader to a correspondence between Thor's experiences and the circumtextual deluding of Gylfi. Expressions such as 'It doesn't have to be told' ('Þá er eigi skylt at segja frá'), 'There's no need to relate it at length' ('Eigi þarf langt frá því at segja') and – an especially loaded phrase, as it is in Daudet's text – 'To cut a long story short' ('Ekki er langt um at gøra') serve to emphasise in both embedded and embedding stories the arbitrariness of narratorial options, which are also figured in each case by the abrupt termination of a threatened storyline. Just as the giant stronghold vanishes from sight when Thor grips his hammer, so too, after Gylfi/Gangleri has been told several more stories about gods and giants, the Æsir and their hall suddenly disappear because Gylfi's questions are pressing too hard; he has apparently won by default the contest of wisdom, but they have cheated him of further narrative knowledge by their disappearing trick. Returning home, he recirculates the tales he has acquired. But the Æsir perpetrate another deception: they assume the names of the gods in the stories they have told him, and thus the migrants from Asia merge with the beings in those myths – which, the extradiegetic narrator finally suggests, have themselves allegorised events in the Trojan war.

The *Gylfaginning* title, then, of this section of the Edda, with its reference to delusion, 'is a reminder that the stories Gylfi hears and evidently believes are not held by the [implied] author to be true' (Faulkes 1982: xviii). Further ironies operate when the circumtextual framing is extended intertextually. Anthony Faulkes has remarked on the 'ancient Scandinavian tradition of composing poems of mythological instruction as dialogues or dramatic monologues' (xxv). Very like *Gylfaginning*, he points out, is another contest-of-wisdom text in which Odin tells stories about the gods in the third person; and there are similar devices in other eddic poems such as *Grímnismál*, where moreover the names of that mysterious trinity High One, Just-as-High and Third are revealed as pseudonyms of Odin himself – and yet so also is the name Gangleri! Indeed this Odin/Gangleri equation is briefly mentioned to Gylfi/Gangleri during his own *Gylfaginning* dialogue with the mysterious trio. There could hardly be a more cautionary insistence on the substitutive and dispossessive slippages that can disconcert a narrative exchange. Through such framings, generically unstable, Snorri's canny text both strengthens and relativises its own position within the discursive mix of medieval Icelandic culture.

Anthony Wilden's remark on ritually exchanged gifts can be applied to stories: they 'do not stand for what they "represent" in some fixed relationship to an unconscious "meaning". They are symbols of the act of exchange itself, which is what ties the society and its neighbours together' (1972: 32). Yet this needs a further brief gloss; for to say that exchange ties a society together overlooks the way a narrative transaction unties discourse as it ties. It enacts continually a rhythm of tying/untying/retying (and so on) because the inescapable effect of substitutive and dispossessive devices is circular: what gets exchanged through narrative is a set of signs that reaffirm the value of such textual transactions themselves – while also forcing them, by challenge and riposte, to be always renegotiated.

III

In the conclusion to his book *Culture and Practical Reason*, the anthropologist Marshall Sahlins sketches a broad contrast between 'bourgeois' and 'tribal' cultures with regard to their modes of symbolic production. The most distinctive thing about our own kind of social organisation, he remarks, is that it is based on structurally separate subsystems (political, religious, educational and so on), which are all subordinated to the requirements of the economy. 'This', comments Sahlins (1976: 212), 'gives credibility to the kind of reflectionist theory which perceives in the superstructure the differentiations (notably of class) established in production and exchange.' Contrastingly, institutional relations form another pattern altogether in so-called primitive cultures, where 'economic, political, and ritual action are organised by the one generalised kinship structure'. Each of these two social orders has its own corresponding symbolic grid. Generally speaking, in tribal culture it is the extensive family network that dominates the meanings attached to interaction between persons, groups, institutions and practices; in bourgeois culture, material production constitutes a primary set of classifications 'figured as the meaningful differences between products' (213), in terms of which individual status and the significance of all sorts of activities may be gauged.

Sahlins himself admits that this schematic contrast is fairly crude, but for present purposes it indicates some of the issues raised by narrative texts that situate their mode of semantic exchange at a point where 'primitive' and 'Western' cultures clash. An exemplary case is Chinua Achebe's *Things Fall Apart* (1976), which frames dispossession in a much more painful light than Snorri Sturluson's tale.

This novel relates a decline and fall – not only of the main character Okonkwo but also of his tribal culture. This process occurs in clearly delineated stages, and an action sequence could be extracted from the text without difficulty, as it is for example by this reviewer, quoted on the back cover in a gesture of circumtextual framing:

> The story is the tragedy of Okonkwo, an important man in the Obi tribe [sic: the name should read Ibo] in the days when white men were first appearing on the scene. . . . Mr Achebe's very simple but excellent novel tells of the series of events by which Okonkwo through his pride and his fears becomes exiled from his tribe and returns only to be forced into the ignominy of suicide to escape the results of his rash courage against the white man.[8]

No doubt the 'plot' could be described more precisely than that, but any action-based summary would fail to indicate how significant for the exchange offered to us is an implicit tension between different sorts of narrative possibility, intratextually framed.

One of the starkest moments in the novel comes in its final paragraph, and could not be rendered into an event within a plot. It is a moment of dispossession at both individual and cultural levels, reframing the story ironically by showing how it could be appropriated for the western genre of a 'report' in which bureaucratic presumption mingles with the specious objectivity of social scientism. Discovering that Okonkwo has committed suicide, the District Commissioner muses briefly and detachedly on the anthropological interest of this episode and its usefulness for the book he is writing on Nigerian tribal customs:

> Every day brought him some new material. The story of this man who had killed a messenger and hanged himself would make interesting reading. One could almost write a whole chapter on him. Perhaps not a whole chapter but a reasonable paragraph, at any rate. There was so much else to include, and one must be firm in cutting out details. He had already chosen the title of the book, after much thought: *The Pacification of the Primitive Tribes of the Lower Niger*.
>
> (148)

If this were the novel's only juxtaposition of different cultural perspectives, it might seem a facile contrast. But other western ways of framing the hero's story have already been suggested intertextually. One important reference to a certain religious heritage of white culture is signalled in the very title, taken from Yeats's poem 'The Second Coming', whose opening lines are printed as an epigraph on the title page:

> Turning and turning in the widening gyre
> The falcon cannot hear the falconer;
> Things fall apart; the centre cannot hold;
> Mere anarchy is loosed upon the world.

This poem goes on to view the periodic transition from one culture to another (pre-Christian to Christian, for instance, or Christian to post-Christian) as necessarily a brutal upheaval; and it evokes the idea that historical patterns are repeated cyclically. An epoch of two millennia, covering the dominant period of ancient Mediterranean culture, is seen as having been overturned by 'a rocking cradle' (through the birth of Jesus) – and now the next two millennia, drawing to a close in their turn, are seen as culminating in the advent of some new disruptive force at a different 'Bethlehem'. For a reader who brings to Achebe's novel that kind of broad mythological understanding, the story of Okonkwo becomes just a turn in the centrifuge of cyclic history.

But that is not the only European historical myth to which the novel alludes. Less emphatically signalled, but relevant, is another view of history and violence: that of the 'survival of the fittest'. It is touched on in a fragmentary manner halfway through the second chapter, within a paragraph describing the stern way in which Okonkwo ruled his household and was ruled in turn by his fear – a fear 'deeper and more intimate than the fear of evil and capricious gods and of magic, the fear of the forest, and the forces of nature, malevolent, red in tooth and claw' (9). The provenance of that last phrase gives a different possibility for framing the story of Okonkwo and his tribe. It comes from one of the most famous nineteenth-century poems, Tennyson's long elegy 'In Memoriam', in lines which attach a particular interpretation to the death of an individual within the context of larger changes. Nature, though 'careless of the single life', is said at first to be 'careful of the type' (which could mean the human species, or a race) – and then even this is retracted:

> 'So careful of the type?' but no.
> From scarpèd cliff and quarried stone
> She [Nature] cries, 'A thousand types are gone;
> I care for nothing, all shall go.
>
> 'Thou makest thine appeal to me:
> I bring to life, I bring to death;
> The spirit does but mean the breath:
> I know no more.' And he, shall he,
>
> Man, her last work, who seemed so fair,
> Such splendid purpose in his eyes,
> Who rolled the psalm to wintry skies,
> Who built him fanes of fruitless prayer,
>
> Who trusted God was love indeed
> And love creation's final law –
> Though Nature, red in tooth and claw
> With ravine, shrieked against his creed –

Who loved, who suffered countless ills,
Who battled for the True, the Just,
Be blown about the desert dust,
Or sealed within the iron hills?

Although they refer to a more personal experience (bereavement) than Yeats's poem evokes, the historical perspective in these lines far exceeds the few thousand years mentioned in 'The Second Coming'. Published just before Darwin's book *The Origin of Species*, Tennyson's 'In Memoriam' expresses a keen and painful awareness of evolutionary processes. In Yeats's poem, written several decades later, the violence that erupts fearfully to mark the coming of a new era is seen as part of a cyclic pattern in human culture; in Tennyson's, the violence belongs to natural processes of evolution, and humans can only hope that a divinely providential scheme underlies the savagery.

In short, two different kinds of narrative structure are indicated by these two mythic allusions: one follows a circular pattern, with periods of anarchy and order in alternation, while the other involves conflict leading to the eradication of some kinds of creature and the triumph of other kinds. Those narrative structures suggest two ways of interpreting what happens in *Things Fall Apart*.

But the text also draws extensively on traditional Nigerian stories and the ritual customs with which they are associated. Not only are there references to an 'endless stock of folk tales' (25), to fables told by women (53, 59, 67–70), to 'masculine stories of violence and bloodshed' (37) – all circulating within the tribal culture and helping to constitute it; there are also references to various other practices which serve intratextually as models for different narrative relations. At one point, for example, it is stated that 'a man's life from birth to death was a series of transition rites'(85). A *rite de passage*, as anthropologists call it, normally has three phases: first, separation from one's previous position in the community; then a 'liminal' or marginal phase, when one is neither one thing nor another; and finally a renewed engagement with communal life, though in an altered position. *Things Fall Apart*, explicitly subdivided into three numbered parts, seems to conduct its protagonist through a sequence similar to this. But what meanings are attached to the different stages of Okonkwo's life? Instead of a reintegrative movement within a stable system, is it not a disintegrative one that he follows, a trajectory emblematic of the decline of his culture?

Each of the novel's three sections culminates by conjoining an act of discourse (a speech to the clan) with acts of social exchange. Chapters 12 and 13, ending Part 1, produce an array of traditional ritual observances and economic transactions: kinship structures (the bride-price), market stories (notably one in which a goat is fraudulently replaced by a log of wood), ritual sacrifice (a magical form of exchange), compensation (an on-the-spot fine for crop damage), various presentations of symbolic gifts accompanied by speeches or songs, and finally the exacting of punishment – Okonkwo's exile – for a deed of pollution. Ending Part 2, chapter 19 brings to a close the seven-year period of Okonkwo's exile in Mbanta, the village of his mother's kinsfolk. The great feast that he holds there is not a matter of measured obligation ('It is not to pay you back for all you did for me in these seven years' (177)); its extravagance underlines the fact that it is an act of symbolic exchange, serving to reaffirm the bonds of kinship and other stable values, and the speech which concludes the chapter makes this explicit. The last few chapters of the novel show that the system of exchange within this culture is changing. A balance between spiritual and material things has been affected by the coming of foreign ways: 'The white man had indeed brought a lunatic religion, but he had also built a trading store and for the first time palm oil and kernel became things of great price, and much money flowed into Umuofia' (126). Correspondingly the system of white retribution has an impact on tribal life; the imposition of fines is based now on a different principle, virtually one of ransom, and there is the humiliation of imprisonment which makes Okonkwo long for the old days of warfare when justice was reckoned by the numbers of dead on each side. Significantly it is at the edge of the marketplace, on the road leading from the white man's court, that Okonkwo kills the messenger. And this requires his own life, which will be followed in turn by 'sacrifices to cleanse the desecrated land' (147). A link is implicitly suggested between the advent of a price-based economy and the kind of cultural measurement implicit in the District Commissioner's prospective account of 'pacification'.

Returning to Sahlins's schematic contrast between the forms of symbolic organisation in western and tribal cultures, one might see *Things Fall Apart* as tracing a particular historical shift from a system of exchange in which storytelling, like everything else, tethers its meanings to networks of family and village interaction to a system in which possession (including dispossession) is the dominant discursive principle. And yet the text's own exchange with its implied readers is positioned in a way that merges these different systems and their respective narrative forms. It is written in English; generically, it is oriented to the European novel; and in other respects, too, from its title onwards, it is overtly affiliated with a western literary tradition. Moreover, an address to an English reader is frequently implied in its narratorial tenor – for instance in explanations of tribal beliefs and customs. On the other hand, much of the narration assumes, or feigns to assume, a local audience already equipped with certain knowledge; the very first sentence states that 'Okonkwo was well known throughout the nine villages and even beyond', without specifying any geographical or ethnic scenario. At least two narrative voices are merged, then, in the narration of *Things Fall Apart* (cf. McEwan 1983: 20–36), and accordingly the exchange that the novel as a whole offers to its readers is a culturally mixed one.

IV

The three texts discussed in this chapter reveal something of the variety of forms that dispossession can take. Several substitutive processes are also illustrated in the story from Snorri's *Edda*: to summarise briefly, we have seen the same character serving different actantial purposes at different times through a magical process of substitution (as Thor's goats are helpers, then providers, then helpers again); we have seen how character doubling tends to dissolve actantial roles ambiguously (as the trickster Loki and his giant-king namesake help to propel the narrative through their relations with each other and with their further counterparts Logi and Skrymir); and we have seen that syncretic substitution is a feature of the set of discursive relationships behind that text. But we have looked in more detail at dispossessive factors: at the way Babette's disturbance of Jack's attempt at narratorial control in *White Noise* simultaneously complicates the enunciative relation of implied reader to implied author; at the way the tale of Thor's visit to giantland similarly embeds a dispossessive model that thematises the circumstances of its own telling, with consequences for the enunciative situation of the *Edda* itself; and at the way the District Commissioner in the final paragraph of *Things Fall Apart* takes control of Okonkwo's story, resituating it within an extratextual framework where its dimensions are curtailed and its meanings belittlingly transvalued. We have noticed, further, that none of these dispossessive acts represented within an utterance is itself immune from being 'framed' in turn within the encompassing enunciation, so that for instance *Things Fall Apart* incorporates the District Commissioner's discourse (merely parasitic in itself, as Serres (1982) would insist) within the novel's more comprehensive exchange of cultural ironies.

The next chapter will consider substitution and dispossession not simply as particular devices that may occur now and then in a text, but rather as qualities that may pervade it and indeed constitute its narrativity. This will involve a scrutiny of a term used uncritically so far, the 'implied author', and an exploration of the idea that a reader may exploit some measure of dispossession at the enunciative level of a text to the extent that the grip of narratorial control is loosened at the level of utterance.

4
VOICE, SEQUENCE AND CONTROL

> The voice grew louder and stronger, rolling ... in repeated echoes.
>
> (Flaubert 1961: 109)

I

That facile slogan 'the death of the author' has distracted attention from more subtle intimations of mortality in the case of the so-called 'implied author'. Who or what is the latter? If, as we have remarked, any utterance presupposes an implicit structure of enunciation, then two participant positions may seem, on the face of it, to constitute a textual exchange: those of an enunciator or message-sender and an enunciatee or message-receiver. (Such, for example is the assumption made by Greimas and Courtés 1982: 105.) In a written narrative fiction, the enunciator's position apparently corresponds to what literary criticism knows as the implied author. The earliest account of this elusive vice-regent figure is given by Wayne Booth, who argues that the governing consciousness discernible in a story, the source of its constituent choices and values, is a projected self-image, 'an ideal, literary, created version' of the person who actually wrote it (1961: 71–5). Taking up Booth's catchy term, a number of other narrative theorists reinterpret the 'implied author' in slightly different ways. Seymour Chatman (1978: 151) sets it within a schematic six-part model:

Real author > Implied author > Narrator > Narratee > Implied reader > Real reader.

That looks attractively tidy, and has often been repeated (e.g. Yacobi 1981: 122; Lintvelt 1981: 25–30; Martin 1986: 154). But its application sometimes proves troublesome. Chatman himself, for example, repeats (while trying to refute) a confusion initiated by Booth himself in stating that not all stories have narrators; this leads him to designate as an 'implied author' the narrator-as-direct-observer in a story such as Hemingway's 'The Killers' (Chatman 1975: 218; Booth 1961: 151). Roger Fowler (1977: 83–4), having identified Marlow as the narrator in some of Conrad's fiction, supposes that the anonymous first-person figure who embeds Marlow's narration must be the implied author – though it would surely seem more satisfactory to recognise that a text may involve more than one narratorial level. Wallace Martin (1986) is similarly perplexed, stating first that 'an implied author ... [sometimes] refers to himself as "I" ' (135) and later that 'the implied author, by definition, never uses "I" ' (154). Nevertheless, however uncertainly defined, the 'implied author' has continued to be invoked deferentially by writers of various persuasions, from Booth himself, who asserts in a later book (1979: 278) that 'a respect for implied authors can be the most important single enabling act of criticism', to Paul Hernadi, in whose study of generic concepts the implied author is saluted as 'a highly valuable contribution to literary theory at large' (1972: 74), and to Catherine Belsey, who in her project of developing a new critical practice finds room for the implied author as an 'extremely useful instrument in the formal analysis of narrative texts' (1980: 30).

While reluctant to discard the notion of an implied author, some recent critics find fault with the way Chatman and others have used it. Shlomith Rimmon-Kenan regards it as an *inferred*, rather than implied, principle of design or set of norms pervading all components of a text. Arguing that the concept must be 'de-personified', she disagrees with Chatman's insertion of it into a communicative chain between author and narrator; it is, she says, a construct 'assembled by the reader' (1983: 87–8).[1] A few others are more sceptical still. Mieke Bal remarks (1981: 42) that the notion of an implied author has proved

> very popular because it promised something which, in my view, it has not been able to deliver: it promised to account for the ideology of the text. This would have made it possible to condemn a text without condemning its author

and vice versa – a very attractive proposition to the autonomists of the '60s.'

Susan Lanser similarly contends that one ignores important cultural functions of a text if one regards an abstractly implied author as the source of textual norms rather than holding the real author directly responsible. She reproaches Chatman for severing aesthetics from ideology in his assertion that 'it makes no more sense to accuse the real Céline or Montherlant of what the implied author causes to happen in *Journey to the End of the Night* or *Les Jeunes Filles* than to hold the real Conrad responsible for the reactionary attitudes of the implied author of *The Secret Agent* ' (Chatman 1978: 149). This, protests Lanser (1981: 50), 'reduces the notion of implied author to that of an unreliable narrative voice'. Yet Lanser, though cautious, does not go so far as to reject the term; nor, as we have seen, does Rimmon-Kenan; nor does Ross Chambers in *Story and Situation* (1984).[2]

But Gérard Genette (1988) does reject it. While not the first to inflict injury on the implied author, he bids fair to administer a *coup de grâce*.[3] Wielding Occam's razor, he insists that there is no apparent instance of an implied author that cannot be more simply identified with either a real author or a narrator. This latter pair is certainly sufficient, he maintains, to account for the production – both real and fictive – of the text:

> A narrative of fiction is produced fictively by its narrator and actually by its (real) author. No one is toiling away between them, and every type of textual performance can be attributed only to one or the other, depending on the level chosen.
>
> (139–40)

Thus, on the one hand, in cases where the teller is positioned omnisciently above and outside the tale, like the one who relates Balzac's *Le Père Goriot* from a level of superior knowledge and without any involvement as a character, the function is not authorial but narratorial; the proper Genettian classification would be 'extradiegetic and heterodiegetic'. On the other hand, with regard to any image of the author derived by a reader from the text, Genette wants us to see it simply as that – an *image* (whether accurate or not) of the *real* author, rather than as a distinct intermediary figure. He cites the familiar observation, made a century ago by Engels and later by Lukács and others, that the reactionary views of Balzac the man yield in some of his fiction to much more enlightened insights into social processes. Genette thinks there is no need to adduce an implied author to explain this; all it shows, he asserts, is that

> the image of the author constructed by the (competent) reader is more faithful than the idea that that author had of himself. . . . Here, therefore, *the implied author is the* authentic *real author.* To play the scientist, we will write IA = RA. In this case, of course, IA – a faithful and thus transparent image – becomes an unnecessary agent. Exit IA.
>
> (143)

Has the time now come, then, to follow up Roland Barthes's announcement (1977) of 'the death of the author' with an R.I.P. for the implied author as well? Perhaps; but while Genette's strictures may seem irresistibly cogent, they cannot dispose of that important problem which the notion of an implied author has been an attempt (albeit unsatisfactory) to solve: where to locate those workings of semantic authorisation by which a reader's interpretive scope is curbed. In other words, how do texts regulate one's reading of them and contrive to establish 'norms' of meaning? Whether an implied author is eliminated or reinstated, that ideological question remains inconveniently to be analysed.

A simple starting point is to recognise that two particular aspects of a narrative text, if linked in a mutually reinforcing way, do tend to solicit for it a unity attributable to the aegis of some superintendant of signification at the enunciative level – tend, that is, to present it as a 'completed artistic whole' for which Booth's implied author supposedly stands as guarantor (Booth 1961: 73–4). One is the control exerted through a narrator's voice, governing the tenor of the speech-act relationship presented within the utterance; the other is the control exerted through sequential arrangement, governing the 'trajectory' of the figures or actants.[4] When these factors are bound together in a tight nexus, a reader may incline to think of them as possessed by a unitary subject, a regulator of meanings assignable to the text, in short an implied author. That is, if no ironic discrepancy is perceptible – as it is in the case of an 'unreliable' narrator (Booth 1961: 159) – between voice and sequence, between the tenor of the narratorial relation and the serial momentum of textual figures, then a reader is likely to construct an implied author with norms equivalent to those of the narrator (Lanser 1981: 151).

Nevertheless, such a notion is unsatisfactory, as this chapter will try to show, unless it can be severed from any assumption of centralised authority. For even a text that is extremely homogeneous in voice and sequence will often seem to be *latently* at odds with itself in this matter of authority. Through intratextual and intertextual framing, it can resist in part its own unitary desires by commenting *sotto voce* on the kind of normative restraint that it is exercising over its semantic potential. We usually think of self-commentary as being the overtly reflexive sort – extending from Sterne's *Tristram Shandy* and Diderot's *Jacques le fataliste* to Calvino's *If on a Winter's Night a Traveller* and Sollers's *Drame* – that has come to be called metafictional. But it can take more oblique forms: discreetly embedded elements of 'unconscious' allegory that serve to alleviate the pressure of control by confessing, as if through Freudian slippage, what it costs.[5] This disclosure, albeit indirect, of the price being paid to subordinate centrifugal voices and trajectories makes it inappropriate to posit a single implied author, for in such cases signification is dispersed among different positions within the text and is therefore able to stimulate correspondingly different readings.

It will be instructive to consider first in general terms how this works through the disposition of those two constitutive factors, voice and sequence, and then how it works through the detail of two very different texts, Gustave Flaubert's *Three Tales* (1961) and Marguerite Duras's *The Vice-Consul* (1987). Although there are no grounds for doubting that Flaubert's three narrators are veracious and trustworthy in what they explicitly relate, a kind of textual unconscious is operative in each case; while the Duras text, by profoundly radicalising relations between utterance and enunciation, presents narrative exchange in a different light altogether.

On the face of it, monologue is an axiomatic precondition of narrative, though not its sole or sufficient property. A narrator speaks, and the storytelling can proceed only for as long as interlocutors and rival narrators keep silent. Their part in a possible dialogue must be silenced in order that a single voice may be heard in the narrative mode. And yet it is not so simple. No monologue can entirely quell those other speakers whose accents hover vestigially or proleptically around the text that would exclude them. For as Bakhtin (1981: 280–2) remarks, every utterance carries the pressure marks of a polyglot linguistic environment; it 'cannot escape the profound influence of the answering word that it anticipates' as 'the speaker tries to get a reading on his own word'.

Now this capacity for internalising counter-texts makes a given text's meanings potentially unstable. In some measure, another 'side of the story' is always ready to take over, to wrest semantic control from its narrator at the level of the utterance and even from its ulterior quasi-authorial custodian at the enunciative level.[6] To the extent that a particular way of telling manages to forestall or fend off that eventuality, imposing ostensible unity through an all-inclusive, 'omnidicent' tone, it dictates authoritatively the terms of that narrative exchange. And on the contrary, to the extent that it fails or declines, wittingly or not, to determine whose side of the story gets heard, it reveals an imbalance of power and so leaves itself open to dispossession.

The second important destabilising factor concerns the means by which textual figures move and stop: this is what I have been calling substitution. To repeat a summary formulation stated in the Introduction: whereas 'exchange' indicates broadly a giving-and-taking of signs between parties, 'dispossession' refers to a wresting or arresting of control over the relative positions of those parties, and 'substitution' to an altering of the relation between the signs themselves. To the extent that a text conceals the fundamentally substitutive operation of narrative sequencing itself – conceals, that is, the way in which metonymic disjunction is made to seem a kind of cohesive continuity – it maintains not only its momentum but also its authoritative control over the values derivable from it in reading.

II

It is only an apparent tautology to say that in the first of Flaubert's *Three Tales*, 'A Simple Heart', the suave narrator does nearly all the talking. While there is an obvious sense in which, by definition, the discourse in any story must be entirely narratorial, few stories are as monologic in effect as this one. More is involved than just a question of the extent to which characters are 'allowed' to speak for themselves.[7] As it happens, dialogue *is* very scanty in this case, but even where it does occur it may be represented in such a way (e.g. by ironic placement) that it remains under the firm domination of the narrator. Volosinov's (1973) perception that a quoting voice variously manipulates a quoted voice is apposite here. A magisterial tone prevails in 'A Simple Heart', homogenising all that it relates and tending to curtail the text's capacity for a 'plural' effect of the sort described by Barthes (1974: 41–2):

> The best way to conceive the ... plural is to listen to the text as an iridescent exchange carried on by multiple voices, on different wavelengths and subject from time to time to a sudden *dissolve*, leaving a gap which enables the utterance to shift from one point of view to another

'A Simple Heart' does much to subdue that potentially multi-vocal mix. For not only is direct speech confined to a few very brief and banal utterances, but reported speech is also parsimonious and given in a summary, generalised manner. Any narrative exchanges among the characters are mentioned only as fragmentary and inconsequential: the Marquis de Grémanville lets drop 'bawdy stories' (22), Liébard relates anecdotal snippets, 'adding moral reflexions to each story' (25), Victor amuses Félicité 'by telling her stories full of nautical jargon' (33). Seldom is the quality of dialogic interchange in ordinary human conversation audibly represented. Instead, when voices are heard they tend mostly to be associated either with mere animal noise or with the reciting of Holy Writ. On the one hand there is the kind of babble that occurs on market days: 'Then the hum of voices began to fill the town, mingled with the neighing of horses, the bleating of lambs, the grunting of pigs, and the rattle of carts in the streets' (22). On the other hand there is the kind of authoritative, univocal story that Félicité hears in church, 'sacred history'; it tells of 'the Garden of Eden, the Flood, the Tower of Babel, cities burning, peoples dying, and idols being overthrown; and this dazzling vision left her with a great respect for the Almighty and a profound fear of his wrath' (29).

When our attention is so directly drawn to the status of particular vocal acts, the effect is to constitute these – speculatively – as embedded figures of the text's own storytelling mode, instances of a *mise-en-abyme* of the enunciation, with the function of stimulating us to consider the position from which that narratorial voice itself speaks and the terms of the semantic exchange it proposes. This aspect of the story has been most fully and subtly discussed by Chambers (1984). Regarding the general significance of *mise-en-abyme* effects in fiction, Chambers argues (29–30) that 'a given segment of text, in specular relationship with another such segment or with the text as a whole, can be conceived as a "model" of the text, or text segment, to which it is compared'; and among the observations he makes about this Flaubert text is that it achieves 'dialogic' effects through a contrast between 'the measured style of the narration' and the occasional flickers of *style indirect libre* that catch the tone of a character's virtual speech. Each style, suggests Chambers, can be read as implicitly commenting on the other. This is valid; but all the same, the narrating voice remains incorporative and predominant. In those passages quoted above, for instance, it is exerting strong control over its representations of other speech acts. And throughout the story it hardly permits the awesome voice of supposedly supernatural authority to blend with ordinary sounds except in a somewhat comical way. Félicité herself brings them together in the rest of the paragraph about her response to hearing biblical narratives:

> Then she wept as she listened to the story of the Passion. Why had they crucified Him, when He loved children, fed the multitudes, healed the blind, and had chosen out of humility to be born among the poor, on the litter of a stable? The sowing of the seed, the reaping of the harvest, the pressing of the grapes – all those familiar things of which the Gospels speak had their place in her life. God had sanctified them in passing, so that she loved the lambs more tenderly for love of the Lamb of God, and the doves for the sake of the Holy Ghost. ... She found it difficult, however, to imagine what the Holy Ghost looked like, for it was not just a bird but a fire as well, and sometimes a breath. She wondered ... whether that was its voice she had heard in the sweet music of the bells.
>
> (29–30)

The two voices, that of the divine *logos* and that of the creaturely world, combine mainly in Loulou. Until his death, this parrot is her quasi-human companion and interlocutor, increasingly so as she grows deaf:

> Imaginary buzzings in the head added to her troubles. Often her mistress would say: 'Heavens, how stupid [*bête*] you

are!' ... Only one sound reached her ears now, and that was the voice of the parrot. ...

They held conversations with each other, he repeating *ad nauseam* the three phrases in his repertory, she replying with words which were just as disconnected but which came from the heart.

(46–7)

After his posthumous glorification at the hands of a taxidermist, the rote-reciter of small talk becomes the deity's virtual spokesman, installed worshipfully in Félicité's room near a picture of the Paraclete so that the two mingle in her mind,

> the parrot being sanctified by this connexion with the Holy Ghost, which itself acquired new life and meaning in her eyes. God the Father could not have chosen a dove as a means of expressing himself, since doves cannot talk, but rather one of Loulou's ancestors'.

(50)

Loulou is thus doubly parodic: not only travestying human conversation through raucous mimicry but also, in Félicité's credulous imagination, coming to represent an interpreter of Sacred History. And accordingly that underlying dichotomy between the too natural 'hum of voices' and the too supernatural 'voice heard in the sweet music of the bells' remains effectively unmodified. By burlesquing both, the narrator seems on the one hand to dissociate himself from any presumption of authoritative (quasi-divine) privilege and on the other to rise so clearly above the level of human (quasi-animal) noise that his own voice is exempt from challenge: monopolising as if by default an intermediate position, quietly claiming sole custody of the significance of Félicité's story, and minimising the risk of being dispossessed of his proprietary role by any alternative interpretations.

This monopoly increases in the last two sections, and Félicité's deafness makes it seem natural that 'the pealing of bells and the lowing of cattle went out of her life. Every living thing moved about in a ghostly silence' (46). At the very end, as Félicité lies dying in her little upstairs room, she cannot hear 'the clear voices of the children, and the deep voices of the men' (55) from the religious procession below as it passes the wayside altar on which lies the stuffed and wormy remnant of Loulou; 'a deep silence' envelops her final moments as the 'gigantic parrot' soars overhead (71–3). Indeed, what can be told about Félicité within the chosen narrative mode of 'A Simple Heart' depends, in a sense, on keeping her quiet. Although the synoptic opening section mentions that 'her voice was sharp', it adds immediately that she seems 'always silent' (18). Ensuing sections confirm this, and constitute in effect the story of her silencing.

We can turn for a while from questions of voice and dispossession to questions of sequence and substitution by way of that same final sentence of section 1: 'Always silent and upright and deliberate in her movements, she looked like a wooden doll driven by clockwork.' Just as the narrator is permitted to dominate this text vocally, so too the joinery of narration moves Félicité along as if she were an automaton, a thing amongst things that are successively placed and replaced so as to produce by figurative means an *effect* of happenings. She herself becomes reified in accordance with her own notion of 'the order of things' (51). This subordination to an object-laden milieu has as much to do with the narrative momentum in general as with the 'nature' of an individual 'character'. For if we consider how one thing follows another in 'A Simple Heart' we find for the most part that it is by juxtaposition rather than by strict consequence, and by summary rather than by enactment. Causal links are absent. Instead there are quick and arbitrary shifts, often metonymic, from one chance situation or happening or figure to another (Hanoulle 1972: 45).

The catalogue of Félicité's misfortunes at the start of section 2 establishes the pattern clearly as being one of substitutive transformation. Her parents die, her sisters disperse, and in their stead (with only a comma intervening to mark the flicker) come successive employers, who abuse her; then Théodore ('God's gift') appears to offer the prospect of a permanent replacement for her suddenly dismantled family, but abandons her overnight – and so it continues through the rest of the story. One after another, those she has cared for all die: Virginie, Victor, Père Colmiche, Loulou, Mme Aubain. And yet this is not elaborated in terms of a psychology of deprivation (*pace* Debray-Genette 1970: 349); the sequencing is rhetorical. Not only does the text contain many constructions such as 'After the Poles it was Père Colmiche' (43) and 'but found one of his friends waiting for her instead' (21); it also makes extensive use of 'Then', and of very brief paragraphs, to manage quick transitions.

Section 1 may seem a mere descriptive prelude to the story proper, almost static in its manner of sketching the interior of Mme Aubain's house and indicating Félicité's situation within it. But an emphasis on subservience to physical and social constraints is particularly important in such details as the position of the house between alleyway and lane, the narrow entrance hall, the pile of boxes and cartons, the permanently closed drawing room upstairs – and, in the middle of the parlour mantlepiece, the clock designed to resemble a miniature temple of the hearth goddess Vesta. Félicité herself, like a true vestal votary, goes to sleep each evening in front of the hearth with a rosary in her hands; and this reinforced insistence on motifs of domestic devotion recurs with variations in later sections of the story, so that the movement of telling is generated by mutual transformations of the homely and the holy. Félicité's 'dog-like devotion' (43) is constant in impulse but its occasions and objects keep changing, through pious observances such as the making of a *reposoir* (altar of repose) with Virginie (30) and a series of other acts of worship up to her offering of Loulou for the final *reposoir*. Among her altarpieces are the *commode*, with its three candlesticks, at which Félicité prays beside Virginie's corpse (39), another *commode* in her own room, 'draped with a cloth just like an altar' (49), and the mantlepiece on which she places the stuffed parrot so that she can see it during her prayers (50). The whole bedroom looks like a cross between chapel and bazaar, full of 'such a quantity of religious bric-à-brac and miscellaneous oddments' (49). By shaping Félicité's story along the lines of a saint's life, with each episode an apparent link in an apparent chain that leads quasi-naturally to a beatific climax, the narrative sequence encourages a reader to overlook the arbitrariness of those rhetorical substitutions that speciously sanctify, in effect, a more and more cramped social situation. When, in the story's last sentence, Félicité imagines Loulou 'hovering [*planant*] above her head', it seems that the heavens are 'opening' (56); but there is an ironic echo, not to be missed, of her first awed impression of the Aubain household: 'she lived there in a kind of fearful awe caused by "the style [*genre*] of the house" and by the memory of "Monsieur" brooding [*planant*] over everything' (21). In its substitution of looming parrot/paraclete for looming patriarch, this trope indicates that she is still subordinate to 'the order of things', walled up soundlessly within her class.

On the one hand, then, the narration of this text comprises various devices that tend emphatically to control the exchange of meanings; but on the other hand, less emphatically, there are undercurrents that complicate (though they may not cancel) those meanings. Trying to decide which hand belongs definitively to the 'implied author' would be silly; the point is rather that 'A Simple Heart' contains intratextually the terms of different reading contracts, none endorsed by any definitive principle of signification. By lending themselves to be framed as allegorising the means through which vocal effects and sequential moves are produced, parts of this text implicitly authorise a reader to question such strategies and ask what is at stake. In this regard the grotesquerie of Loulou's metaphorisation, both as ridiculous vocal intermediary and as culmination of the series of sacred/profane inversions, is especially revealing. He can serve as a figure for textual self-reflection, a covert admission that the mimetic mode in terms of which the narrator tries to control voice and sequence must itself be sacrificed if the text is to become available to us for interpretation. Dying of his own debility (unlike comparable figures in the other two tales), Loulou cannot exert posthumous power except over that epitome of the naively literal reader, Félicité, who – as Shoshana Felman (1978: 159–68) has remarked – accepts at face value the identity of words and things, and is subjugated by the illusions of 'a realist reading'. Being reluctant to identify our own reading position with that of such a simple heart, 'whose intelligence was so limited' (36), we find ourselves outside 'the little circle of her ideas' (46) – and therefore able to question the authority with which the narrator presumes to make such condescending pronouncements. The *represented* enunciation, at the narratorial level within the utterance, can thus be at least partly divested of its power.

III

'The Legend of St Julian Hospitator', second of the *Three Tales*, opens in a manner reminiscent of the first section of 'A Simple Heart': again the main character is situated within an enclosed dwelling – very emphatically so this time, the château being ringed by several concentric features (Debray-Genette 1971: 48–9;

Brombert 1966: 223) – and again the pattern of the main character's life is synoptically foretold in the early pages. But from the outset this story shapes setting and character in a more schematic way. Indeed the narrative mode throughout the 'Legend' forsakes the pretences of realism and shows its manipulative hand. The issue of narratorial control comes right into the open in section 1 because the exposition of character and circumstance extends beyond mere conspectus, such as we get in 'A Simple Heart', to become insistently predictive. By supernatural means, Julian's parents are presented with a pair of prophecies about his future: his mother learns that he will become a saint, while his father, separately, is told that his son will be associated with much blood, much glory and an emperor's family. The two sorts of trajectory adumbrated by these two ghostly voices are incidentally illustrated, straight afterwards, by two corresponding sorts of story: pilgrims visit the castle with tales of their journeys to holy places, and warriors visit with tales of battles and wounds.

This pair of predictions about Julian, each reinforced by a brief sample of the genre appropriate to it, indicates proleptically two sorts of narrative ordering. Prediction, a device of strict control, requires the virtual sacrifice of possible alternative developments. A catch in this case is that the prophetic utterances appear to be discrepant; and they become well nigh incompatible when the second one, enigmatically referring to bloodshed, is amplified in explicit terms near the close of section 1 by a talking stag that Julian has wantonly shot. While a distant bell tolls (a motif associated in all three stories with divinely inspired speech), the beast curses him and predicts that he will kill his own parents. For a prospective saint, this poses a severe vocational embarrassment. For a reader, it offers part of a reflection on the narrative method generally. Much of section 1 has been taken up with accounts of Julian's obsessive bloodthirst and his incremental acts of cruelty. The killing of the deer comes at the end of a long hunting episode, which has been preceded by a series of sadistic brutalities towards smaller creatures. The slaughter may be read as acknowledging in disguised form this text's own violent suppression of the voices of social interchange. It is significant, for instance, that the talking stag belongs to a family group, 'a stag with a doe and its fawn' (67), that mirrors Julian's own. And a human analogy is explicit not only in the description of the stag but also in the emphasis on the hind's voice – 'a deep, heart-rending [*déchirante*], human cry [*voix*]'. (Soon afterwards, when by accident Julian almost kills his own mother, she too utters a cry that is *déchirant*.) That the animals are, in a sense, substitutes for people in the story's figurative scheme is plainly indicated in section 2, when Julian goes on another, more nightmarish hunting foray and is eluded by silent animals: 'His lust for blood took hold of him again, and since animals were lacking he would gladly have slaughtered men' (78).

The climax of section 2 articulates a horrific fulfilment of the stag's dire prediction, though not until other forecasts have come to pass: Julian does spill much blood (other people's) in battle, he decapitates a Caliph, he releases an Emperor from prison, he marries the Emperor's daughter, and he settles down with her in another castle. To carry out the requirements of his legend he must kill his parents – which, all unwitting, he does. Immediately he hears an echo of the voice of the prophetic stag.

The third and final section of the 'Legend' emphasises Julian's alienation from common humanity. Those people to whom he tries to tell his story shun him. Conversely he feels a revulsion from them:

> The craving to take part in the life of other men impelled him to go down into the city. But the bestial faces of the people he met, the noise of their work, and the triviality of their conversation froze his heart.
>
> (81)

So the voices of ordinary people break in briefly, but only to be silenced at once. Then in one of those abrupt, unmotivated shifts that abound in the 'Legend' as they do in 'A Simple Heart', Julian resolves to devote his life in utter humility to the service of others. This typifies the narrative structure generally; arbitrary substitution rather than interlinking of events is what produces the momentum. Instead of the bonds of causality, instead of entailment, there is just an alternation from one component story (a career of bloodshed) to the other (a career of saintliness), or a superimposition of one upon the other (Sherzer 1974: 64; Daniels 1972: 229–38). So Julian now takes up his dwelling in a crude little hut near a riverbank and acts as a ferryman for travellers. One dark and stormy night a voice resonant with echoes from elsewhere in the *Three Tales* summons him from the opposite shore: 'this penetrating voice had the sound of a church bell' (84). Julian fetches him and rows him across; his passenger is a hideous leper, to whom Julian gives food and drink. And then, at the leper's command, he puts him in his bed and warms him with his own body; whereupon the wretch is transfigured and ascends through a burst-open roof to the heavens as the risen Christ with Julian, speechless as ever, in his arms.

It has not escaped critical notice that the description of the leper establishes very specific verbal links with the prophetic stag and with Julian's father, so that the climactic embrace can be seen as a reconciliation of father (God) and son (saint) in which, as Berg (1982: 59) notes, family roles are partly transposed: 'Julian is obedient like a son, provident like a father; the leper is authoritative like a father, weak like a son'. But be that as it may, the narrative is functioning here in a way that cannot be reduced satisfactorily to a parable of familial psychology. Within the text's economy of figures, the leprous father, whose earlier disguise was that of an animal and who is now described as having skin 'colder than a snake' (86), can also be regarded as a screen for that excluded beastlike social world. And one is led to ask, then, whether this embrace amounts to a convincing act of inclusion. For embraces may merely disguise inequality rather than remove it, as with that moment in 'A Simple Heart' where the shared pain of bereavement impels Mme Aubain and Félicité to clasp one another 'in a warm embrace, satisfying their grief in a kiss that made them equal' (42), says the narrator – and yet the basic exchange rate between maid and mistress, emphasised at the start of the story, remains unaltered: one of them gets a mere hundred francs a year for doing all the work, the other sits in an easy chair and enjoys a comfortable income. Similarly, the embrace that concludes the 'Legend' does not alter Julian's reclusive disengagement from humanity at large. And this can be read as an implicit admission of the story's own omissions. No social element has, after all, been directly incorporated into the representation of Julian's experiences. The terminal embrace is simply gestural; and indeed since the leper is himself an outcast he mirrors Julian, who, far from overcoming his own alienation, is therefore embracing the very image of it. The narrator, ordering the hagiological outcome in accordance with divinely sponsored dictates, has kept semantic control only at the cost of sacrificing much of the human world, as figuratively acknowledged in the slaying of parents and animals.

If Félicité's 'simple heart' was regulated by a kind of bovine placidity, Julian's 'cruel heart' [*cœur féroce*] (67) represents a wilder animality which, like Félicité's heart, is as much a social product as a natural attribute. Julian is born into a cruelly controlled society, repressive, divisive and brutal. That can be glimpsed as background in the story but is never addressed by it. It is a world in which social privilege and religious prerogative attempt to maintain control by setting the rest of humanity as far away as animals. Young Julian studies Holy Writ while 'high up in a turret where there was no noise to disturb' (60); beasts of burden are sometimes seen below. Yet such isolation deprives *him*, too, of a voice. Only once in the entire story does he speak directly – when setting out on the hunting expedition from which he will return to kill his parents 'roaring like a wild beast' (79).

The narrator adds a brief postscript: 'And that is [*voilà*] the story of St Julian Hospitator, more or less [*à peu près*] as it is depicted on a stained-glass window in a church in my part of the world' (87). The effect of this is simultaneously to claim and disclaim a certain sort of authority. The *voilà* implies definitiveness, and yet distances what has just been told from its teller: there it is, there you have it. And the *à peu près* indicates a space for enunciative dispossession, casually stepping outside the official version's constrictive frame in the very act of citing it. And yet this is readable as a somewhat facile gesture, one that hardly erases, any more than does the transfigurative explosion of Julian's hermit-hut, the imagery of containment with which the 'Legend' began.

IV

And now to the third of the *Three Tales*, 'Herodias'. Considering how different in some respects is the manner of this last tale, its opening passage has a remarkably symmetrical resemblance to the openings of 'A Simple Heart' and the 'Legend'. Again the accent falls at once on strict enclosure: this time, the walled and fortified citadel of Machaerus, surrounded by an abyss. (The word *abîme* is thrice repeated in the expository preamble.) Within it is the palace of Herod Antipas, Tetrarch of Galilee; beyond the palace is a heap of houses where the common folk live, linked to the fortress by a wall that follows the 'uneven ground' [*les inégalités du terrain*] (89) – a reminder of those 'differences in level' which signify social inequality in Mme Aubain's house. Even more emphatically than with Julian's two castles, this citadel represents an attempt to control by exclusion. At the beginning of the story Herod stands looking out over the ramparts, full of apprehension because of barely subdued political conflicts all around him. Jewish factions, Arabs, Romans: all menace his precarious control.[8]

On this morning, all seems quiet at first. And then a disruptive element intrudes: 'Suddenly a voice in the distance, which sounded as if it came from the depths of the earth, made the Tetrarch turn pale' (90). The voice is that of Jokanaan (John the Baptist), imprisoned secretly in an underground dungeon. Loth to have him killed but fearing the disorder that his prophecies betoken, Herod summons his servant Mannaëi and asks for an account of the visit that a couple of men had made recently to John's cell. In words whose pertinence as self-commenting textual allegory will become plain later, Mannaëi reports: 'They exchanged some mysterious words with him, like thieves when they meet at crossroads in the evening. Then they went off towards Upper Galilee, saying that they would return with great tidings [*une grande nouvelle*]' (91). Mannaëi also tells Herod of an enigmatic utterance by John: 'If He is to wax, then I must wane!' (92). It is clear, though inexplicit, that he refers to Christ; we shall return shortly to the import of this allusion. Herodias appears next and expresses vengefully her desire to have John's voice silenced, for he had once shamed her by denouncing her in public as an adulteress. The incident is recalled in terms that unmistakably echo the descriptions of prophetic phantom, stag, father and leper in the 'Legend': 'His eyes flashed, his voice roared' (95; cf. 59, 67, 79, 84). Section 1 ends with a conversation between Herod and Phanuel, one of John's followers, which is interrupted by a message that the Proconsul Vitellius is soon to arrive at the citadel. Section 2 recounts the arrival of the Romans and a tour of inspection during which the secret cell of John is revealed. The prophet's mighty and fearsome voice is raised in a tirade that foretells the overthrow of the present régime and stirs the hearts of those Jews who are present: 'The people were reminded of the days of their exile and all the catastrophes of their history' (107). Repeatedly it is the power of his speaking that is emphasised: 'The voice grew louder and stronger, rolling and roaring like thunder, and as the mountains sent it back, it broke over Machaerus in repeated echoes' (109). And while claiming to prophesy on God's behalf, John also declares 'I will roar like a bear, bray like a wild ass' (108) – and others, too, associate him with animals (92, 95, 106).

In section 3, which is largely taken up with the great feast that evening, John becomes the subject of heated disagreements among different social groups. Meanwhile word has spread among the people that John is imprisoned in the palace, and a noisy crowd gathers at its gates. The abyss is filled with ant-like figures, 'swarming [*fourmillait*] in a dark mass' and shouting John's name (118). But inside the fortress, at her mother's instigation, Salome performs her voluptuous dance; Herod's desire is inflamed and he offers her whatever she wants; her demand, to which he accedes, is for John's head; and the gruesome act of exchange is carried out.

That is not quite the end of the story, but we can pause there to recapitulate. Herod, a figure of insecure power, is trying to control John, a figure who speaks with supreme confidence on behalf of divinely sanctioned power – as Herod himself recognises. To release him would be too dangerous: 'One does not release wild beasts' (98). For here in one man's voice are the accents of animal and God, and here also are two sorts of prophecy (similar to those that occurred in the 'Legend'), foretelling on the one hand death and judgement and on the other a new harmonious order (107). Although John is eventually killed at Herod's behest, this will fail to quell the power of his message; we know as much because the story alludes pointedly to other stories circulating beyond its own borders. Already section 3 has directly dramatised a variety of responses to the prophetic voice: different ethnic, religious and political groups at the feast have exchanged views on the resurrection; the populace has begun to swarm with excitement as John's words spread among them; Herodias has tried to silence him utterly. And then in an all-important epilogue the two nameless disciples return from Galilee, bringing Phanuel the long-awaited answer. Though unspecified, it is clearly the news that Jesus is indeed the Messiah heralded by John, whose words about waxing and waning, echoed here at the end, Phanuel now understands. In effect it is a principle of narrative power that is being announced: one storyteller must be dispossessed of a voice in order that another's may be heard, and yet that dispossession itself can enter into what is heard.

The kinds of exchange control differ somewhat from one of

Flaubert's tales to another, and a reader needs to frame them as an intertextual group in order to recognise the generic inflections that are involved. Each of the three has its own predominant means of combining narratorial voice with narrated sequence in order to authorise implicitly a particular mode of interpretation. Each also produces, as latent self-commentary, its own *effigy* of that seemingly authoritative way of telling – and once having elevated that effigy, it contrives to sacrifice it. In 'A Simple Heart', as we have seen, it is Loulou who embodies this reflexive textual figure, and he is soon reduced to the status of a stuffed absurdity. And whereas Loulou, even while alive, is a mere reciter of Félicité's own limited language, his counterpart in the 'Legend' is more potent, being independent of the main character, speaking in triplicate (stag, father, leper) as a patriarchal judge (67) and surviving violent attempts to silence it; and yet it remains dissociated from ordinary human exchanges. In contrast, the embedded model of enunciation in 'Herodias' is the voice of John himself, which not only spreads far and wide while he lives ('The speeches he had addressed to great crowds had spread far and wide, and were still circulating; [one] heard them repeated everywhere, and they filled the air'; 95) but also continues to relay stories after his death ('He has gone down to the dead to proclaim the coming of Christ'; 124). These mark differences in genre. Through Loulou, 'A Simple Heart' comments on the *realistic* mode in which it represents a silent saint-as-simpleton who accepts the social order passively; through its spectral judge-figures, the 'Legend' comments on the *mythic* mode in which it represents a silent saint-as-paradox who transcends the social order evasively; through John the Baptist, 'Herodias' comments on the *historiographic* mode in which it represents a vociferous saint-as-messenger who helps reshape the social order actively.

Intertextual framing has also a wider scope, as we can see if we notice how the efficacy of John's prophecies is associated with motifs of resurrection and growth. During the feast, one man claims that John is Elias reborn; and we know – through the vast circulation of texts regarded as 'history' – that the Messiah whose advent John foretells, and about whom stories are already being told at the feast, will himself eventually generate further stories of miraculous survival. (By way of contrast, another of those at the feast quotes the pagan Lucretius on the body's mortality: 'Nec crescit, nec post mortem durare videtur' (It neither grows, nor is seen as surviving death; 116). Thus it is the anticipated gospel that, by virtue of its emphasis on the indefinite transmissibility of narration and on the paradox that authority may grow more powerful for being executed, becomes this text's most comprehensive *mise-en-abyme*. Before his death, John's 'voice grew louder and stronger' while he prophesied (109); and his aphorism, repeated as the last quoted statement of the story, concerns the Word that will expand through his own demise.

The final sentences give us a glimpse of the three men setting out on the road to Galilee, taking turns at carrying John's heavy head, just as earlier (91) they had promised to be the bearers of *une grande nouvelle* – 'great tidings' (but *nouvelle* also means the literary genre of the short story). This portable relic is what the sacrificial demands of the story cannot dispose of entirely: as if the beheading of a unificatory implied *author* had allowed the textual *authority* of this triune group of tales to persist more variously, available to be reappropriated because severed now from any single nexus between narrating voice and narrated sequence. And we, as readers, find that we are sharing in this process of resurrecting and re-porting the capital left-over.

V

Before one gets very far into a reading of Marguerite Duras's *The Vice-Consul* there is little room for doubt that voice, sequence and control will be insistently problematic in this text. The opening sentence, a startlingly abrupt chiasmus, not only initiates a story but embeds it at once within a represented act of enunciation: 'She walks on, writes Peter Morgan.' The story of her walking proceeds immediately, and 'she' turns out to be a young Asian beggar, pregnant, cast out of her home by her mother. But we hear no further mention of the one who is telling her story until the second section (spatial breaks frequently segment the text, though there are no numbered chapters); and again only that briefest of identifications is given – 'writes Peter Morgan' (13). Reticence concerning the situation of the framed story's narrator may seem for a moment to be dispelled a few pages later, whereas in fact a reader's bearings are about to be thoroughly disturbed. The third section (a mere page long) begins, 'Peter Morgan has stopped writing' (18), and goes on to relate with apparent omniscience that 'Peter Morgan is young. He wants to shoulder the misery of

Calcutta.' His thoughts are seemingly laid open to view: 'A swarming ants' nest, thinks Peter Morgan. Dinginess, horror, the fear of God, misery and yet more misery, he thinks.' Following this, the section ends with an early-morning glimpse (focalised through Peter Morgan as observer) of the French Vice-Consul for Lahore emerging onto his balcony overlooking the Calcutta street where the beggar-woman sleeps; Peter Morgan leaves the scene. The focalisation then shifts at the start of the next section to the Vice-Consul as the previous scene is replayed – and several lines about the beggar-woman that have just been presented to us as 'what [Peter Morgan] knows' (18) now recur verbatim (20) – but as if rendering what the omniscient narrator knows, or perhaps what the Vice-Consul knows (since he seems for a while to be the focaliser). This is extremely disconcerting because it confuses the line between utterance and enunciation.

In retrospect it becomes clear, if one has not at first noticed this, that the instability of voice is already there from the opening page, with its merging of shifty pronouns and its lack of definite attribution or address:

> I need some signpost to lead me astray. Make your mind a blank. Refuse to recognise familiar landmarks. Turn your steps towards the most hostile point on the horizon, towards the vast marshlands, bewilderingly criss-crossed by a thousand causeways.
> She does so. Day after day she walks...

There is a simultaneity and even an implicit analogy between this kind of movement and the act of writing, as the book's opening sentence suggests; and correspondingly the act of reading such an errant text involves disoriention, so shifty are the deictics. Often we are unsure who is speaking, and where we stand in relation to the vocal mix. Thus, as the text proceeds to follow the Vice-Consul through his morning routine there are fragments of unattributed, untethered speech, such as this:

> In the garden, a voice can still be faintly heard asking: When the gentleman is at home, do you ever hear music played on the piano? Scales? A tune clumsily played with one hand? The voice of someone very old replies: Yes, long ago, at night, yes, a child used to pick out with one finger a tune...
> (23)

Apparently this is some kind of a memory trace, but partly dramatised and anonymous like the words of a chorus in a classical Greek play. It lasts for a paragraph, after which the narration seems to revert to omniscience – and yet, while voice stabilises temporarily, there are still oddities of sequence: for instance, the section ends with an unassimilated image of a bicycle propped against a tennis-court fence; we are simply told, 'It belongs to Anne-Marie Stretter' (25). Both Mme Stretter, who is the French Ambassador's wife, and her bicycle are among the substitutive figures by which this text progresses. As far as Anne-Marie Stretter's function is concerned, for example, it is not only that she subsequently merges with other women in the memory or imagination of her admirer Charles Rossett (151); what also occurs is that Rossett's private linking of her with his particular dream fantasy of 'a rosy-cheeked reader who reads Proust' (33) slips osmotically into the Vice-Consul's later description of the wife that *he* imagines his aunt will find for him – 'a rose-coloured reader, with rosy cheeks, reading Proust' (168).[9] Because of such slippages, Anne-Marie comes to seem something other than just an enigmatic character; she is hardly a character at all, in the usual sense, so much as a fluid image serving to effect transitions from one passage of the text to another. She is herself a figure for the desire to understand and be understood (97–9) and for the impossibility of understanding; significantly, she is often imagined to be reading (71, 159), but one 'cannot see what she was reading' (84). And the narrative function of her bicycle, similarly, is neither a 'syntactic' action-based one (it is not used for anything, except to be looked at and mentioned by some of the men) nor a 'semantic' one (it does not represent anything thematically, unlike the bicycle tied to a tree in Achebe's novel *Things Fall Apart*[10]); it is simply a textual device for forwarding the narration, and in itself it is disturbingly resistant to interpretation, just as she is. There are more than half a dozen further brief references to her bicycle, and they mostly emphasise its inscrutability and that of the men who refer to it (e.g. 35, 61, 108). While not *standing for* anything in a symbolic or paradigmatic sense, it does have the syntagmatic function of *standing in for* the missing connections between people, for the lack of any consequential dealings with one another. Thus it draws attention to the fact that the narrative sequencing works through metonymic disjunction, which in this case, unlike that of Flaubert's *Three Tales*, is not disguised as smooth cohesion. Non-sequiturs and inconsequentialities are strongly marked here: they not only occur in direct conversation (60, 114 *et passim*) but are often mentioned explicitly – for instance, in the beggar-woman's story, which seems to show 'no correlation between cause and effect' (146), at the reception, where onlookers see that 'nothing is going to happen, nothing' (95), and at the resort hotel, when Rossett 'loses the thread of [Anne-Marie Stretter's] narrative' (152).

Correspondingly, the lack of a dependably unifying voice is quite overt throughout this text. Several *mise-en-abyme* elements indicate that the 'whole story' cannot be told, and especially that no speaking position can comprehend the vast and intricate social problems of Asia. India itself, an amalgam of the 'many different Indias' (125) experienced by different people, seems a figure for the impulse to produce fiction rather than the capacity to accomplish it; Peter Morgan's options in his novel-in-progress are discussed sceptically by others (144–7), the Club Secretary longs fruitlessly to write a novel about what he has seen and heard in the cities of Asia (56), and the Ambassador had once tried in vain to do so (106). The Secretary and the Vice-Consul swap personal stories (56), the latter licensing a wider circulation of what he relates (67); but an air of improvised fictioneering hangs about it all, and the phrase 'tell or invent' is applied in each case (69). There are frequent confessions and allegations of lying (e.g. 102, 112, 138, 154). Much of what we learn about the titular character and about the Ambassador's wife is explicitly presented as a tissue of unsourced and unverified rumours (e.g. 24, 73). Words derive no simple guarantee from a speaker's identity; the Vice-Consul's voice is described by others as 'grafted on to him ... not his voice, but someone else's' (103); even his laugh is 'like the sound track of a dubbed film, utterly lacking in conviction' (87) – an anticipation of the radical method that Duras uses to disconnect voice from actor in her film *India Song*, which reworks elements of *The Vice-Consul*. And in addition to all these enunciative uncertainties there are specific instances of narrative dispossession affecting both the beggar-woman's story and the Vice-Consul's story. The most sharply marked occurs in the final section, when the Secretary and the Vice-Consul are again reminiscing drunkenly about the days of their youth in France. Previously we have learned that the former went to school near Arras in the Pas-de-Calais and the latter at Montfort in Seine-et-

Oise. Now, at the end, they appear to take over one another's histories; for instance the Vice-Consul tells tales that supposedly refer to *his* days in Arras. (There has been an anticipatory hint of this interchange: 76.) Any shred of confidence that a reader may have tried to preserve in the authority of any narrating voices is shown to be unfounded, for the effect is retroactive.

This dispossessive shift extends to the relation between the beggar-woman's story and the story of those associated with the diplomatic circle. Having known since the opening sentence that Peter Morgan is writing about this beggar who haunts the street near the Embassy, we later discover that a major episode in that story, concerning her selling of her child, was told to him by Anne-Marie Stretter, though the woman in her account was probably not the same one (54); and for the rest, in an act of cultural dispossession stemming from his desire 'to shoulder the misery [*prendre la douleur*] of Calcutta' (18), Peter Morgan is replacing the beggar's lost experiences [*à la place de ce qui a disparu*] with memories and inventions of his own (54–5). In this light the relative status of the two storylines can hardly be clear. Murphy (1982: 104) refers to that which deals with the Vice-Consul as the 'primary *récit* ' (A) and says that it frames the other one (B); but while this view is encouraged not only by the title but also by the fact that Peter Morgan as a character in A is the narrator of B, on the other hand the text begins with B and later tells us that Anne-Marie Stretter from A will also figure in B (147). As Willis (1987: 106) remarks, 'it is as if the framing story – Peter Morgan's narrative of the beggar-woman, with which the text opens – were continually invading, and becoming enfolded inside, the *framed story*'. The beggar-woman 'transgresses diegetic boundaries' (Borgomano 1981: 484)

What kind of narrative exchange, then, does this text offer its readers? It is not so much an exchange of meanings as a thwarting of the desire for it. This is implicitly suggested by the nature of several transactions that occur within the text, from sexual dealings (between the beggar-woman and the fishermen near the beginning, and between Anne-Marie Stretter and Michael Richard near the end) to familial relations, especially the treatment of daughters by mothers. Marcelle Marini (1977), in her extensive analysis of this novel, attaches exemplary importance to the way it dramatises the mother–daughter pair. In particular she sees the episode at the Vinh-Long market as crucial: there the beggar-woman, having received a coin from a passing white woman, persists in trying to hand over her baby to her, and eventually succeeds. Now for Marini this moment is not only an overcoming of the beggar's own banishment by her mother, it also represents quasi-mythically a distinctive feminine mode of exchange, one that refuses the primacy of a patriarchal order and institutes an alternative form of genealogy such as is envisaged theoretically by Irigaray.[11] But the significance of this hand-over in Duras's text seems more elusive than that, by no means amounting to the 'new system' of relations that it symbolises for Marini (1977: 257). Its ambiguity is underlined in a conversation between Peter Morgan and his friends: 'Finally, the exchange, if that's what it was, or, to put it another way, the giving up, was not, in the long run, very different from any other exchange or surrender. And yet it did take place' (146). Rather than symbolising a 'restitutive gift' (Marini 1977: 258), the beggar-woman's way of passing on her child can be seen as a disengaging and mobilising act, similar to Anne-Marie Stretter's rotation among the men at the reception (and elsewhere) or to the continual transfer of stories among unstable enunciative positions. None of these dealings clinches a contract; they effect a circulation.

This can be seen in certain symmetries between Anne-Marie Stretter and the beggar-woman (and indeed the Vice-Consul), not in their actantial roles but in their figurative aspects. Though at opposite extremes socially, and seeming to perform different functions in their respective stories, both women move beyond the pale of safety: one of them sleeps at night, during her long trek, 'where the tigers are' (37) outside the fires that protect villages, and later among the outcast Calcutta lepers; the other swims at night in the sea, 'beyond the wire fencing designed to keep out the Delta sharks' (160). In this they resemble the Vice-Consul of Lahore, whose very designation suggests in French his beyond-ness (*là*, there; *hors*, outside). The beggar-woman seems to shadow Anne-Marie Stretter (159) as if she is her counterpart, and in one of the last scenes of the novel the two female figures almost coalesce in Charles Rossett's imagination: having just left the resort hotel, hearing the beggar-woman's song from somewhere nearby, he sees Anne-Marie emerge from the hotel and walk towards the beach, realises he has lost his desire for her and imagines that she is losing her memory (159–61); then he is accosted by the beggar-woman (who herself is a figure for forgetting: 145) as she emerges from the waters of the lagoon, and although he flings down coins for her she does not stop for them but pursues him until he takes refuge behind the hotel fence; and her song, again bringing Anne-Marie Stretter to his mind, is heard once more (163–5).

This novel links music with loss – loss of erotic or maternal love, loss of origins – and with the impossibility of a completely meaningful exchange. The recurrent motif of the beggar-woman's song is a simple incantation, hardly distinguished from her repetition of the name of her natal village, Battambang, where her mother cast her out. The strange word itself is not a communicative sign but a vestige; 'everything else has evaporated' (146).[12] Comparably, the piano tune of 'Indiana's Song' is associated with the Vice-Consul's mother, who herself is said to have played the piano and to have 'walked out and left him' (23, 74–5, 96); and it 'evokes the memory of that lonely, dark, abominable act' (79) which lost him his position in Lahore. In a similar way the Schubert piece that Anne-Marie Stretter plays, with its compellingly repeated melody (128–9), is linked with her conjectural past as a 'beloved child of Venice' (149) and with her Venetian mother (85). Each of these musical elements, connoting severance and residue, is a figure for the substitutive process by which the text moves along.

The last section of *The Vice-Consul* leaves us with that eponymous personage talking disjointedly to the Club Secretary, whose stories he has now appropriated as his own. He expects that in his new posting in Bombay he will continue to be the object of others' curiosity, always being photographed. Of himself he has 'nothing more to tell' (169). This final image of him can be read as a figure for the implied author of Duras's ultimately non-specular text, frustratingly elusive because of the apparent relinquishment of exchange controls. He is, as Peter Morgan remarks bluntly, 'only interesting in his absence' (116), and the prefix in his title announces his ersatz status: 'in place of' or 'acting as substitute for' another, a deputy's deputy, with no authority vested directly in his own person, since it is not he but the full Consul who represents a sovereign state. Having 'shattered the mirrors' in his residence at Lahore (127), the Vice-Consul cannot be seen as a reflection. His motives are impervious to scrutiny; just as the title of his own theme-tune Indiana Song is illegible (22), so too it is 'impossible' for others to read him (59). It is therefore inappropriate to impose, as Bal does (1974: 15), a psychological explanation on his behaviour.[13]

These elements in *The Vice-Consul* demonstrate the aptness of a remark by Willis (1987: 3) that Duras's texts 'exemplify a resistance to consumption and disposability', in offering a reader only 'repetition and intertextual circulation'. It is perhaps true that such resistance may in its turn be caught up within a system of exchange, as Barthes suggests (in an image reminiscent of this novel) when he asks provocatively, during a discussion of mercantile pressures on contemporary literature, 'Is today's writer the residual substitute for the beggar ... [being] unproductive, but provided for?' – and answers that even a seemingly parasitic or gratuitous role gets drawn into a 'circuit of expenditures' (1975: 23–4). According to Barthes, no attempt to deny the marketing of signs can avoid being recuperated eventually by that economy. Nevertheless at the micro-level, for a reader of *The Vice-Consul* who is attentive to intratextual and intertextual framing, it remains the case that any wish to invest in a stable semantic exchange will be blocked or deflected; no interpretive effort can get a secure purchase on this novel because it is so disjunctive within itself and because its narrative components are transferred to and from other texts by Duras[14], which variously transvalue them.

We have seen that the notion of an 'implied author' attempts to contain semantic negotiations within the field of a unitary subject. The following chapter will look at the way in which linguists try to analyse textual 'unity', and at what occurs when a cluster of texts signed by different writers participate in a game of challenge and riposte. Among the issues to be raised is the gendering of narrative exchanges, and its relation to what one of these texts calls 'paragovernment'.

5
FICTIONS OF CHALLENGE AND RIPOSTE

'In other words, you lack theory,' he said, 'you have no coherent critique. . . . Your behaviour is purely interaction'.
(Moorhouse 1977: 111)

The essential feature of text . . . is that it is interaction . . . It is perhaps the most highly coded form of the gift.
(Halliday 1978: 139–40)

His story he gives me is an impossible object. . . . [E]ach detail is persuasive, representational, but as one's eyes focus back to see the whole construct, the pulsing, shift, alternating impossibilities are apparent.
(Wilding 1978a: 48)

I

The importance attached by Bourdieu (1977) to the tempo of exchanges and to the opportunities that these provide for strategies of challenge and riposte was mentioned in the Introduction. Similarly, Lyotard (1984) has drawn attention to the spatio-temporal dynamics of repositioning in a communicative situation:

Each language partner, when a 'move' pertaining to him is made, undergoes a 'displacement', an alteration of some kind that not only affects him in his capacity as addressee and referent, but also as sender. These 'moves' necessarily provoke 'countermoves'.
(16)

In narrative, the moves and countermoves can become very intricate when one storyteller claims to be correcting or completing a prior text, and even more so when the question of priority itself is contested. The present chapter compares four rivalrous texts, each purporting to give the 'true' account of something allegedly misreported by one or more of the others.

At the heart of this matter is the notion of textual unity. We saw in chapter 4 that it tends to accompany the 'implied author' postulate; here it will be scrutinised in terms drawn from sociolinguistic analysis, for its exponents commonly take a 'text' to be 'any passage that forms a unified whole' (Halliday and Hasan 1976: 1). This definition is a little too innocent, because the verb 'forms' could seem to imply, deceptively, an autotelic process that virtually elides human agency. A sharper definition would regard a text as *being formed* in such a way that it has an *ostensible unity*, whose intended function is to curtail meaning. As a preliminary gloss on that last clause, here are some remarks from the book *Language and Control* (Fowler and Hodge et al. 1979: 63):

> All language is addressed to someone, and involves an addressee as well as an addresser; it is relational. We suggest that communicative relationships are generally asymmetrical, in the sense that one participant has more authority than the other(s); that differences of class or status are at issue in discourse; the relationship is more or less competitive, a negotiation for power.

In *written* language, especially fictive texts, this negotiatory process is likely to be mediated in complex ways. In the absence of a direct speaker/listener relationship, surrogates intervene. As previous chapters have shown, within written narrative fictions the imprint of authority tends to be most potent – but also most at risk, most open to scrutiny – in two areas of selection: voice (exerting control as to whose side of the story is told, and thus trying to secure itself against dispossession) and sequence (exerting control as to how and where, through substitutive processes, the story moves and stops).

In that light, the sociolinguistic concept of text as a verbal 'exchange of meanings' (Halliday 1978: 139–41) can become clearer. This Hallidayan formulation may seem valuable in emphasising that signification is structurally produced through a process of exchange; but its weakness is that it does not emphasise how readily the semantic content invested by one participant may be transvalued or subverted by the other. Indeed, Halliday states explicitly that a text is the kind of gift which 'does not in the slightest degree impoverish the giver' (1978: 140). Freadman (1987: 92–3) shows through a witty analogy with tennis why that view is inadequate. The players, she remarks, do not exchange balls, they exchange shots; and the distinction, she suggests, is very much like that between 'exchanging meanings' and exchanging *signs* :

> Player A plays a shot. . . . Player B is, let's say, the 'receiver', but to *receive* a shot s/he must return it, play, that is to say, another. The same shot, then – Player A's serve – has a *different value* for each of the two players: a 'good shot' may win a point for its player, but, well received, it may turn against s/him, its speed, its turn, or its angle enabling an unexpected return.
>
> To suppose that discursive interaction is the giving and receiving of *meanings* is like describing a game of tennis as the giving and receiving of balls. To suppose, on the contrary, that it is the playing of shots is to allow the value of those shots to be subject to play, and the meaning of the interaction to be the upshot of the perpetual modification of each shot by its return.

Plainly, the possibilities for making shots are not unrestricted: not only are there limits to individual skill, and once the ball is in play a shot is constrained by the shot to which it is a 'return', but also what any tennis player may do at any given point is formally determined by the rules of the game.

These conditions and conventions, which both permit and shape the shot-making, correspond broadly to 'register' in the Hallidayan schema. Register comprises a triad of enunciative variables: field, tenor and mode (Halliday 1978: 31). 'Field' refers to the particular set of actions into which a given text is being inserted, 'tenor' to the relations between participants in the textual exchange, and 'mode' to the way in which the communication is being channelled – basically in oral or written form, rhetorically organised to fit the occasion. In brief, then, the three semiotic structures that constitute a discursive situation are indicated by these questions: What is going on? Who is taking part? What role is the language medium playing?

The general utility of this tripartite schema is not in doubt. But while it may be applied neatly in studies of 'unmarked' cases and norms – of oral language development, of routine conversations, or of writing that is fairly limited in scope – it needs a more subtle inflexion to deal with the way literary texts (i.e., those read as literary) often complicate their situational structures. For instance, with regard to *tenor*, one has to consider how the readability of certain narrative fictions may depend on a presupposition 'that a given segment of text, in specular relationship with another such segment or with the text as a whole, can be conceived as a "model" of the text, or text segment, to which it is compared' (Chambers 1984: 29). Enunciative aspects of an utterance are inscribed in such a way that, among the various textual devices proposing guidance to the reader, there may occur a form of embedding or *mise-en-abyme*, which 'implies the representation, internally to the fictional framework, of a situation involving the major components of a communicational act (emitter–discourse– recipient) – and very frequently the mirroring within a story of the storytelling relationship itself: narrator–narration–narratee' (33). An example from Chambers (mentioned in chapter 1 above) is the embedded narrational situation in Balzac's 'Sarrasine', where

> a narrator with specific qualities (e.g. maleness) is using his storytelling as a means of influencing (specifically, seducing) a narratee, also endowed with specific qualities (e.g., female- ness) – an act whose performance and outcome are deter- mined by the precise relationship of power, knowledge, and desire distributed between the two.
>
> (34)

Now it is plain that a function of these embeddings of tenor is to limit a reader's interpretive freedom; but it is equally plain that they cannot be guaranteed to do so with complete efficacy. For the reader must decide, as Chambers remarks, 'whether a specific embedded feature is a model or an antimodel of the text in question, or something in between' (35) – and furthermore *may* decide to reject the implied how-to-read directive anyway. In the very act of constructing an appropriate tenor – by allocating, for instance, a particular set of satisfyingly differential roles for narrator and narratee within an embedded storytelling situation – a text runs the risk of revealing how the confidence trick is performed, how arbitrary is the conferral of dominant storytelling rights, how much it requires a relinquishment or suppression of alternative sides of the story, and hence how adjustable or even reversible the balance of narrative power might be.

Questions of tenor can thus become complicated by questions of mode. The counterpart in written narration to those auxiliary signals, such as intonation and gesture, by which the teller of an oral story may try overtly to make the telling more 'telling' must be less directly interpersonal. The governance of meaning is therefore less secure in writing, more liable to interpretive variation; and any would-be reinforcement of the narrating position can have a recoil effect. That is, the desire to authorise pre-emptively one kind of tenor relation rather than another may induce resistance by drawing attention to what it wishes to overrule. Apart from recent work by Chambers (1984) and Maclean (1988), proper consideration of this means by which texts implicitly propose plausible positions for transacting their semantic business has seldom been closely examined in literary theory. There is still much to be discovered about how narrative contracts are inscribed and how they may leave room for dispossessive positional shifts.

For another reason as well, the interpretability of literary storytelling tends to be less stable than in most other language situations. As has been argued in earlier chapters, the process of figurative shuffling also runs counter to any attempt to fix significance within a unifying frame. At issue here is the question of modal connectedness. In discussing aspects of mode in 'ordinary' language use, those who take a systemic-functional approach tend to emphasise syntactic and semantic ligatures. Analogously, structuralist narratology tends to emphasise interlinked action sequences. But another way to analyse the rhetorical mode of a narrative text, as we have seen, is to emphasise points of severance or cleavage; that is, to trace the way narration proceeds by juxtaposing differential and discrete figures in an illusory sequence, a series of metonymic substitutions.

II

Discourse analysts usually confine the term 'substitution' to a particular form of cohesive relation between linguistic items, where one expression may simply replace another in a sequence. There are problems in that view, as Brown and Yule (1983: 201–4) have remarked. However, as understood in the present study, substitution is a much more extensive and variable set of devices; indeed it exceeds all that Halliday and Hasan (1976) call 'cohesion'. It can figure in any of the three functions that Fowler (1981) identifies as constituting textual structure: cohesion, progression and localisation. 'Cohesive' features are those by which a text seems to hang together, achieving consistency among its lexico-grammatical components; 'progressive' features, in Fowler's usage, lead the reader onwards in a spatial or temporal sense, for instance by adverbial means, by contiguities or by tense markers; and 'localising' features depart in a marked way from the ongoing textual norm, arresting the reader's attention by some device that draws attention to itself, such as repetition. These functions can overlap, and are likely when they do to produce an effect of what the present study calls substitution, an effect which often contributes more importantly to serial narrative structure than does any interlinking of events.

Here is a short and simple example, from the beginning of a modern Australian story:

> The hotel was shoulder to shoulder. I was shoulder to shoulder with Hestia in the square-shaped bar which we stood around and which read, left to right: the shoulder chains and leather of the greasy bikeheads; shoulder to shoulder with the pale turtle necks of the camp bikeheads; the starch of the blue psychiatric nurses; the hunch of domino players; the semi-non-conformist middle class with red and blue dot peasant neckerchiefs, some daring to wear beads; radicals in battle dress, back (or shoulder) to Hestia and me, shoulder to shoulder. We are as much our fringe as our core.
> Perhaps.
> We also stand shoulder to shoulder within ourselves.
> 'He wiped his feet on me and then broke my back', she said.

The *localising* device here, a tenfold repetition of 'shoulder' in the first five sentences, is obvious enough. Also involved is a metonymic *progression*, a reading of the bar from side to side, from shoulder to shoulder. *Cohesion*, too, is at work, tying sentences together by such relations as pronouns, both anaphoric ('we' and 'she' have preceding referents) and cataphoric ('he' anticipates its referent). But it is interesting to note that the first-person plural pronouns are not stable in reference. The 'we' in 'the square-shaped bar which we stood around' is more particular than in 'We also stand shoulder to shoulder within ourselves'; for the latter has a generic (i.e. purportedly universalising) quality, emphasised by the shift from past to present tense, and moreover its predicate is metaphorical, like the gnomic utterance about fringe and core. There is, then, in that pronominal slide and that troping movement of 'shoulder', a process of change under way, something not explicable by a straightforward linguistic account of co-reference, nor for that matter by any sequence of events. In terms of orthodox literary analysis we could only say lamely that this is a passage of description or exposition, a setting of the scene. But already the text is developing its strategy of control, conveying an ideology through a style. For this juxtaposition of segments is not only the narrational method, generating an illusion of motion by substituting one figure for another, seriatim; it is also the 'real' social structure that it represents as a series of side-by-side signs whose value (e.g. fringe or core) differs according to where one stands – or on whom.

It is this rhetorically produced illusion of narrative movement, not any plottable action, that gives space for the story to occur. There is something similar in any mobile narrative trajectory, which might then be seen as analogous to the paradoxical flight of Zeno's arrow, neatly summarised in deconstructive terms by Culler (1979: 162–3): 'At any given time the arrow is at a particular spot. ... The motion of the arrow is never given as something simple and present which could be grasped in itself; it is always already complex and differential, involving traces of the *not-now* in the *now.*'

But meanwhile, back in the hotel, what of Hestia? The quoted passage opens a text entitled 'The Oracular Story'. This is the rest of its first page:

'He wiped his feet on me and then broke my back,' she said.
'You've done that to others.'
'That doesn't help, saying that.'
'I thought you were beyond emotional attack.'
'Oh yeah, I forgot,' she said.
She was crying. I placed a hand on her black denim shirt,

'Hey come on – they love dancing well who dance among the thorns.'

'That sort of dance isn't my style anymore,' she said, 'or the thorns.'

'Love is . . . lawless?'

'He said to me – let's have a little predictability in our life. Keep away from the whirlpools. Have a few people to dinner. Milton wanted to try another way of living. He wanted to try open fires and classical music.'

'A nice brochure.'

'That's why you had to leave the Big House.'

'Oh – is that why.'

'But he's still your friend.'

'And now he's thrown you out,' I said. 'Young cocks . . . love no coops?'

If one attempted to summarise the rest of the story as a sequence of events, it would probably go something like this: after further pub talk, Hestia swallows a fistful of nembutal tablets; the narrator takes her home, by which time she is apparently asleep; he strips her, puts her to bed, and after becoming aroused at the thought of Milton's previous access to her, rapes her while she sleeps; a few days later he is at her place when Milton arrives and a hostile conversation occurs during which Hestia laughingly tells Milton what the narrator had done while she was unconscious; the narrator then suggests to Hestia that she take some more tablets and go to bed with him again; time elapses, and he next reports bits of conversation with Hestia as they swim in a lake, have breakfast in a secluded cottage, ride motorbikes along bush trails, make love (while both conscious, this time) and talk some more. But such a summary, merely abstracting a set of successive happenings, tells us very little about the motor on which this text runs or the way it operates as a transaction – about the field within which it should be placed, about the tenor of relations between its participants, and about the mode through which its language is shaped.

Field, tenor and mode invade one another here. One might say that the field of 'The Oracular Story' seems to be libertarian life in a modern city; but that is much too imprecise. To say more exactly what is 'going on' must be to examine its triangulation of intercourse, which – being verbal as much as sexual – is intricated with questions of both tenor (Who is saying and doing what to whom?) and mode (How is it being said and done?). For instance one could note, framing its mode circumtextually, that this item of text is a story surrounded by other stories, most immediately (though not only, as we shall see) in a book called *Tales of Mystery and Romance* by Frank Moorhouse, published in Sydney in 1977 and bearing in its material presentation all the conventional signs of fictionality. ' The author states that no identification is intended with living people', according to a prefatory guarantee; but this is two-edged. It might seem that the tenor of this exchange can be described simply in terms of 'author' and 'reader' roles, the former being in this case identifiable with a certain Moorhouse who writes and does certain other things as a known semi-public personage in the Australian literary world. And yet the announced fictive status of the text requires us to understand its tenor a little more carefully. It would be just as incautious to assume that the narrating 'I' inscribed within the utterance is directly equivalent to the enunciating subject designated by that authorial name on the book's cover as it would be to assume that the signature Frank Moorhouse plays no part in the exchange. What occurs between author and reader in a case like this does so through textual intermediaries, and the precise angle of refraction may prove indeterminable.

Besides, the mode is duplex. As the title explicitly indicates, speech will be highlighted – but through written representation. The story is 'oracular' in that it consists very largely of portentous pronouncements by the narrator – though these are mostly embedded within dialogue, and whatever sense we invest them with has to be gauged with an eye to the rhetorical particulars of the reported conversational exchanges. Much of the dialogue, especially towards the end, is taken up with stooge questions from Hestia and authoritative-sounding answers from the unnamed 'first person'. His statements tend to be abstract and sententious, with an almost catechismic quality, as if he were glibly quoting in a chain of factitious substitutions:

> 'What of the future of the world?'
> 'Destruction of the species.'
> 'When?'
> 'A date has been calculated but not released.'
> 'Will any survive?'

'A handful will escape to another planet.'
'What is the purpose of life?'
'The loss of consciousness through immersion. Most people do it very well.'

(114–15)

'I do have answers', the narrator tells Hestia – and what he adds next, by way of advice to her, could as well comment on his own discursive procedure: 'Make an arbitrary decision. Respond then to the challenges set in motion by the arbitrary decision' (112). His answers *per se* do not matter, as he finally admits; they merely bespeak his arrogation of authority.

The rhetorical device by which the story concludes is a sudden switch from the succession of questions and answers to a final imperative. Hestia is speaking:

> 'Where do you get your new certainty, your new answers?'
> 'I'm tired of people who pretend *not* to have all the answers.'
> 'Do the answers matter?'
> 'No.'
> 'Fuck me,' she said, 'fuck me you oracular bastard.'
>
> (115)

Such a finale seems unlikely to mark a new active role for Hestia; all she demands, apparently, is that he do *to* her what he is obviously intent on doing, and the transitive direction of the verb maintains her in a passively compliant position. That is, this arrangement of language has an ideological dimension. As represented, her closing line is not in any substantial sense an answer to his answers, not a resolution of any of the human conundrums broached in the story and not a sign of resistance to the narrator's demands – as it would have been if she had retorted, 'Fuck *you* . . .'. In short, no dispossession occurs. She merely yields to him, as orifice to oracle; and this makes it uncomfortable that the title slyly suggests an analogy between the narrator's dealings with Hestia and the text's dealings with a reader.

To clarify what such an analogy involves, we can usefully turn again to the book by Chambers (1984), discussed in chapter 1. It argues that 'the maintenance of narrative authority implies an act of seduction':

> This is never more the case than when the narrative content

is acknowledged to be fictional, that is, non-informative (in the conventional sense of the term): the 'point' of the narration can only lie then in its obtaining from the narratee a specific type of attention (to which the information divulged may certainly be germane but cannot be essential).
(51)

Narration, Chambers demonstrates, is frequently and variously thematised within texts as a strategically duplicitous act of seduction, not least in the ways in which it may disclaim any such intent. That insight is plainly pertinent to our consideration of 'The Oracular Story', in which seductive moves are of several sorts. One might read it as a tale of the progressive capitulation of Hestia to the narrator, through the stages of being involuntarily subjected to his will, subjecting herself voluntarily, and asking to be subjected. But there is more to it than that, because both sexual exchange and narrative exchange involve a third party. Milton is the obscure object of desire for the narrator as well as for Hestia. If the narrator's utterances to Hestia have the instrumental function of gaining him access to her body, that physical access in turn has the instrumental function of gaining him vicarious contact with Milton. As he grotesquely puts it when speaking to her, 'You are the vessel from which we [Milton and I] both drink' (115) – and yet she is more than their receptacle. Through her relations with the two men, she becomes a *sign* to be exchanged, a sign whose different value for each of them the narrator tries to control and fix by careful placement of his narrative 'shots'. Hestia turns into a figure for his own act of narration: not a reciprocated meaning, but a point to be won. In so far as she is also a player, it is as a stand-in or surrogate. Milton is the obliquely positioned 'receiver', the one whose textual and sexual attention the narrator seeks.

III

But the boundary between text and context, between story and situation, between participants and onlookers, can be indefinite. The narrator need not be left in possession of the 'field' he has staked out. And if among readers of 'The Oracular Story' there is someone who may see himself as partly corresponding to the fictive Milton, then the solicited exchange has another dimension, its account of sordid seduction serving as a piquant ploy in a kind of semantic contest with private overtones.

This would be idle conjecture were there not, in fact, a published story by another hand in which Milton materialises as narrator to attempt a revision of registers, a usurpation of the teller's authority, a feat of dispossession. Here is the deft first paragraph of 'The Nembutal Story' published in Michael Wilding's *The Phallic Forest* (1978), a book that is dedicated to Frank Moorhouse[1]:

> Reading his story the incident of the nembutal she swallowed in the pub seemed indisputable. It was as he had told me it had been, some years ago now, three years back, and the other people who had been there weren't in his story, but the incident itself, the swilling down the handful of tablets and the attempt to swallow another ten or so at a second gulp, this was as he had told me. What he hadn't told me at the time was that he had taken her back home, undressed her, put her to bed, lubricated her cunt with KY jelly and fucked her while she was unconscious. Had I simply read that page, not knowing there was any incident it was based on, I would have thought it just another of his decreasingly pleasant stories, with their fading distinction between fictional creation and compulsive fantasy. His need to fuck someone unconscious displayed there, convincingly displayed; and I might have wondered if he had done that. Knowing there was a basic incident, my feelings were somewhat more complex. Though it is another girl he's been having a scene with who the fucking while unconscious definitely happened to, that was the time Henry Bosco raped me was how she put it as we lay there, and she asked me not to tell anyone about the rape, which she couldn't substantiate anyway, particularly not to tell him whom she had never told. And now perhaps one sees why, suspecting perhaps his fascination with such a possibility, wanting to get her to lace her drink and fuck her when she passed out, that after all was what he put in Part II of the story he gave me to read, suggesting to Wesley she swallowed some nembutal and gin and they did it again. And what's in it for me? I think he had her say.
>
> (44–5)

The 'Nembutal' narrator makes male manipulation and rivalry the acknowledged field of these textual exchanges. He tries to achieve ascendancy over the 'Oracular' narrator in three ways: seeking greater complicity with readers through use of an intimate monologue uninterrupted by dramatised dialogue; introducing a more complicated and puzzling sexual geometry with the references to the unnamed 'new girl', to 'Henry Bosco' (an anglicised form of the name of a French regional writer), and later to others; and problematising in a more radical way questions about reliability, ascertainability and authorised versions.

Even from such a brief sample as the quoted opening paragraph, it is apparent that this narrative riposte will not purport to divulge what 'really' happened. Rather its procedure is to suggest that fact and fiction always commingle inextricably, making it impossible to retrieve even what it teasingly calls 'the basic incident'; and that any exchange will involve a struggle for control over what is being transacted. There is hardly anything in this story that unequivocally recounts a palpable action, even in passing. Instead it dwells speculatively on the elusiveness of any secure knowledge of any set of events.

This is underlined by certain discrepancies at the textual level between 'The Oracular Story' and the story to which 'The Nembutal Story' refers. A reader who can see that the latter has some dependence on the former may well think it odd that 'Hestia' has become 'Wesley' and that the later story talks about 'Part 2' of the earlier story – which has no such division into parts; or that, further on, the narrator says: 'In his story she is unhappy because a character called Milton has fucked her brother'(47) – yet 'The Oracular Story' mentions no such brother. These incongruous details can be simply explained. There was an earlier version of Moorhouse's tale. It differed in several details and was segmented into three short parts under the general heading of 'The Oracular Stories', which circulated as part of a booklet called *The Illegal Relatives*, written by Moorhouse and produced, with obscene graphics, by an underground publisher. Wilding's text refers to that version. A yet more complicated textual history is traceable for this pair of stories, taking into account their circulation in manuscript, their public readings, their links with other stories – for instance with 'Wesley's Brother at the Wake for Jack Kerouac', which appeared in an anthology edited by Moorhouse (1973), their appearance in successive issues of a periodical co-edited by Moorhouse and Wilding and later in an anthology edited by Wilding (1978b).[2] But these details do not fundamentally alter the problematic of their interrelation. For regardless of origins and recensions, those discrepant elements noted above can serve to illustrate the point that no textual unity is of fixed compass. The visible, tangible, circumtextual limits of its embodiment in a particular cluster of pages do not mark a story's ultimate boundaries. It can never be more than provisionally complete, since 'there is an unlimited number of other narratives that can be *constructed in response* to it or *perceived as related* to it' (Smith 1980: 221).

Moreover this point is fortified both by the cunning way 'The Nembutal Story' moves along and by the playful way it blows the gaff on its own narratorial credentials. Much of the momentum comes from quick shifts, often in mid-sentence, as one half-told incident or half-glimpsed character gives way abruptly to another. These function as unstable ironies; each successive mention, on that first page or so, of the 'incident', or of what has been 'told' about it, moves us nearer to a *mise-en-abyme* of the most paradoxical sort. The regression accelerates in the dizzying substitutions of that single sentence in which we learn of an apparent replica of the rape, said to have 'definitely happened' in this case yet also said to be unsubstantiated, involving another (unnamed) woman and another (improbably named) man, as well as the same two men (that is, those sexual and narratorial rivals, Milton and 'him'), featuring narrative prohibitions (broken here in the act of being reported during a more literal kind of embedding). No plot emerges from 'The Nembutal Story'. Rather, resorting again to Fowler's terms, it can be noted that one of the main 'progressive' (i.e., story-forwarding) elements in the narration is a 'localising' (i.e., attention-focusing) effect of deviations from normal 'cohesive' usage. The first couple of sentences exemplify this, with their awkward juxtaposition of references to 'his' (the Oracular narrator's) oral and written versions of 'the incident', made even more productively awkward by that irregular grammar at the very start, with its dangling participial phrase: 'Reading his story the incident of the nembutal she swallowed in the pub seemed indisputable.' Other syntactical slippages, as the story continues, tend even more to let one part of an utterance slide away from another, making readers increasingly dependent on the teller at the same time that he disarmingly casts doubt on his own authority to tell. Unlike the Oracular narrator, this one acknowledges that he is unreliable – and thus ingratiates himself with us, appearing to be, as candid parasite, more trustworthy than the narrator of the host text.

By foregrounding in this fashion the inescapably substitutive nature of narration and the compulsion of narratorial authority to risk dispossession, Wilding's text emphasises the need to refine some tenets of discourse analysis. It is quite true, as Ruqaiya Hasan declares, that 'the central notion in the definition of the text is that of unity' (Halliday and Hasan 1985: 70; Hasan 1980: 75); but in practice, linguists have not always paid due attention to the problematic nature of this notion and to its ideological aspect in particular.[3] In the pair of stories discussed here, arbitrary ways of framing a 'whole construct' turn out to be under challenge. Narrators may bid for control either by rhetorical closure (as in 'The Oracular Story', which confines its dialogue to exercises in micro-terminal domination and then rounds itself off with a specious air of finality) or, less palpably and perhaps more shrewdly, by an illusion of textual freeplay (as in 'The Nembutal Story', which appears to open itself to a virtual semantic infinitude through self-ironising references to suspect gifts such as the Trojan horse and to optical illusions such as Escher's graphics). What the Nembutal narrator says about his rival's account of the elusive 'incident' amounts also to a dissolving of any *histoire* into a figment of *discours*: 'His story he gives me is an impossible object ... each detail is persuasive, representational, but as one's eyes focus back to see the whole construct, the pulsing, shifting alternating impossibilities are apparent' (48).

IV

Whether seemingly closed or open, however, a story strengthens its particular brand of narratorial authority only by suppressing, more or less tacitly, alternative sides of the story. The nembutal mode of narration, no less than the oracular, disguises rape as seduction. Female acquiescence or even silence is a precondition in these cases for what the male narrators want to tell each other. Hestia/Wesley is a drug-subdued decoy in a game of masculinity, or a vessel from which each narrator drinks, having filled her with their own words. 'I cannot deal with her emotions', says the Nembutal narrator defensively, 'they are for her to write about, that option is always open to her'. She is a figure of the narrative hearth, as the mythic associations of her name indicate; she guards the place where desires are kindled, including the desire to tell and the desire to be told. 'The Oracular Story' underlines this point: 'I was slumped in Hestia's fireplace corner dozing, some days later, when Milton and three radical students manoeuvred in' (110). By a pleasant coincidence, which Henry Bosco's namesake would appreciate, the French meanings of *foyer* – both hearth and focus – serve as a reminder that one narrator's sign may be refocalised by another narrator. New narrating positions may, after all, be found. 'What of politics?' Hestia asks the Oracular narrator, who replies in these terms:

> 'For people like us, no person can represent us. The only electorate is the electorate of personal activity. Nothing guarantees freedom.'
> 'Are you therefore unrepresented in the power arrangements?'
> 'There is a para-government.'
>
> (114)

If a text represents certain power arrangements, by the same token its particular strategy for governing semantic exchange may be alternatively para-politicised and transvalued in its turn. By observing precisely how a text works on us, we can put it to work again. By pinpointing the kind of elision that shapes it, we can recirculate it in a modified, differently selective form. By moving a story on further, we can reactivate and extend its substitutive process, dispossess it of the authority that it invests in any one ideological position.

This is the gist of two further stories, to which we shall soon turn: Amy Witting's 'A Piece of this Puzzle is Missing' (1978) and Louise Dow's 'Written Off' (1987). Both try to bring about a more basic dispossession than Wilding's text attempts. For while offering a riposte to 'The Oracular Story', 'The Nembutal Story' does not take an oppositional stance towards it; rather, it situates itself complicitly as a ludic move in a shared entertainment, taking up and attempting to cap the narrative line initiated by Moorhouse, intensifying its doubleness of mode (oral/written, invention/true record).[4] It may up the ante, tighten the screw, tease the fibres, muddy the waters, but it does not fundamentally challenge the rules of the game. In other words, the para-political relation between 'The Oracular Story' and 'The Nembutal Story' is very similar to that between components of an ongoing multiphase 'group oral narrative', as Toolan (1988) describes it:

At first glance the group story appears to be an admirably democratic storytelling mode, built on a heightened degree of interdependence. The division between tellers and listeners falls away, as does anxiety over tellability, and a spirit of benevolent mutual indulgence may prevail: all are contributing to a story that each already knows. But, in some ways, and with more scope than usual, a competitive rivalry may shape the several contributions to the telling, there may not be full agreement on the point, on whom among the storytellers comes out of the story well, and so on. In some ways, given the general familiarity with the broad story outlines, the exercise may become more oral-literary, with great attention paid to the most effective and entertaining methods of verbal expression. ... In practice ... a group story may become more a series of hypotheses or conjectures about what might have been the case. ... And the more that a group's talk becomes an unordered set of overlapping conjectures, the more the talk returns from narrative mode to that of ordinary conversation or gossip.

(173–4)

Chambers (1986: 213) remarks that gossip serves to define a group's constituent members and their values by identifying a scandal and excluding a scapegoat. It involves 'not just a display of worldly experience but also linguistic display. The successful gossiper must have a talent for the memorable turn of phrase, the wry paradox, the penetrating remark, the formulation so esthetically pleasing that it resists critical analysis' (214). The exchange of gossip has a close affinity with certain literary fictions, for when these masquerade as truthful they 'can become a form of symbolic, sometimes actual, victimisation' (215). The Nembutal narrator speculates that 'The Oracular Story' may have been intended to victimise: that is, to implement a scheme (aired in conversation) for destroying the nerve of those who read it.

> Two considerations: firstly, is his story a round in his psychic battle, a trial with live ammunition, designed not for publication in the magazine we are producing, but for the promotion of unease, for the releasing of uncertainties, a story written for me, my psychic destruction. Yet secondly, more charitably, more hopefully, might it not be the materials for my story about his proposal, my story about the submis-

sion of stories for the destruction of editors and publishers' readers. Is this a gift from him, providing material for me to write about, a gift like his giving himself to Wesley, unsolicited, unexpected, imposed. Beware of Greeks bearing gifts, of course, what Trojan horse did Homer put through her gate, how can I be unsuspicious? When I finished reading his story and he came back with the beer ready to discuss the magazine with our designer, I said, I'll tell the true account of the nembutal incident; at which we both laughed, at those private meanings of the word true.

(49–50)

At the same time when these stories were first appearing, Moorhouse and Wilding had in fact just begun to co-edit an innovative periodical, *Tabloid Story*, whose distinctive features are pertinent to a circumtextual framing not only of the pair of texts that we have been considering but also to Amy Witting's response to them. All three were published there. From a detailed account (Wilding 1978b) of how *Tabloid Story* began and developed, the following particulars are of special interest here.

Dissatisfied with the meagre openings for experimental prose in Australia's established literary quarterlies, a group of Sydney fiction writers in the early 1970s 'came up with the idea of producing a packaged short story magazine as a supplement to other host journals' (295). A different host was arranged for each successive issue: an airline in-flight publication, a national weekly, student and suburban newspapers, and so on. The aim was 'to provide space for the variety of stories that weren't being catered for' in the staid quarterlies (302), such as fiction in 'the confessional, revelatory mode – less defined by its manner than by its materials – sexuality, drugs, inner city bohemian life styles, despairs and ecstacies' (305). It is hardly surprising, then, that *Tabloid Story* often found it difficult to negotiate with prospective sponsors whose readerships were less adventurous than the supplement's editors wished to be. After several other troubles, a great hue and cry erupted over the eighth issue, provoked mainly by Amy Witting's 'A Piece of this Puzzle is Missing', which the state Minister for Education declared in parliament to be the work of 'a scribbler on lavatory walls'. The host for *Tabloid Story* no. 8 happened to be *Education*, the journal of the New South Wales Teachers' Federation, and *Education*'s luckless editor found himself deluged with letters of protest from hundreds of outraged school staff quick to express their 'disgust' with Witting's story in particular. Talk of obscenity charges abated when it transpired that Witting not only had some claim to literary standing (having been published more than once in *The New Yorker*) but was also the author of language textbooks and a senior teacher, nearing retirement age, at a respectable girls' school. The major irony of this episode remained unknown to most people until years later: her story had been written in protest at the 'callous and mindless sexism' (Hospital 1989: 80) that Witting saw in a couple of stories published in the first two issues of *Tabloid Story*: Moorhouse's 'The Oracular Story' and Wilding's 'The Nembutal Story'. Her counter-strategy was simply 'to tell the story from the girl's point of view, and to do it in their idiom – one of flip, value-free sex and violence' (80). Submitted under an androgynous pseudonym, 'A Piece of this Puzzle is Missing' was accepted by those whose work it sought to parody. Thus *Tabloid Story*, arch-parasite, became an unwitting host to a Witting riposte.

With hindsight one can see that her story's title, 'A Piece of this Puzzle is Missing', may hint at its undeclared intertextual component (recalling the reference in 'The Nembutal Story' to those *trompe-l'œil* 'triangles whose dimensions bend'). It may also suggest that stories like 'The Oracular Story' and 'The Nembutal Story' are themselves incomplete puzzles, in that they exclude the female character's feelings. 'A Piece of this Puzzle is Missing' tries to supply this lack and thereby to offer an implicit critique of certain narrative structures in which – applying terms used by Irigaray (1985) – women are passive and undifferentiated objects of exchange relations. Hestia/Wesley, surrogate seducee of 'The Oracular Story'/'The Nembutal Story', becomes the unnamed first-person narrator of 'A Piece of this Puzzle is Missing'. (The men are renamed Alan and Breen.) In 'The Oracular Story'/'The Nembutal Story', her body had been a text inscribed by males; here in 'A Piece of this Puzzle is Missing' she begins by adopting this same role of being put upon and written upon, but finally discovers her own voice and uses it to reject that role in a forthright way. Preoccupied with what can be said, with what can be written, and with the modal differences, she observes that the language used on paper by her male writer-companion Alan is bolder than anything he says to her in person: whereas profanities litter his stories, anatomical euphemisms clutter his conversation.

Yet in neither mode will he permit the expression of feelings. Her own problem, she records, is the counterpart (or consequence?) of that: she keeps finding herself in bed with someone she doesn't like, submitting to things she doesn't like, because 'of not being able to fight people off with words' (161). If she tries to resist Alan and his demands for anal penetration ('The arsehole having no gender . . . he might be thinking of Breen'), her 'tongue goes limp' (158). What *she* wants, it soon becomes clear, is to be loved; but when at last she manages to tell him so, Alan is appalled. Speechless, he departs in a hurry. She expects that he will return once he has found a way to relexicalise her 'dirty words' of love, but she is now ready for him with the language of physical elimination, in both writing and speech:

> I've printed a notice with letters three inches high: PISS OFF. But that's a last resort. I'm hoping to be able to say it. If I can say it, it hasn't been a complete waste of time.
> Piss off. Piss off. Piss off.
>
> (163)

As a short story, 'A Piece of this Puzzle is Missing' stands firmly on its own feet. But how well it works as parody is another matter. By the simplest empirical criterion, it failed to control the terms of its immediate reception: wishing to indicate something that she deemed scandalous in the writing of others, Witting brought invective upon her own writing instead. 'A Piece of this Puzzle is Missing' missed its targets. This was partly because they were obscured by the incongruities of its circumtextual framing; readers of that *Tabloid Story* supplement, as their indignant letters showed, could not see beyond the lack of fit between the inserted material and 'a journal that purports to be the official voice of the N.S.W. Teachers' Federation'.[5] But the text does virtually nothing to signal its desire for intertextual framing. Reference to 'The Oracular Story' and 'The Nembutal Story' is so discreet as to be illegible and therefore inefficacious: nothing of the nembutal incident survives, the names are unrecognisably different, there are no specific verbal echoes; in short, too much of the puzzle is missing.

That trio of stories – 'The Oracular Story', 'The Nembutal Story' and 'A Piece of this Puzzle is Missing' – appeared in *Tabloid Story* in 1972, 1973 and 1974 respectively, reappearing together in *The Tabloid Story Pocket Book* of 1978. Published in 1987, Louise Dow's story 'Written Off' can be seen as a belated postscript rejoinder to the Moorhouse and Wilding texts. Whether she knew of Witting's much earlier rejoinder is unclear; however, her own takes a less oblique line, so that the intertextual framing of 'The Oracular Story' and 'The Nembutal Story' is made unmistakable to anyone who knows them. One sentence is quoted directly, there is specific reference to the nembutal-swallowing incident, and the male characters are provocatively called Frank and Michael.

'Written Off' begins promisingly. The wordplay of its title is both an indication of the way Hestia/Wesley is treated in that initial pair of stories and an admission that the present story is playing off theirs. In conjunction with the title, the first sentence has a nice piquancy: 'It's me they've been talking about all this time, as though I didn't exist.' But the implied awareness of modal slippage (written off ... talked about) is not carried through in any way, and indeed the tale seems to fall awkwardly between two narrative options: most of it remains vicariously dependent on the borrowed situation without inflecting it in any inventive way, and on the other hand the narrator announces a bulimic preoccupation which has nothing to do with the rest, though it might have had the potential for being developed towards an independent text. In addition to this structural weakness, the writing becomes tediously strident: for instance Frank is not only 'horribly jealous', he is a 'horrible man', and the narrator arrives at a 'horrible realisation' that she was raped.

In discussing the agonistic element of language transactions, Lyotard (1984) remarks that it is pragmatically important for a participant not to remain circumscribed within the other's terms of exchange. For 'everyone knows', says Lyotard, 'that a countermove that is merely reactional is not a "good" move. Reactional countermoves are no more than programmed effects in the opponent's strategy; they play into his hands and thus have no effect on the balance of power' (16). If 'Written Off' demonstrates this failure, the confused reception of 'A Piece of this Puzzle is Missing' shows that a more independent move may simply encounter a different kind of problem. Is there some other parapolitical narrative means by which a 'female voice' can be raised on the subject of exclusive exchanges? This is one of the questions pursued in the course of the next chapter, which also reconsiders the issue of textual unity, with particular reference to two stories by Katherine Mansfield.

6

'ALWAYS A SACRIFICE': EXECUTING UNITIES

> The truth is, one can only get *so much* into a story: there is always a sacrifice. One has to leave out what one knows.
> (Mansfield, in Murry 1983: 221)
>
> Sacrifice is the archaic form of exchange ... a magical exchange, unquantified, irrational.
> (Vaneigem 1983: 57)

I

It is ironical that in general critical usage the one word 'unity' slides among so many diverse meanings. Some of these need not be lingered over here, because they appear to indicate no more than an evaluative gesture. When one critic asserts that Katherine Mansfield's stories of late Victorian life in New Zealand are 'unified by the selecting eye of a great prose artist' (Gordon 1974: xiv), no precise textual analysis is involved. When another inverts that kind of judgement by declaring the form of the typical Mansfield story to be 'all too unified' (Bayley 1976: 33), mere impression is still posing as aesthetics.

More careful applications of the term 'unity' cover broadly two different senses, sometimes distinguished (artificially but conveniently) by the terms *cohesion*, which has to do with the linkage and sequential intelligibility of parts in relation to other parts, and *coherence*, which has to do with the integrity of all parts in relation to a framed whole. The former, as noted in our previous chapter, falls within the province of linguists. It can be traced through co-reference, conjunction, ellipsis and other syntactic devices or dependencies, especially those that work at a discursive level, beyond the span of a sentence. In an extended sense cohesion is also the province of much structuralist narratology, because of a favoured (some would say specious) analogy between (1) those articulated constituents of the text's linguistic medium and (2) interlinked 'events' of a supposedly underlying plot, thought to form what Todorov (1969a: 19) calls syntactic unity (*l'unité syntaxique*).

Despite their logical difference, it is fairly common for assertions about cohesive ties to merge with assertions about coherential structures. Edgar Allan Poe's view of the short story genre, still influential after a century and a half, is a case in point: his formulaic pronouncements take it for granted that a chain of sequential 'incidents' is requisite for achieving the all-important 'unity of effect or impression'.[1] In other cases, coherence is seen as deriving rather from particular symmetries, recurrences and resonances in a text's imagery. C.A. Hankin (1983) exemplifies this way of reading in her book on Mansfield. Of the twelve-part story 'Prelude', Hankin says: 'Unifying these episodes ... is the repeated appearance of objects and activities which have symbolic meaning' (117). And on the companion story 'At the Bay', she comments: 'The pervasive motifs of the sun and sea (or water) provide a unifying framework' (227). A more sophisticated version of this kind of reading posits what Greimas and Courtés (1982) call 'figurative or thematic isotopy' (52–3): an isotopy is a set of recurrences, iterating paradigmatic categories (perhaps sea/sun, perhaps inside/outside, perhaps male/female ...) along a syntagmatic chain. Thus it 'constitutes a reading grid which makes the surface of the text homogeneous since it makes the elimination of ambiguities possible' (163–5).[2]

But it should be obvious that neither linked events nor patterned figures *per se* can guarantee an effect of coherence, for this depends ultimately on the reader's framing of the 'text as a whole', and it is through the pervasive influence of a seemingly homogeneous attitudinal 'voice' that a reader is likely to be persuaded, if at all, to regard events as conjunctive or figures as isotopic. Consider the implications of some remarks in an essay by Susan Gubar (1983) on the fiction of Katherine Mansfield. Gubar declares that in the story 'Prelude' the aloe plant 'symbolises women's intimation of their own regenerative powers', and she sees in the text other instances of what she calls 'the transformative character of the female imagination', associating this with the childbearing body (37). For Gubar, accordingly, a very specific interpretive frame is applicable:

> Mansfield's 'Prelude' is a story not only about the move of a family from one house to another but also about the move from imagining the womb as a store, a cavity, a hump, a riddle, or a bleeding wound to imagining the womb as a transforming matrix of primordial change.
>
> (34)

'The move from imagining' one thing to imagining another: who is presumed to be doing this moving, this imagining? Gubar argues that it is the story's womenfolk *and* its narrator, collectively; she virtually identifies the point of view with a commonalty of female characters. In keeping with this view, Gubar comments that Mrs Fairfield, Beryl, Linda and Kezia represent phases of female growth: 'The ages of women are shown to be blessed by imaginative vision, filtered through family concerns, in a matriarchy, if that word can refer to a country admittedly not owned but governed and graced by women's rituals.'

Gubar does not present her interpretation as idiosyncratic or in any sense partial. Presumably she would claim to derive authority for it from the putative dominance of a certain narratorial voice in the text, deemed to emanate from an implied author and to convey an ideology to which the critic herself readily assents. And indeed, it is not hard to detect among the various discourses constituting 'Prelude' a particular strand that may seem at first to be privileged above others. It emerges in passages such as the following, where the reader is apparently being encouraged to share a position of superior knowledge:

> Pat the handy-man sprawled in his little room behind the kitchen. His sponge-bag, coat and trousers hung from the door-peg like a hanged man. From the edge of the blanket his twisted toes protruded, and on the floor beside him there was an empty cane bird cage. He looked like a comic picture.
>
> (Section 4)

> 'Here, half a moment', said Burnell [to Pat], 'Hand me those two parcels'. And he said to Linda, 'I've brought you back a bottle of oysters and a pineapple', as though he had brought her back all the harvest of the earth.
>
> (Section 7)

'ALWAYS A SACRIFICE'

... she spoke to her mother with the special voice that women use at night to each other as though they spoke in their sleep or from some hollow cave ...

(Section 11)[3]

Plainly, since no character or focaliser is present while Pat sleeps, the observer to whom he 'looked like a comic picture' must be narratorial; plainly the use of 'as though' in describing Stanley Burnell's attitude lays claim to a wiser point of view than his; plainly that 'special voice' of woman to woman is what Dällenbach (1989) would call a *mise-en-abyme de l'énonciation*, an allegorical echo of the restrictively knowing tone with which the narrator speaks at certain moments. But how much totalising force is exerted upon the text by these means? To what extent does an implicit adoption of that 'special voice' control the play of other voices?

Some current theories of reading tend to support the general assumption behind Gubar's account of what this story is 'about' – the assumption, that is, of interpretive closure, of a process whereby the text virtually requires the reader to construct a particular fixed meaning for it. Most notable are those concepts of ideology and the subject that emphasise the subjection of readers (or viewers) to an inscribed position. Most narratives, so it is said, observe the conventions of classic realism, which supposedly offers a specious vantage point as the condition of its ostensible coherence; readers are placed in a passively compliant role, a 'fixed relation of watching', which governs their sense of the way the story forms a meaningful whole.[4] But even those texts that Barthes (1974: x) has taught us to regard as *lisible* ('readerly', encouraging smooth access from signifier to signified) are seldom so singleminded. The voice of closure and would-be coherence in Mansfield's 'Prelude' can neither subsume without residue all that is told nor silence entirely all that is not told. Although signification may have the shape of a circuit, resistance continues to occur within it. A reading such as Gubar's overlooks the ways in which this story resists its own main ideological current.

That image, for instance, of the aloe itself is more changeable than the quoted commentary by Gubar recognises. Near the end of the story, in the eleventh of its twelve numbered mini-chapters, there is a powerful evocation of this strange garden plant through the eyes of Linda Burnell, the materfamilias. As Linda looks at it and walks around it, she imagines it as 'a ship with the oars lifted', its tall central stem a budding mast. In reverie she sees herself being rowed away in this ship, escaping all the demands of domesticity and motherhood. Here the image of freedom from oppressive responsibility moves the narrative forward not so much by any event or new situation as by inflecting the previous metaphorical presentation of this plant in section 6. There, Linda's young daughter Kezia sees the aloe for the first time. Its context in that earlier passage is a description of the garden as divided by the driveway into two contrasting parts: one dark, bushy, disorderly, frightening, and the other neatly planted with camellias, roses, pansies and other bright flowers. Separating these two opposed aspects of nature is not only the drive but a kind of island in the middle of it, made of banked-up grass and surmounted by the aloe – huge, thorny and ancient. Kezia asks Linda what it is; her mother tells her its name and sees it herself as almost animate:

> Linda looked up at the fat swelling plant with its cruel leaves and fleshy stem. High above them, as though becalmed in the air, and yet holding so fast to the earth it grew from, it might have had claws instead of roots. The curving leaves seemed to be hiding something; the blind stem cut into the air as if no wind could ever shake it.

Later this sinister image is radically altered by the passage in section 11 where Linda associates the aloe with her impulse to escape. No longer becalmed in air or fixed to the earth, the plant comes to seem a fast-moving ship. This figurative transformation typifies much of the story's method of moving itself along. One metaphoric development becomes a kind of substitute for another, yet not in such a way that the second effaces the first. The aloe retains *both* metaphoric aspects, holding their contradictions together and apart.

When functioning discursively, which is to say beyond lexical and sentential levels, metaphor is usually regarded – especially in its metonymic form – as a linking device or 'isotopic connector' (Greimas and Courtés 1982: 191–3). There should be no need here, by the way, to justify this treatment of metonymy as one form of metaphor. The famous dichotomy established by Jakobson (1956) between metaphoric (selecting from a substitutive repertoire) and metonymic (combining through contiguous relations) is a further instance of that binary compulsion, already discussed, by which an act of reading differentially produces each term as the other's 'other'. The matter has been discussed at length elsewhere, and Maria Ruegg's remarks (1979) suffice to indicate the point of most immediate relevance here. Metaphor and metonymy, she notes, 'both involve a *kind* of substitution (of one signifier for another) and both involve some degree of semantic contiguity which provides the necessary link between the two signifiers' (145).[5] Through its activity, then, of superimposing sense B on sense A, metaphor-as-metonymy apparently 'joins' one element of the signifying sequence to another. But this notion, too, needs refinement. Whereas the standard summaries usually describe the metonymic as a 'mode of connection' (Bowie 1979: 129) or a 'combinative' device (Hawkes 1977: 77), closer inspection shows that its substitutive procedure, ostensibly forming a juncture, is always working through an elision.

Section 11 of 'Prelude' deserves further attention in this regard because its picture of the aloe cannot be disengaged from a complicating context of metonymic variations that have a somewhat *disconnective* effect. In particular, the way in which the women's imaginations are characterised as separate from one another rather than (as Gubar thinks) communally merged is by representing the place each occupies in her domestic situation through imagery drawn from the adjacent garden. Various details evoke the contiguous yet dislocative relations between house and garden, and simultaneously serve to specify the way those relations differ for each of the three women. Beryl plucks floral items to adorn herself (she wears a bunch of pansies in the front of her dress) and her painting of the clematis cluster also suggests that nature, for Beryl, is to be used for ornamental purposes. Her sister, Linda, in contrast, responds to flowers and plants with a sensuous langour; for her, the drawing-room smells of lilies and the garden through which she walks in the moonlight is full of the colours of camellias, the scent of verbena and the stark splendour of the aloe itself. Their mother, Mrs Fairfield, sees the garden in terms of practical domesticity; she regards fruit trees and bushes as sources of provisions for the pantry, just as at the beginning of section 6 she had been looking out from the kitchen window at the vegetable patch and grape vine.

In that earlier section the garden had exhibited the contrasting, segmented aspects of wildness and cultivation, with 'many little paths on either side'. Similarly now, among these women there are marked differences of attitude towards domestic life and what lies beyond it. In section 11, as so often elsewhere, the story can be seen as progressing simply by juxtaposition – not integration – of these differences. Even within one character's mind, incongruous attitudes may co-exist, as in Linda's compartmentalised ambivalence towards her husband: 'There were all her feelings for him, sharp and defined, one as true as the other. And there was this other, this hatred, just as real as the rest. She could have done her feelings up in little packets and given them to Stanley.' To Linda, standing there beside the aloe, her vague dream of escape seems 'more real' than the prospect of going back into the house where her husband and sister are playing cribbage – which is presented as another image of movement without co-ordination.

> The cribbage pegs were like two little peoeple going up the road together, turning round the sharp corner, and coming down the road again. They were pursuing each other. They did not so much want to get ahead as to keep near enough to talk – to keep near, perhaps that was all.
> But no, there was always one who was impatient and hopped away as the other came up, and would not listen.

Not only is this a metonymy in itself, a figure by which the pegs indicate that the players are temperamentally out of phase, but it may also be read as suggesting the metonymic nature of the text's own relay, its way of moving by fits and starts. Such a figurative context in this penultimate section is far from encouraging a reader to interpret the image of the aloe as a fixed symbol – whether signifying 'women's intimation of their own regenerative powers' (Gubar's phrase) or anything else of a unifying sort. It suggests severed, rather than shared, understandings: just as, at the start of the section, the carving knife which Stanley uses on the roast duck is 'dividing ... with nice precision', so too the grassy mound on which the aloe grows appears to be 'dividing the drive into two arms'.

II

The placing of characters in relation to several doubtful boundaries or dividing lines is a preoccupation running through much of this text (and even more through its companion piece 'At the Bay', to be discussed presently). Who is beyond this or that pale, who belongs where, who may move where, who may speak from where: these questions are raised from the very outset, for 'Prelude' begins with a statement of exclusion: 'There was not an inch of room'. The immediate literal reference in this opening sentence is to the tightly packed buggy, so full of the Burnell family's possessions that the two youngest children cannot be fitted in. 'We shall simply have to cast them off', exclaims their mother as her daughters stand forlornly in front of the vacated house. Already there are indications that one cannot adequately summarise 'Prelude' as 'a story ... about the move of a family from one house to another': Gubar's précis smoothes over the extent to which the move accentuates divisions in the family – and correspondingly in the 'story'. As its dozen numbered sections move to and fro between various family members, the arbitrary selectiveness of narration is underlined: shifts in focalisation do not always coincide with the sectional breaks. The story has twelve marked beginnings and the same number of endings, as if to signal that, whatever is packed into any part of it, there must be innumerable omissions. It is truistic that 'stories, to be stories, must leave things out' (Danto 1965: 12). But it is noteworthy that some stories include an indication of this selectiveness by giving prominence to imagery of intratextual framing and other *mise-en-abyme* elements.

Consider a simple recurrent motif, figuring in nearly every section of 'Prelude', that associates windows with points of view. To cite a few instances: in section 1, Linda's perception of her children is juxtaposed with that of her neighbour Mrs Samuel Josephs, 'who had been watching the scene from behind her drawing room blind': in section 2, Kezia's fancies and fears are depicted in relation to different tinted windows of the house; in section 4, Kezia and her aunt Beryl, at bedtime, separately imagine themselves being watched through the window – the little girl by hundreds of cats sitting in the sky, the young woman by an admiring voyeur lurking in the garden; in section 5, the contrast between Linda's escapist desires and her husband's material complacency is pointedly made in relation to his waking of her by rattling the blind as he stands at the window; in section 6, old Mrs Fairfield's contented sense of harmony between family tasks and the natural world is pictured as she stands looking out of the kitchen window, and then is interrupted by her irritable daughter Beryl. And so on, right through the story. How is this motif interpretable? No doubt one could see it as betokening the text's confidence in its own illusion of transparent realism, assuring the reader that its world of meanings is fully and directly visible. This would be to endorse that theory of meaning according to which a text places its reader in a 'fixed relation of watching'. On the other hand, by the very insistence of this repetition the text draws attention to differences of station, alternative perceptions, shifts from frame to frame. One could notice that some of the windows have blinds: a cautionary paranomasia. And one could notice that the story's final section substitutes for the window a mirror in which Beryl sees herself (both indulgently and critically) and in which Kezia finally acts out with her cat a small parody of self-regard.

Moreover, while this specular element, framing what is *seen*, admits the arbitrary nature of 'focalisation', another element bears a similarly reflexive relation to what is *said* or 'vocalised'. Most apparent in the final section, it gives an ironic qualification to the apparently privileged perspective noticed earlier. For section 12, instead of confirming those sharply exclusive class-based and gender-based valuations observable in previous passages, undercuts them by the device of Beryl's letter to her friend Nan.[6] The tone of this letter is recognisably akin to that of some of the narrator's own earlier remarks, and therefore when Beryl herself judges her epistolary manner to involve distortion, the reliability of the general narrator is – by the same token – called into question.

> Beryl leaned her elbows on the table and read it through again. The voice of the letter seemed to come up to her from the page. It was faint already, like a voice heard over the telephone, high, gushing, with something bitter in the sound. Oh, she detested it today.

This 'voice', with its woman-to-woman falseness, surely requires one to be sceptical about any suggestion of unequivocal privilege in that other 'voice', mentioned in section 11: 'the special voice that women use ... to each other.' Indeed, far from indicating a reliable ground or unificatory principle, this narrative mode has already put its own credentials in doubt at the end of section 10. Alice, the servant girl, has been making the afternoon tea while reading something called *Dream Book*, which is propped against the butter dish. It is a particular kind of semiotic manual, one that

'ALWAYS A SACRIFICE'

(like Gubar's interpretation) arbitrarily reduces shifty signifier to fixed signified, and it is comically situated here in such a way that it could hardly fail to be seen as an 'anti-model' of Mansfield's text: 'To dream of spiders creeping over you is good. Signifies large sum of money in near future. Should party be in family way an easy confinement may be expected' As Alice is reading and buttering, the imperious Miss Beryl comes into the kitchen, speaks to her cuttingly, and exits. Then the narrator takes up Alice's focal position: 'But what Alice really hated Miss Beryl for was that she made her feel low. She talked to Alice *in a special voice* as though she wasn't quite all there' (italics added).

What price, now, that other 'special voice'? The price of exclusiveness. And indeed the narrator keeps insisting on this point; as Alice takes the scones to the ladies the snippet of conversation she hears, while utterly trivial in any usual sense, is significantly yet another image of excision: '"The only thing to do", she heard, as she opened the dining-room door, "is to cut the sleeves out entirely..."' And immediately after that, trenchantly, section 11 begins as follows:

> The white duck did not look as if it had ever had a head when Alice placed it in front of Stanley Burnell that night. It lay, in beautifully basted resignation, on a blue dish – its legs tied together with a piece of string and a wreath of little balls of stuffing round it.
> It was hard to say which of the two, Alice or the duck, looked the better basted; they were both such a rich colour and they both had the same air of gloss and strain.

By figuratively identifying the servant's situation with that of the headless duck, this passage recalls the quasi-Lacanian spectacle of section 9, in which the children had witnessed the decapitation itself.[7] (In order to do so they ventured to an ultra-marginal spot: 'At the bottom of the orchard a gate was set in the paling fence. On the other side a steep bank led down to a bridge that spanned the creek, and once up the bank on the other side you were on the fringe of the paddocks.') After executing the bird, Pat the handyman had set the body back on the ground and it had waddled some distance, to the children's wonder. Now, in the carving dish, the duck 'did not look as if it had ever had a head'. And the text, similarly, has been so well cooked that anyone bent on its consumption would never notice what is missing. But once aware of the self-referential framing elements, a reader may recognise in this culinary item a figure by which the text can confess the way it has executed its own ostensible unity. For the decapitee is said to resemble Alice ('It was hard to say which of the two ... looked the better basted'), and she signifies narrative possibilities not developed in this story: 'She had the most marvellous retorts ready for questions that she knew would never be put to her.' Thus the text comes to include what the narration has sacrificially excluded.

III

Not only is 'At the Bay' something of a sequel to 'Prelude' as far as character and situation are concerned, but it also has the same overtly marked subdivisional structure. Again there are twelve sections, and while they comprise a 'natural' temporal unity – the span of a single day – the multiplied starting and finishing points emphasise the factitiousness of any selections and of any particular sequential arrangement. Furthermore, this questionability of demarcation lines is recurrently and variously thematised within the language of the text.

The opening passage accentuates misty indistinctness, obscuring two boundaries in particular: the margin between sea and land, and the one between domesticated area and surrounding bush.

> Very early morning. The sun was not yet risen, and the whole of Crescent Bay was hidden under a white sea-mist. The big bush-covered hills at the back were smothered. You could not see where they ended and the paddocks and bungalows began. The sandy road was gone and the paddocks and bungalows the other side of it; there were no white dunes covered with reddish grass beyond them; there was nothing to mark which was beach and where was the sea. A heavy dew had fallen. The grass was blue. Big drops hung on the bushes and just did not fall; the silvery, fluffy toi-toi was limp on its long stalks, and all the marigolds and the pinks in the bungalow gardens were bowed to the earth with wetness. Drenched were the cold fuschias, round pearls of dew lay on the flat nasturtium leaves. It looked as though the sea had beaten up softly in the darkness, as though one immense wave had come rippling, rippling – how far? Perhaps if you had waked up in the middle of the night you might have seen a big fish flicking in at the window and gone again . . .

The problematic nature of categorical differences, adumbrated here, is a pervasive motif throughout the story, and continues to be specifically linked with uncertainties of voice and focus. To regard it just as a 'theme' or 'isotopic connector' would be to miss the point that, by adverting to it repeatedly, in ways that will be noticed shortly, the text is calling into doubt the grounds of its own structural relations.

The remainder of this first section consists of a whimsical account of the early morning activities of various domesticated animals: a flock of sheep, the sheepdog, the Burnells' cat. They are described in a manner that has not appealed to the taste of all readers; the humanising of the animal risks cuteness, and the description cannot justify itself in terms of plot. But by initiating a series of human/animal transpositions it does function structurally; that is, it announces the text's method of articulating a story about the instability of differential categories. 'Description' here is not surface ornamentation attached in an ancillary way to events. Nor does it evoke a static sense of place that might be taken to confer unity on a few vignettes, for 'the whole of Crescent Bay was hidden' at the start, and the picture will remain pointedly incomplete. Certainly the locative title indicates a kind of placement, but then 'At the Bay' turns out not to be an innocent phrase. What is this liminal world where different categories, and different story-fragments, come into restless proximity?

It is not, at any rate, a world of clear-cut and consequential actions. Just as 'Prelude' is true to its title in leaving its characters and readers 'waiting for something to happen that just did not happen' (like Linda at the end of section 5), so also much of 'At the Bay' is teasingly uneventful. In particular its early sections move discontinuously from one lightly limned scene to another in ways that may seem to do little more than collocate sketches of a particular social microcosm: an upper-middle-class household near Wellington in colonial late-Victorian New Zealand. But the text goes on to acknowledge discreetly the partiality of its representations, to reveal that the *real* can be rendered textually only insofar as particular social constraints and compensatory strategies are exemplified in the positions from which a story is told and from which it permits responses.

These self-reflexive implications, however, are hardly manifest in the first few sections. After the day-break opening, section 2 merely relates an early morning encounter in the water between the brisk businessman Stanley Burnell and his brother-in-law Jonathan Trout. Nothing much *happens* that could be said to contribute to any chain of action; it is just a brief mini-episode, which at first neatly characterises the two men as temperamentally opposite but goes on to suggest amusingly that neither is in his element.

Section 3 shows how Stanley's fussy and blustering insistence on domestic order inflicts on the household the very disarray that he deplores. Again he is portrayed by juxtaposition; this time it is mainly his mother-in-law whose attitude rubs against his. The door through which in the previous section he had dashed towards the beach and through which he now dashes off to work is for old Mrs Fairfield an aperture whereby the natural world can be admitted into the house in a domesticated form: on the table sits an old salad bowl filled with nasturtiums, while the sound of the sea enters and the sun streams on to walls and floor. In contrast to her calmness, Stanley gets into a great lather of agitation because things and people will not stay in what he deems to be their proper places. His notions about rules, roles and hierarchies are not sufficiently respected, he feels, by the women-folk, who 'took it for granted that it was your job to slave away for them while they didn't even take the trouble to see that your walking stick wasn't lost'. His daughters, though obediently subdued in his presence, run 'into the paddock like chickens let out of a coop' as soon as he leaves, and the female adults breathe freely:

> Oh, the relief, the difference it made to have the man out of the house. Their very voices were changed as they called to one another; they sounded warm and loving and as if they shared a secret. Beryl went over to the table. 'Have another cup of tea, mother. It's still hot.' She wanted, somehow, to celebrate the fact that they could do what they liked, now.

But there will be reason, later, to notice – as was the case in 'Prelude' – that this womanly tone is not always so warmly inclusive as it seems for the moment. And as for those children, though temporarily out of their coop they are still not unbounded, as the beginning of the next section shows: young Lottie, trying to keep up with her siblings, gets on to the stile and cannot get off, 'half in the paddock still and half in the tussock grass'.

This fourth section goes on to introduce two other lots of

children, playing down by the water's edge. First there are the Samuel Josephs, who in their natural state are described as 'leaping like savages' but whom we now see being strictly programmed by their family's lady-help; she 'kept order with a whistle that she wore tied around her neck, and a small cane with which she directed operations'. And then there are the Trout boys, the elder of whom has already learned to mimic adult ways of manipulating others – establishing a hierarchy of command and requiring ritual vows of obedience ('Promise not to tell').

What people may tell or do at the bay depends very much on the position each occupies *vis-à-vis* its lines of demarcation. Yet even the natural margins continue to seem as unstable as they did at the beginning of the story; this is especially so later, in section 7, where the sea is imagined as merging with the life of the land and even incorporating the houses. The shoreline becomes a place of mysterious mirrorings and transpositions: boundaries dissolve and change is insidious.

> Over there on the weed-hung rocks that looked at low tide like shaggy beasts come down to the water to drink, the sunlight seemed to spin like a silver coin dropped into each of the small rock pools. They danced, they quivered, and minute ripples laved the porous shores. Looking down, bending over, each pool was like a lake with pink and blue houses clustered on the shores; and oh! the vast mountainous country behind those houses – the ravines, the passes, the dangerous creeks and fearful tracks that led to the water's edge.

What this troubled marginality means in social terms is clear in section 5, where Beryl, down on the beach, meets the sinister Mrs Kember, who is notorious for declining to abide by conventional distinctions. 'The way she treated men as though she was one of them, and the fact that she didn't care twopence about her house and called the servant Gladys "Glad-eyes", was disgraceful.' Her husband Harry is reported to be similarly outrageous: 'How did he live? Of course there were stories, but such stories! They simply couldn't be told. The women he'd been seen with, the places he'd been seen in ... but nothing was ever certain, nothing definite.' There could hardly be a plainer indication than this of the ambiguous nexus between narrative capacity and the limits placed on a given social exchange. The Kembers' transgressions simultaneously curtail and generate stories, because in such a constricted cultural environment where few things are fully tellable there is an appetite for gossip and innuendo. To Beryl, it is the sexual *indefiniteness* of the Kembers that is disturbing:

> 'I believe in pretty girls having a good time', said Mrs Harry Kember. 'Why not? Don't you make a mistake, my dear. Enjoy yourself'. And suddenly she turned turtle, disappeared, and swam away quickly, quickly, like a rat. Then she flicked around and began swimming back. She was going to say something else. Beryl felt that she was being poisoned by this cold woman, but she longed to hear. But oh, how strange, how horrible! As Mrs Harry Kember came up close she looked, in her black waterproof bathing-cap, with her sleepy face lifted above the water, just her chin touching, like a horrible caricature of her husband.

Fascinatingly compressed into those few sentences is a subtle insight into the uncertain narratability of gender relations. Beryl's longing to be told more about women's opportunities is struggling against her revulsion from the coldness of the woman who can tell; and furthermore, the female narrator disconcertingly metamorphoses – as she recedes – into animals (turning turtle, swimming like a rat) and – as she approaches – into a caricature of her male counterpart. What the story seems to be inviting readers to contemplate here is an issue that has emerged recently in anthropological theory with Sherry Ortner's question, 'Is female to male as nature is to culture?' (Ortner 1974). As Gillian Gillison (1980: 143) remarks:

> This formula ties the origin and meaning of gender, not to the interaction between men and women, but to the theory of how culture is different from and superior to nature. The way a people conceptualise their relation to animals or to the uncultivated environment becomes the true subject matter of gender.

The displacement of difference here (cf. Brown 1983) is metonymic, and 'At the Bay' and 'Prelude' are rich in examples of its narrative extensions. For instance, one aspect could be traced in sections 9, 10 and 11 of 'At the Bay', which successively show the children at play ('Round the table there sat a bull, a rooster, a donkey that kept forgetting it was a donkey, a sheep and a bee'), then Jonathan Trout and his sister-in-law Linda reflecting on 'the difference' between his life and that of others while he compares himself to an insect and she compares him to a fowl and a weed, and then a sly transition from a talking cat to a talking husband who has previously been described as a 'trapped beast'. But worth particular emphasis here is the fact that the nature/culture metonymies serve to frame the narratorial shifts with an intra-textual rationale. If such oppositions as human versus animal, or the-bay-as-settlement versus the-bay-as-unsettling-border-of-wilderness, cannot be firmly maintained in the language of the text, then by the same token a teller's authority to tell becomes very precarious, very partial. One of the things at stake in these stories is a renegotiation of the cultural domain through an enfranchisement of female narration, since culture is a set of processes for acquiring and displaying what counts as knowledge (Crick 1982: 287), and narrative is a primary mode through which those processes occur. Yet passage after passage hints at a recognition that every storytelling act, including women's oppositional narration, requires suppression or distortion of other such acts.

It seems to Linda in section 6, reflecting on Stanley's way of imposing himself, that 'her whole time was spent . . . listening to his story', and in section 10 it is to the self-absorbed ramblings of her brother-in-law Jonathan that she must attend – a point he at least admits when he breaks into song with the words

Would ye hear the story
How it unfolds itself . . .

But whose story is this text as a whole unfolding? While women are mostly represented in 'At the Bay' as lenders of sympathetic ears, nevertheless the narration itself would no doubt be regarded by most readers as spoken by a female voice;[8] and in the eighth section it gives us a critical reflex of its own narrative mode, acknowledging in effect how close it comes to repeating the accents of those exclusively self-absorbed male stories. Undeniably there is a snooty tone in this section. It presents the servant Alice and her shopkeeper acquaintance Mrs Stubbs in a belittling light that excludes them from what Gubar (1983: 48) calls 'the euphoric community of women at the bay'. Here is how Alice is described as she leaves the house for her afternoon out:

> She wore a white cotton dress with such large spots on it, and so many that they made you shudder, white shoes and a leghorn turned up under the brim with poppies. Of course she wore gloves, white ones, stained at the fastenings with iron-mould, and in one hand she carried a very dashed-looking sunshade which she referred to as her *perishall*.

Yet immediately afterwards this merciless view of Alice is attributed to a particular observer:

> Beryl, sitting in the window, fanning her freshly washed hair, thought she had never seen such a guy. If Alice had only blacked her face with a piece of cork before she started out *the picture would have been complete*. And where did a girl like that go in a place like this?
>
> (italics added)

To be sure, the ensuing section does not remain formally within Beryl's point of view: but that brief association of an uncharitably satirical 'female' eye with Beryl watching from her window is enough to put the perspective implicitly within a wider one, and to raise doubts about the 'completeness' of the 'picture' that the narrator is purportedly providing.

This last point is comically reinforced through a *mise-en-abyme* a few paragraphs further on in the course of a Dickensian conversation during which Mrs Stubbs shows Alice some 'pictures'. One is a portrait of her late husband. 'That's 'im', says his widow, illustrating her account of his demise by pointing at a photograph under which is the ludicrous caption, 'Be not afraid – it is I'. Plainly this simulacrum is *not* "im' in person, just a framing of his absence; and plainly it is not he who speaks – or can be imagined as ever having spoken – the words attributed to him here, which indeed are quoted from an incongruous scriptural context. In this cluster of simple ironies, whereby a 'person' is textually present only as a framed figure and a first-person assertion of identity is no more than a caption chosen by others, there is a virtual confession of the way texts may exclude even that which they claim to have selected for representation. Also on display is a studio photo of the shopkeeper herself:

> Mrs Stubbs sat in an arm-chair, leaning very much to one side. There was a look of mild astonishment on her large face, and well there might be. For though the arm-chair

stood on a carpet, to the left of it, miraculously skirting the carpet border, there was a dashing waterfall. On her right stood a Grecian pillar with a giant fern tree on either side of it, and in the back-ground towered a gaunt mountain, pale with snow.

There, in burlesque résumé, their artificial dichotomy deconstructively exposed, are the story's main metonymies. 'Nature' (waterfall, fern, mountain) and 'culture' (armchair, carpet, pillar) take shape as a hodge podge of tokens, discrete and incongruous parts of a contrived frame for the stiffly posed human figure. Absurdly exaggerated though their correlative arrangement is in this case, its specular relationship with the text that encloses it is unmistakable. Neither 'natural' nor 'cultural' is itself a homogeneous category, in 'At the Bay' any more than in 'Prelude'; and the lines that sometimes seem to separate one from another may also turn out to be indistinct. Far from providing secure reference points or sources of value for any human exchange, they seem to confound the desire for meaning. This is underlined in the final section of 'At the Bay', where the ludicrous emblems of pillar and fern reappear transformed into realistic terms. Beryl is at the window again. It is night time. Her narcissistic fantasies materialise in the person of Harry Kember, prowling past. In response to his invitation, she steps over the window sill – but stops short of the garden's edge; the tall fuschia bush, which falls 'over the fence in a shower' and has 'a little pit of darkness beneath', is too sinister in its sexual allure. And what options, anyway, would she have beyond the pillars of domesticity? Her own earlier jibe about Alice has turned back on her own situation: where could a girl like that go in a place like this? In its implications the question is no less specifically social for remaining rhetorical. So it is too with the question that Harry Kember flings out when she retreats: '"Then why in God's name did you come?" . . . Nobody answered him.' The story ends, as it had begun, with the indecipherable murmur of the sea. Similarly section 6 had recorded Linda's realisation that the flowers and bushes around her have no answer to her question about reasons for 'the common lot of women'.

The disconnective metonymies through which the text has kept unfolding 'the story' do not offer any secure placement, then, whether 'natural' or 'social', for any narrator, whether male or female, servant or shopkeeper, parent or child. Our next chapter examines a very different kind of text, in which the autobiographical narrator's ambition is to reconcile natural and social in the story of his own unfolding character. What place is there for the traditional concept of 'character' in an inquiry into narrative exchanges? Chapter 1 quoted Genette's remark that one should 'decompose the study of "characterisation" into the study of its constituting devices'; are substitution and dispossession among those devices?

7
THE CHARACTERS OF DANGER AND DESIRE

> How shall I trace the history, where seek
> The origin of what I then have felt?
> Oft in those moments . . .
> what I saw
> Appeared like something in myself, a dream,
> A prospect in my mind.
> (Wordsworth, *The Prelude*, 2. 365–71)[1]

In the 1815 preface to his *Poems in Two Volumes* Wordsworth names 'Narrative' first among the 'various moulds' into which poetry may be cast, and goes on to list 'divers forms' that it takes, from epic to metrical novel. What they have distinctively in common, he observes, is that 'the Narrator, however liberally his speaking agents be introduced, is himself the source from which everything primarily flows' (Owen and Smyser 1974: vol. 3, 27). Wordsworth's definition sensibly ignores that series of plotted events which modern narratology in the Aristotelian line has usually regarded as the axiomatic *sine qua non* of storyness. His primary emphasis, more Platonic in its affiliations (Bialostosky 1984), comes down firmly instead on the quintessential act of telling, dispersed though it may be through several 'speaking agents'. That none of these agents, nor the narrator, need be a character in the ordinary structuralist sense (an amalgam of 'relatively stable' person-like traits that intersect with a 'chain of events'; Chatman 1978: 127) will become clear from a consideration of *The Prelude*. The story told in this poem does not concatenate a sequence of happenings involving homogeneous personal subjects; rather, it traces the irresolute interaction of discursive figures – figures of motion, figures of governance –

143

which carry the marks of a particular sociocultural dilemma.

To regard its poet-narrator as a single unified personage who follows one trajectory is to miss much of the rhetorical play that constitutes the very narrative movement itself. And yet that is often how *The Prelude* is read. Undeterred by the knowledge that it comprises several versions of different scope composed over a half-century span during which countless bits of textual tissue were excised or transplanted, and that whichever version one reads is partly an editorial artefact, some of Wordsworth's critics have been remarkably confident in accepting at face value the poem's own self-unificatory gestures. Abrams (1974), for example, asserts that 'a supervising idea . . . controls Wordsworth's account and shapes it into a structure in which the protagonist is put forward as one who has been elected to play a special role in a providential plot' (76–7); one that Abrams describes as a 'quest' and also as a 'pilgrimage' – merging these and other terms, in a homogenised journey-model, the 'controlling idea' as he insistently calls it (102).

Now the pattern indicated by Abrams and others is certainly salient, and may appropriately be called a 'controlling idea', for control is indeed of prime concern in shaping the story. But to see this text as so single-minded is to repress much of it. Abrams speaks on behalf of a widespread critical orthodoxy whose general hermeneutic principles Hirsch (1967) has theorised most explicitly. Obedience to the 'controlling idea' (that same revealing phrase) of a literary work is urged with eloquent anxiety by Hirsch. A reader must submit, he contends, to 'the intrinsic genre that compels the determination of one meaning instead of another' (102). What Hirsch refuses to concede is that any such determination is not an inherent textual given but a function of particular framing acts in which a semantic restriction must be artificially imposed if the reader wishes to favour one of the registers that bear on a text. *The Prelude* is an instructive case of a text's own anticipation of this struggle for and against control. Repeatedly displaying discursive contradictions, it consists largely of efforts to efface them by proposing holistic, programmatic rereadings of its structure – only to bring in yet further contradictions in the process.

From the outset it is self-revisionary. Here, in the 1805 text, is how it begins:

THE CHARACTERS OF DANGER AND DESIRE

Oh there is a blessing in this gentle breeze
That blows from the green fields and from the clouds
And from the sky; it beats against my cheek,
And seems half conscious of the joy it gives.
O welcome messenger! O welcome friend! 5
A captive greets thee, coming from a house
Of bondage, from yon city's walls set free,
A prison where he hath been long immured.
Now I am free, enfranchised and at large,
May fix my habitation where I will. 10
What dwelling shall receive me, in what vale
Shall be my harbour, underneath what grove
Shall I take up my home, and what sweet stream
Shall with its murmurs lull me to my rest?
The earth is all before me – with a heart 15
Joyous, nor scared at its own liberty,
I look about, and should the guide I chuse
Be nothing better than a wandering cloud
I cannot miss my way. I breathe again –
Trances of thought and mountings of the mind 20
Come fast upon me. It is shaken off,
As by miraculous gift 'tis shaken off,
That burthen of my own unnatural self,
The heavy weight of many a weary day
Not mine, and such as were not made for me. 25
Long months – if such bold word accord
With any promises of human life –
Long months of ease and undisturbed delight
Are mine in prospect. Whither shall I turn,
By road or pathway, or through open field, 30
Or shall a twig or any floating thing
Upon the river point me out my course?

    Enough that I am free, for months to come
May dedicate myself to chosen tasks,
May quit the tiresome sea and dwell on shore – 35
If not a settler on the soil, at least
To drink wild water, and to pluck green herbs,
And gather fruits fresh from their native bough.
Nay more, if I may trust myself, this hour
Hath brought a gift that consecrates my joy; 40

> For I, methought, while the sweet breath of heaven
> Was blowing on my body, felt within
> A corresponding mild creative breeze,
> A vital breeze which travelled gently on
> O'er things which it had made, and is become   45
> A tempest, a redundant energy,
> Vexing its own creation. 'Tis a power
> That does not come unrecognised, a storm
> Which, breaking up a long-continued frost,
> Brings with it vernal promises, the hope   50
> Of active days, of dignity and thought,
> Of prowess in an honourable field,
> Pure passions, virtue, knowledge, and delight,
> The holy life of music and of verse.
>
>   Thus far, O friend, did I, not used to make   55
> A present joy the matter of my song,
> Pour out that day my soul in measured strains,
> Even in the very words which I have here
> Recorded. To the open fields I told
> A prophesy; poetic numbers came   60
> Spontaneously, and clothed in priestly robe
> My spirit, thus singled out, as it might seem,
> For holy services. Great hopes were mine:
> My own voice cheared me, and, far more, the mind's
> Internal echo of the imperfect sound –   65
> To both I listened, drawing from them both
> A chearful confidence in things to come.

Sketching the situation from which the poem will proceed, those opening lines adduce two biblical analogies, one filtered through an intermediate text. The narrator comes (echoing Exodus 13.3) 'from a house / Of bondage' (6–7), like the Israelites freed from Egypt. Yet he also solicits comparison with earlier wanderers, primal rejects dismissed from a commodious garden rather than delivered from a confining city, and here (15–19) the intertextual framing works through a cluster of adaptations from the last lines of *Paradise Lost*; in addition to the modified resonance of 'The earth is all before me', those key words *rest, guide, choose, wandering* and *way* are all repeated from Milton's final sentence (cf. Reid 1976). Then which situation is the prelude to *The Prelude*?

Is the speaker initially emancipated or expelled? Insistence on 'valid interpretation' would require an exclusive choice, just as for Hirsch 'an interpretation of *Hamlet* which views the hero as a dilatory intellectual is not compatible with one that views him as a forceful man of action thwarted by circumstances' (128). In that perspective, the discovery of formal unity depends on securing a unified personality for the central character. *The Prelude*, however, makes no such security available, and instead of permitting the speaker's orientation to be determined either way, this passage presents disjunctively a metonymic paradox: the mind will 'mount' – or be mounted, since the phrasing in line 20 may suggest both senses – in such a way that descent from Eden can be substituted, as if synonymously, for ascent from Egypt. Active and passive at once, the equivocation in 'mountings of the mind' foreshadows fuller indications that the balance of power in this text between 'the mind' and its surroundings is unstable.

Besides, there are different overtures of control here, not entirely concordant. Who is the inscribed narratee, recipient of the (proleptically) received version of this story? That is, to whom is *The Prelude* being related? A direct vocative greets the creative breath itself in line 5: 'O welcome friend!': it is an aspect of the natural world that is addressed. Yet an odd shift soon takes place, moving the breeze from second to third person, so that at line 55 the repetition 'O friend' marks a difference: the amicable auditor is now human. Later to be named as 'Coleridge', he is already being enlisted as a controller of meaning in the poem – an intratextual reader of exemplary competence for whom (so the story goes) the story is being told, for whom (as the final line of Book 1 puts it) 'this labour will be welcome', and for whom the narrator *wishes* to present 'a theme / Single and of determined bounds' (1. 668–9). 'Coleridge' functions less as a particular person than as a virtual reading position, designed to replicate the narrator's own and to seem interchangeable with the sympathetic attentions of his natural environment. Accordingly, a few lines further on, the initial utterance is said to have been addressed not only 'to the open fields' but also to a further audience in the speaker himself, listening to his voice and to its internally refracted doublet (64–7). Nature and narrator become each other's 'speaking agent'.

Remarkable, then, in this poem's preamble are the two kinds of operation that can disturb the would-be control of any narrative exchange. One is that process of figurative substitution whereby B replaces A rhetorically, as here an Edenic trope purportedly becomes equivalent to an Exodus trope and therefore generates a need for further narration in order to account for the apparent discrepancy. The other is that process of positional alteration, verging on interlocutory reversal, whereby the narrator's orientation towards his story and audience keeps shifting. Both processes are involved in the change of weather that comes over the scene here (41–54). Having fanned the story into its sense of possible beginnings, the breeze that was apostrophised directly from line 5 onwards now veers back into the third person, and also into the past, engendering as it does so an unruly counterpart, an exorbitant gust *within* the poet. Yet the 'power' it betokens is no more immediate for that, since it is one of promise rather than fulfilment: 'the hope of active days', not present activity. That it has 'made things' is asserted, but it brings a disconcerting recognition of things merely desired. (A refrain of 'hopes' then develops; within the next 100 lines there are 'Great hopes', 'hopes /Still higher' and 'lofty hopes', all precariously situated.) Between lines 54 and 55 there is a pause, and the breeze, which *had* seemed a sign from which to proceed, now recedes further in time: 'Thus far, O friend, did I, not used to make / A present joy the matter of my song, / Pour out *that* day my soul in measured strains' – where the sense of 'strains' is doubly eloquent, tense as well as tuneful, qualifying the subsequent profession of 'chearful confidence in things to come'.

But what kind of figure is this 'I', and what 'course' is he taking through the poem? An impulse to censor inconsistencies of character and trajectory, to bring the play of meanings under tighter control, is often apparent in post-1805 revisions of *The Prelude*, and so it is unsurprising that the reference to Exodus was dropped from the opening lines. But the repressed returns after all; the indefiniteness of this narrative journey soon reasserts itself when, after a breather, the happy hiker of 1850 takes up his travels as follows:

> casting then
> A backward glance upon the curling cloud
> Of city smoke, by distance ruralised;
> Keen as a Truant or a Fugitive,
> But as a Pilgrim resolute, I took,

Even with the chance equipment of that hour,
The road that pointed toward the chosen Vale.
It was a splendid evening, and my soul
Once more made trial of her strength, nor lacked
Aeolian visitations; but the harp
Was soon defrauded, and the banded host
Of harmony dispersed in straggling sounds,
And lastly utter silence! 'Be it so;
Why think of anything but present good?'
So, like a home-bound labourer I pursued
My way beneath the mellowing sun, that shed
Mild influence; nor left in me one wish
Again to bend the Sabbath of that time
To a servile yoke. What need of many words?
A pleasant loitering journey, through three days
Continued, brought me to my hermitage.
(1850, 1. 87–107)

This is very far from adumbrating the unified journey described in Abrams's commentary. 'Quest' can hardly encompass the self-substitutions of that disconcertingly multiple figure: truant, fugitive, pilgrim, labourer and hermit. It is important to recognise sociolinguistic traces in these tropes by considering the enunciative stance from which they are being presented as if equivalent. A proper explanatory account of what is involved here would need to be historically situated in terms of language registers; a few general points will suffice now. What exactly is the discursive field of that vocational heroism which has subscribed to 'the hope / Of active days, of dignity and thought, / Of prowess in an honourable field'? Part of it is quasi-priestly: the poet-narrator has dedicated his spirit to 'holy services'. But upon that commitment he superimposes both industriousness and indolence at once, recognising no discrepancy between the paradigms of a manual worker stepping restward and a loiterer on a three-day ramble. Through this odd cluster of images can be glimpsed a particular configuration of changes in the economy of late eighteenth- and early nineteenth-century England: a set of tensile social relations – ostensibly, alliances – between artist and artisan, between the trades of religion and poetry, between rural worker and leisured gent. To subsume these, in one's reading, as facets of a unified character is to comply with the text's own overt ideology and to pass over what

Jameson (1981) would call its 'political unconscious'.

That this matter is indeed political can be seen in the poem's frequent but uneasy use of a term such as 'labour', which as the eighteenth century came to its end was undergoing a process of critical semantic enlargement. To the basic earlier meanings of manual effort and of onerous travail, writers such as Adam Smith (whose *Wealth of Nations* is directly mentioned in *The Prelude*: 12. 76–80) had begun to add the more abstract sense of labour as 'the real measure of the exchangeable value of all commodities' (Smith 1937: 30), and soon after the turn of the century there emerged distinctively the reference to labour as a social class (Williams 1976: 145–8).[2] Meanwhile literary personification of 'Labour' in relation to landscape occurs as early as Goldsmith's *The Traveller* (1764), which declares that 'Nature ... / Still grants her bliss at Labour's earnest call'. Wordsworth allows himself a comparable sentimentality in the picture he paints of his native region in 'Home at Grasmere' (cf. Darlington 1977): there is a noble independence, he avers, about those who work their own land:

> Labour here preserves
> His rosy face, a servant only here
> Of the fireside or of the open field,
> A Freeman therefore sound and unimpaired
> (ll. 359–62)

Very similar to that in some respects is the self-representation at the beginning of *The Prelude*: in the 'open field' (30, 59) the poet-figure is 'free' (7, 9, 33), 'like a peasant' (110). And yet such assertions are shadowed by his awareness that 'a servile yoke' (113) needs to be avoided. Although he may declare himself no longer burdened by 'the heavy weight of many a weary day' (24), he must still share, in so far as his situation recalls the one at the end of *Paradise Lost*, in Adam's curse; the prospect of 'long months of peace ... long months of ease' (26–8) is parenthetically acknowledged to be doubtful. When intervals of ease do occur further on in the poem, they will detract from his seeming resolution to 'dedicate' himself to 'chosen tasks' (34); for instance he confesses having spent his student days in 'good-natured lounging' (the phrase is borrowed from Thomson's *Castle of Indolence*), and something of the same tone carries over into the account straight afterwards of vacation-time 'sundry wanderings' in rural regions (6. 199–213).

The narrative project of *The Prelude* finds itself awkwardly situated in a cultural limbo. The landscape amidst which the speaking figure is at something of a loss, or a loose end, is at once literary and socioeconomic. He belongs neither to the sweating peasantry whose virtues he will extol nor yet to the select company of 'Milton and Shakespeare, labourers divine' (5. 165). After picturing himself in the preamble as being 'singled out' for the 'holy services' of poetry, and as having 'told a prophecy' to 'the open fields', he must later renew his sense of special election in the face of reminders that many others toil with less privilege.[3] Book 4, for example, records the occasion when, walking home at sunrise after dancing away the night, he experiences an intense moment of confirmation that he is 'a dedicated spirit' – and sees, in a flicker of latent irony, 'labourers going forth into the fields' (4. 336–44). Again, in the poem's penultimate book, winding his testimonial towards the climactic claim that he is indeed part of a band of 'poets, even as prophets, each with each / Connected in a mighty scheme of truth' (12. 301–2), he feels a need to dissociate himself from the view that natural gifts require for their growth 'Retirement, leisure, language purified' (12. 189–90), and is nagged by

> an anxious wish
> To ascertain how much of real worth,
> And genuine knowledge, and true power of mind,
> Did at this day exist in those who lived
> By bodily labour, labour far exceeding
> Their due proportion, under all the weight
> Of that injustice which upon ourselves
> By composition of society
> Ourselves entail.
>   (12. 97–105)

In the convolution of that last clause there seems more than a smidgin of guilt, and the rest of the poem is often troubled about the relation between the work that it is producing and the work that is done by those who labour more arduously. The closing lines of Book 1 can express hope of 'honourable toil' (1. 653), hope too that at least to the poem's direct addressee 'this labour will be welcome' (1. 674); but pulling against that are strong fears: fear that dreary burdens will come from 'labour in excess' (12. 197), as in the pageant figure of 'Labour, his own Bond-slave' (3. 630), and above all, fear that nothing of substance will result – that the effort

NARRATIVE EXCHANGES

to tell 'some variegated story' may prove baseless, evanescent, fugitive, until 'the whole beauteous fabric seems to lack / Foundation, and withal appears throughout / Shadowy and insubstantial' (1. 226–8).

The allusion that these lines make to Shakespeare's *The Tempest* is strengthened by their later revision, in which the 'unsubstantial structure melts ... mist into air dissolving' (*1850*, 1. 225–7). Several words are echoed here from the famous speech (previously alluded to in Wordsworth's 'An Evening Walk'[4]) that comes after the end of the masque in Act 4; the actors, says Prospero,

> Are melted into air, into thin air;
> And, like the baseless fabric of this vision,
> The cloud-capped towers ...
>   shall dissolve,
> And like this insubstantial pageant faded,
> Leave not a rack behind.
>   (4. i. 150–6)

There will be more to say soon about relations between *The Prelude* and *The Tempest*. Meanwhile the dual function of this kind of intertextual allusiveness is worth brief general comment. By incorporating quotations from a prestigious prior text written by one of those 'labourers divine', the later text is able both to keep up, and to control somewhat, its rhetorical momentum. While in one sense a curbing device, the use of allusion also allows meanings to run on. A few lines from Book 8 catch this doubleness succinctly, coming in a passage which mainly emphasises the stabilising influence on the poet's mind of his familiarity with landscape forms:

> These thoughts did oft revolve
> About some centre palpable, which at once
> *Incited them to motion, and controlled,*
> And whatsoever shape the fit might take,
> And whencesoever it might come, I still
> At all times had a real solid world
> Of images about me
>   (8. 599–605; italics added)

(As it happens, the italicised line includes another glance at that same masque scene from *The Tempest* : 'Incite them to quick motion' (4. i. 39) is Prospero's command to Ariel, regarding subject spirits of the natural world.) The poem's apparent assertion at this point is that an ideal quasi-gravitational balance allows human ideas to circle around figures of the physical world. But the passage is deeply ambiguous, as Clarke (1962) has remarked:

> The primary meaning of 'images' here seems to be 'Nature's image-work': the young poet is surrounded by pictures, but real solid pictures. However, given the context, a comparison-and-contrast with *mental* images seems also to be implied: 'the images were pictures, as all images are, including images in the mind; yet they were *not* images in the mind, for they were solid.' As so often in poetry the effect of this denial of a meaning is that the meaning denied begins to assert itself as a positive value, thus: 'The images were solid *and yet* were optical appearances'. Moreover we have learnt a few lines earlier that the 'forms distinct' steadied the mind and the thoughts revolved 'About some centre palpable' as though both thoughts and forms were operating in a space at once mental and physical. When therefore the metaphor of the circle ('About some centre . . .') is covertly repeated ('. . . a real solid world / Of images *about* me') the reader tends to assume that the relationship between the images and the self, like that between the forms and the thoughts, is not purely external: in other words 'about me' is not interpreted simply as 'outside and independent of me' but also as 'centred upon me' and even perhaps, in some sense, 'dependent upon me'.

This kind of 'ingenious double-talk', as Clarke calls it, can accordingly be read (reverting to the terms used earlier) as framing intratextually the instability of narrative control itself; for that same rotation of figures and speaking agents which produces storyness may also involve a risk for the narrator of being dispossessed of his power. In attempting to secure his own speaking position the narrator affixes it to those natural images as if to a centre of gravity, and yet that exposes all the more his inability to determine what 'shape the fit might take'. In narration as in social arrangements it may turn out that (to apply phrasing used later of French politics) 'power' has 'reverted' to 'Nature', creating an 'open space / For *her* to move about in, uncontrolled' (*1850*, 11. 31–4). Far from being an isolated instance of shifty roles, that Book 8 passage has numerous parallels elsewhere in the poem. The lines referred to above about the 'insubstantial' fabric of his 'variegated story' (1. 220–8) show much the same tendency; discussing them, Ferguson (1977: 129) comments that 'nature as an external presence appears strangely locked into an unsatisfyingly symbiotic relationship with the poet's "human nature" as the movement from the internal to the external begins to be a slippage'.

Shifts already noted in the initial series of images, especially in the fluidity of the protagonist's self-characterisation *vis-à-vis* his supposedly 'natural' interlocutors, are therefore part of a more general fluctuation between two different language registers. One of them draws upon the local speech of a rustic environment, using simple and regionally particular locutions that approach 'the language of conversation in the middle and lower classes of society'.[5] Alternating with that, the other register draws on an elevated cultural heritage for which the sonorous blank verse patterns, elaborate syntax and rich diction of Miltonic and Shakespearean poetry serve as a stylistic synecdoche. The narrator is placing himself and his implied readership partly within that formal, prestigious tradition in the very act of declaring a certain measure of independence from it. In relation to the literary mainstream he is both free and enclosed from the outset, making gestures of linguistic self-confidence alongside gestures of limitation and deference. This cultural situation, intricately linked to several social changes, underlies the motile relations between *The Prelude* and a number of established literary genres and rhetorical practices: philosophical verse essay, effusive ode, elevated epistle, distended lyric, Miltonic epic, pastoral idyll, rustic rumination, topographical sketch – elements of these all mingle in ways that to Augustan taste would have seemed indecorous if not downright incongruous, along with newer forms, notably the intimate 'conversation poem' recently invented by Coleridge (whose 'Frost at Midnight' is quoted directly at the beginning and end of the two-part proto-Prelude (*1799*, 1. 4 and 2. 497; cf. *1805*, 1. 278 and 2. 467). Against that varied background the irresolute wanderer of Wordsworth's poem, a figure not only released but also evicted, allegorises his historical situation as writer and as countryman.

Now this use of a conflicted language, marked by 'the strife of phrase' (12. 267), corresponds broadly to two different ways of representing the physical world. The differences are especially

THE CHARACTERS OF DANGER AND DESIRE

distinct in lines 271ff. of Book 1 – those with which the earliest version of the poem (1799) had begun: 'Was it for this . . .?' On the one hand there are several specifications of a localised landscape, the narrator's native district: Derwent, Cockermouth, Skiddaw and so forth, are all named, while very particular details focus the imagery: alder shades, a mill race, sandy fields, yellow grunsel. On the other hand this passage brings in the poem's first general reference to 'Nature' (with a capital) – a term which, carrying a traditional freight of philosophical and literary connotations, enters Book 1 as a personified figure only half a dozen times but becomes a more frequent presence in later books.

It is commonly said that Wordsworth's concept of Nature is variable. Another way to put it would be to say that, in the virtual absence of human agents from this poem, 'Nature' serves as the self's (or selves') mobile and mobilising *other*. This is more than just a matter of having several distinct aspects, fostering alike by beauty and by fear, as soother ('the calm / Which Nature breathes among the hills and groves': 1. 284–5) or prosecutor ('I heard among the solitary hills / Low breathings coming after me': 1. 329–30). For just as the 'I' often shifts between 'now' and 'then', from the one writing at the present moment of enunciation to the one whose past experience is recollected within the utterance, so too the forces of external nature enter variously into the telling as well as into the story that is told. The enunciating subject and the subject of the utterance are each such a congeries of contradictory selves ('It is shaken off, / That burthen of my own unnatural self' (1. 22–3); 'I seem / Two consciousnesses' (2. 31–2); 'Having two natures in me' (10. 868); 'Thus strangely did I war against myself' (11. 74) that no single identity can quite manage to amalgamate them, and this blurring of distinctions extends also to the relative roles of self and other as actants. Within the narrated past, declares the narrator, 'the earth / And common face of Nature spake to me' (1. 614–5); and this speech has also been present during the act of composition: 'In progress through this verse my mind hath looked / Upon the speaking face of earth and heaven / As her prime teacher' (5. 11–13).

Then who is whose 'speaking agent'? Who is in charge here? Does narrative motivation come from the individual mind or from capacities beyond it?

NARRATIVE EXCHANGES

> Ye motions of delight, that through the fields
> Stir gently ...
> Oh that I had a music and a voice
> Harmonious as your own, that I might tell
> What ye have done for me.
>   (11. 9–10, 20–2)

While natural 'forms and images' are impelled by 'everlasting motion' (1. 430–1), they may also need to provide 'a frame of outward life' to 'fix . . . those phantoms of conceit' (1. 128–30) at times when the poet's inventions become 'unruly' (1. 145–6). The roles alter, the characterisation of narrator and Nature keeps oscillating; and these instabilities in their relationship generate narrative movement – a movement which cannot be adequately summarised as a 'quest'. The narrator sometimes conflates different journey structures, for example in describing himself as 'a pilgrim gone / In quest of highest truth' (11. 391–2); but that is all the more reason for narrative analysis to distinguish them. Normally a pilgrimage is understood to be open to any willing traveller, and to have a known route and destination. In contrast, the term 'quest' tends to signify something undertaken by a dedicated individual, or at most a select few; while the goal is envisioned, its precise location and even its form are seldom known exactly in advance; and the problematic itinerary makes a quester more dependent than a pilgrim on signs and more subject to detours and redirections.

Early in Book 1 there is a paradigm for the unstable relationship between narrator and Nature. As the 'gentle breeze' addressed in the poem's first line veers from second to third person, from present to past, and from outside to inside ('I . . . felt within / A corresponding mild creative breeze': 41–3), it metamorphoses sharply from a zephyr into 'A tempest, a redundant energy, / Vexing its own creation' (46–7).[6] *Redundant?* In Dr Johnson's dictionary this word is defined as 'superabundant, exuberant, superfluous'; and so its use here, oddly linking wind with mind, reveals that tacit deconstructive logic which Derrida (1976: 141–64) calls supplementarity. Nature is deemed to be a plenitude, with the human imagination a mere adjunct. Yet as an independent source of creative power the latter can exceed or overflow the former, whose total governing capacity is thereby called into question. Versions of this supplementary paradox recur. In the following lines from Book 2, for instance, despite a seemingly careful insistence that power *came* to the poet rather than being produced by him, it remains unclear how something 'universal' can be accompanied by a 'superadded' element:

> that universal power
> And fitness in the latent qualities
> And essences of things, by which the mind
> Is moved by feelings of delight, to me
> Came strengthened with a superadded soul,
> A virtue not its own.
> (2. 343–7)

An analogous paradox is writ large in the very structure of *The Prelude*. Never formally completed by publication in the author's lifetime, never supposed in any case to be complete in itself, and yet coming by default to stand in lieu of the building to which it would have been a mere portico, this supremely supplementary poem manages to have it both ways. It can intimate an ideal unity without taking responsibility for accomplishing it, and indeed while still a foreplay, *praelusio*, it can verge on a *praeteritio*, proceeding to tell that which it disclaims a capacity to tell. As 'circumspection' mingles uncertainly with 'infinite delay' (1. 242), the poem's provisionality allows it to go on postponing the execution of a finished script. And so, in its drive towards and against completion, this text can remain

> a canopy
> Of shapes, and forms, and tendencies to shape,
> That shift and vanish, change and interchange
> (8. 720–2)

– never letting its reader confront the ultimately awful state of repose where

> every motion gone,
> The scene before him lies in perfect view
> Exposed, and lifeless as a written book.
> (8. 725–7)

It is a startling image: to be brought to book, as it were, is to become inert; to be made textually complete is to die. In contrast, shifting shapes are seen here as part of a vivid process, 'Like a magician's airy pageant' (734: that *Tempest* masque again), a 'spectacle to which there is no end' (741) and which is momentarily free of worries about evanescence – though they will return later in a context where Prospero's magic ('by simple waving of a wand, / The wizard instantaneously dissolves / Palace or grove': 11. 79–81) becomes an image of a sceptical spirit that threatens the 'mysteries of passion' (11. 84).

Lying 'in perfect view . . . lifeless', the image of a book is often regarded in *The Prelude* with ambivalence. Among many examples of the poem's two-way argument with its own condition is the passage where, having just remarked 'How books mislead us' (12. 207) in representing 'the differences, the outside marks by which / Society has parted man from man' (217–18), the narrator goes on to declare that his theme is

> the best of those who live
> Not unexalted by religious faith
> Nor uninformed by books (good books, though few),
> In Nature's presence.
>
> (12. 241–4)

And indeed, Book 5 – itself entitled 'Books' – culminates in a grand affirmative fusion of natural present with literary past, asserting that the receptive individual can

> Receive enduring touches of deep joy
> From the great Nature that exists in works
> Of mighty poets. Visionary power
> Attends upon the motions of the winds
> Embodied in the mystery of words.
>
> (5. 617–21)

Discussing these lines and some that follow them, Armstrong (1982) remarks that their syntax holds in suspension, as so often in *The Prelude*, two different sorts of relationship between mind and world: for example, 'visionary power "Attends upon", works on or waits dependently upon, "the motions of the winds", an active and a passive agent' (65–6). But either way the preoccupation is with the powerful embodiment of 'motions' in language.

Book 1 gives special prominence to this vital narrative principle of momentum that stems, as seen already, from substitutions in the sequencing of the utterance and dispossessive shifts in the modelling of the enunciation. Its function emerges most clearly in those familiar passages (reproduced as Appendix B to this book) which relate the formative childhood experiences of trapping, climbing, rowing and skating. Remarkably enough, the word 'motion' itself has explicit climactic emphasis in each of these episodes,[7] but more importantly their sequence plays out the reiterative and interactive elements of narration, signalling issues of textual exchange and control by leading straight into an engagement with *The Tempest*.[8]

In the first three of the four passages, the figurative structure is strictly symmetrical. It is not just that each records a moment of epiphany amidst a craggy landscape; more than that, an isomorphic pattern governs their image-sequences and what Greimas and Courtés (1982: 5–6, 162) would call the 'investments' of their 'actants'. In the first (1. 310–32), the narrator's own agitated, iterative pursuit of natural creatures ('from snare to snare, I plied / My anxious visitation, hurrying on, / Still hurrying hurrying onward') culminates in his being 'O'erpowered' by a 'strong desire' to *take* what others have caught, whereupon initiative is taken from him and he himself becomes the object of imagined pursuit. Those 'sounds / Of undistinguishable motion' mark the reversal.

In the second passage (1. 333–50) the narrator again has a predatory role, wanting this time to take eggs from a raven's nest; but as he clings to the ridge he is himself arrested – his ear assailed by the wind's 'strange utterance', his eye startled by the 'motion' of the clouds. Once more, then, the motive agency shifts, by a kind of dispossession, from the human figure to more powerful agents. (In the 1799 version of these passages, the word 'powers' is actually used in each case to designate these: 1. 35 and 73.)

The third passage (1. 372–426) follows the same narrative program of repetition and reversal. The narrator takes someone else's boat, propels it across the lake 'lustily' (desire is never far from the surface in these passages) – and then turns hurriedly back, admonished by the apparent uprearing of the cliff, which continues afterwards to 'move' uncannily through his mind. A kind of ripple effect develops, marked by even greater use of reiterative phrasing than in the first two passages. Just as 'the voice of mountain-echoes' accompanies the skiff, so the high incidence of repetition amplifies the lines, particularly those that refer to the moving boat (386, 387, 390), the horizon's bound (399, 406), the huge cliff (406, 409), the willow-tree cavern (375, 395, 414), and the dual doubling of 'struck the oars, and struck again'

(385) followed by 'I struck, and struck again' (408). As before, the pivot of the episode is a sudden usurpation of the boy's volition and movement, this time by the 'voluntary power' and 'measured motion' of the cliff figure.

A significant element in these three passages becomes clearer by contrast with the fourth, the ice-skating episode (1. 452–89). Superficially the now familiar pattern seems to be replicated, as human movement is appropriated by the natural environment; but there are important differences. For one thing the activity is no longer entirely solitary. Though the boy does at times separate himself from the crowd, his perceptions have a shared context in 'games confederate' – which, moreover, are not acts of stealth or rapacity: he and his friends are only playing at hunting ('imitative of the chase'), and the echoes contribute accordingly to their pleasures. Most strikingly, instead of the *taking* that occurs in each previous instance, there is now a *giving*; and so a different relationship, implicitly figured as a reciprocal exchange, is established with the surrounding landscape:

> When we had given our bodies to the wind,
> And all the shadowy banks on either side
> Came sweeping through the darkness, spinning still
> The rapid line of motion, then at once
> Have I, reclining back upon my heels,
> Stopped short – yet still the solitary cliffs
> Wheeled by me, even as if the earth had rolled
> With visible motion her diurnal round.
> (1. 479–86)

The narrative sequence still involves an impressive transfer of movement to the natural world (typified by modulating from 'I wheeled about' (458) into 'the solitary cliffs / Wheeled by me'), but it is not admonitory, not disturbing; rather it induces tranquillity. Instead of needing to be subordinated to the disciplinary powers of nature, the narrator can stand and watch the hills stretching 'feebler and feebler' behind him; he is an untroubled still point in this turning world. And instead of the semiotic opacity of those earlier encounters, evident in phrases like 'sounds ... undistinguishable' (330–1), 'strange utterance' (348) and 'undetermined sense' (419), the scene he contemplates this time seems in no way difficult to decipher.

An invocation of natural forces then follows, one that works intertextually in a way that the earliest version signals most clearly:

> Ye powers of earth, ye genii of the springs,
> And ye that have your voices in the clouds,
> And ye that are familiars of the lakes
> And of the standing pools, I may not think
> A vulgar hope was yours when ye employed
> Such ministry – when ye through many a year
> Thus, by the agency of boyish sports,
> On caves and trees, upon the woods and hills,
> Impressed upon all forms the characters
> Of danger or desire, and thus did make
> The surface of the universal earth
> With meanings of delight, of hope and fear,
> Work like a sea.
> (1799, 1. 186–98)

Discreetly but substantially, in their repetitive phrasal rhythms and their apostrophic conventions as much as in details of diction, these lines allude to the long crucial speech by Shakespeare's Prospero which begins:

> Ye elves of hills, brooks, standing lakes, and groves,
> And ye that on the sands with printless foot
> Do chase the ebbing Neptune
> (*The Tempest*, 5. i. 33ff.)

Fortified as they are by a thick spread through the poem of recurrent motifs from the same play (island, tempest, dream, music, drowning, charm, enchantment, power), the specific stylistic parallels here are strikingly insistent, though a little subdued in later versions of the passage. Implicitly, taken in conjunction with those other allusions discussed earlier, they invite a reader to compare this poet of *The Prelude* with that magus of *The Tempest*. On the face of it the two figures stand here in sharp contrast, since Prospero is speaking of a power to administer his own will to and through the spirits of nature – 'by whose aid / (Weak masters though ye be) I have bedimmed / The noontide sun, call'd forth the mutinous winds, / And 'twixt the green sea and the azur'd vault / Set roaring war' – whereas Wordsworth's speaker hails the spirits of nature as 'powers' who employ 'ministry' over himself. The Shakespearean magus apparently dominates the communicative situation; the Wordsworthian poet is apparently subservient to it. Yet that is not the whole story. On the one hand, Prospero is invoking his 'potent art' of control only to renounce it henceforth:

> But this rough magic
> I here abjure; and when I have requir'd
> Some heavenly music (which even now I do)
> To work mine end upon their senses that
> This airy charm is for, I'll break my staff,
> Bury it certain fathoms in the earth,
> And deeper than did ever plummet sound
> I'll drown my book.

Instead of controlling physical and spiritual forces in order to *take* revenge on those who wronged him, he will *give* Ariel (the lightfoot labourer) and Caliban (the servile drudge) their freedom, give Miranda to Ferdinand, and give a pardon to the miscreants. On the other hand, the Wordsworthian narrator will proceed to claim an active role, equivalent and complementary to that of nature. Although in the present passage it is nature's power that can imprint 'the characters / Of danger or desire' and 'make / The surface of the universal earth / With meanings of delight, of hope and fear / Work like a sea', *The Prelude* later declares that the relationship between nature and the responsive individual can be reciprocal:

> From Nature largely he receives, nor so
> Is satisfied, but largely gives again;
> For feeling has to him imparted strength,
> And – powerful in all sentiments of grief,
> Of exultation, fear and joy – his mind,
> Even as an agent of the one great mind,
> Creates, creator and receiver both,
> Working but in alliance with the works
> Which it beholds.
>
> (2. 267–75)

What makes such passages particularly revealing to the narrative analyst is their implicit function as an embedded microtype, or compact model, of the text's own ambiguous relationship with its potential reader. In this they simply accentuate what is latent everywhere in the poem, for there has been an intratextual doubling of auditors all along. Just as in that opening section of the poem the speaking voice addresses both the natural world (in the form of an inspirational breeze) and an ideal fellow-traveller (in the form of a particular human friend), so here too the exchange indicated by the apostrophe to natural spirits accompanies, and serves as image for, a friendly reader's participation in the collaborative task of constructing and endlessly reconstructing narrative meanings, 'working but in alliance with the work'. In the same way that the creative-and-receptive mind engages with Nature, the addressee and the speaking subject can supposedly become 'joint labourers in the work', as the poem's final paragraph asserts (13. 438).

This can be seen as inscribing what Friedman (1979) calls 'Wordsworth's chimerical political economy' – virtually a myth of symmetrical exchange by which real social inequalities are glossed over as spiritually active virtue is attributed to those who are materially subordinate.[9] Friedman detects this value system not only in the Convention of Cintra pamphlet but also in several poems; it reveals, he argues, a Tory humanist ideology based on the tenet that interdependent class relations are mutually rewarding, with 'affective power' supposedly compensating for a lack of 'effective power' and vice versa (285). 'Working in alliance' is thus a principle of control, as much for interpreting a text as for maintaining a social order. At the beginning of Book 9 the narrator represents his own shaping of the text as conjoined by an inclusive pronoun with a reader's traversal of the text:

> As oftentimes a river, it might seem,
> Yielding in part to old remembrances,
> Part swayed by fear to tread an onward road
> That leads direct to the devouring sea,
> Turns and will measure back his course – far back,
> Towards the very regions which he crossed
> In his first outset – so have we long time
> Made motions retrograde.
> (9. 1–8)

This fear of inundation, of an unconfinable surge of meanings, has special prominence in Book 5, whose three main episodes involve motifs of engulfment (cf. Hartman 1964: 227). It is important that drowning figures occur in a 'Book'-length section, entitled 'Books', within a potential 'book' in the usual fuller sense of that word. Few things indicate so strongly an impulse to control the flow of signification as does the circumtextual framing apparatus of a completed volume, palpably containing parts within a whole. *The Prelude* never became an authorised unit of that kind. A 'perfect view' of its text remained latent. In that circumstance there is more than a little of Prospero's spirit of renunciation; the speech quoted above ends with his declaration, 'I'll drown my book'. On the other hand, such relinquishments of control are less than final. Prospero hands over his power only after determining in large measure the bounds within which his subjects will be able to interact. What is more, he retains the right to command their attention: the play concludes not with this abjuration of his book-based 'potent art' but with a promise of further narration: he will tell 'the story of my life', he says. Identically, Book 1 of *The Prelude* ends with its narrator's promise that he will 'forthwith' tell 'the story of my life' (1. 666–7), and in its later books the text continues to be governed substantially by those very devices through which control is ostensibly handed over. After all, the intertextual relation that this Wordsworthian narrative establishes to a Shakespearean predecessor-text is itself one means of investing the narrator with cultural authority.

And yet *The Prelude*, not being a text for theatrical performance, has no dramatis personae. Its gestures towards the medium in which Prospero is both player and playmaster are the merest flickers in the poem's vast series of moving images, and its narrator need not be regarded as a person-like 'character' at all.[10] 'I', like 'Nature', is just a naming, not a warrant of identity; it is among the rhetorical stratagems that solicit unity for the narrative, but there are many countervailing tendencies towards a dispersal of selves.

Character, at least in this kind of narrative, may be thought of quite literally: as script, as figure or mark of writing. The narrator and his 'speaking agents' are precipitates formed from the narrative medium, putative subjects of the verbs that activate it, ways of designating a nexus between motion and control. Lettering, labelling, 'written paper', is an explicit metonymy for 'the story of the man' and a 'type / Or emblem of the utmost that we know' in the anecdote about the blind beggar (7. 615–20). The same point is insisted on in other Book 7 passages (221–2 and 309–10) and in some of the best known 'spots of time' (cf. Chase 1986: 13–31). A murderer's name carved into the ground at Penrith is all that

THE CHARACTERS OF DANGER AND DESIRE

remains of him: 'the characters were fresh and visible' (*1850*, 12. 240); 'characters of the great apocalypse' typifying a vista 'without end' are envisioned in the French Alps (6. 570–2); and in the passage from Book 1, discussed above, the narrator is hailing 'powers' that are said to have

> Impressed upon all forms the characters
> Of danger and desire, and thus did make
> The surface of the universal earth
> With meanings of delight, of hope and fear,
> Work like a sea.

The syntax reveals that its attributions and substitutions of agency are nearly circular: earthly powers that haunt the landscape have printed characters on all forms and thus have made the earth's surface 'work with meanings'. Where exactly is the locus of power? It is hard here to distinguish subject from object; and there is a similar ambiguity about the referent of that resonant phrase 'the characters / Of danger or desire'. What is dangerous, and what is desired, in this economy of narrative figures?

An answer indicated by the foregoing analysis is that *both* motion and control are *both* feared and wanted. For without some substitutive movement of 'characters' there would be no narrative; and without some scope for dispossessive shifts the narrator's authority would be too rigidly dominant, and ultimately might 'substitute a universe of death / For that which moves' (*1850*, 14. 160–1).

8
WAITING TO BE TOLD

There are now several questions is there anything that is not narrative and what is narrative what has narrative gotten to be now. When one used to think of narrative one meant a telling of happening in successive moments of its happening the quality of telling depending upon the conviction of the one telling that there was a distinct succession in happening, that one thing happened after something else and since that happening in succession was a profound conviction in every one then really there was no difference whether anyone began in the beginning or the middle or the ending because since narrative was a progressive telling of things that were progressively happening it really did not make any difference where you were at what moment you were in your happening since the important part of telling anything was the conviction that anything that everything was progressively happening. But now we have changed all that we really have.

(Stein 1969: 17)

I

How different is the role of storytelling in Western culture today from its role in earlier periods? We have seen that Wordsworth attempted during an era of great upheaval to elide the social and economic tensions that shaped *The Prelude*, fabricating a unified persona and an ideal of reciprocity which could not be sustained. What strategies are to be found in more recent fictions of exchange? Jean-François Lyotard has argued influentially that we now find ourselves inhabiting a 'postmodern condition' in which 'the grand narrative has lost its credibility, regardless of what mode of unification it uses' (Lyotard 1984: 37). What is this 'grand narrative' and what does it have to do with other sorts of stories? Is 'postmodern' more than a modish motto as far as the study of narrative is concerned?

Lyotard's primary emphasis is on the changing nature and function of knowledge in the technocratic society that has emerged since the mid-twentieth century.[1] Instead of the personal 'use value' that traditionally inhered in it, knowledge is being turned more and more towards relations of mere exchange, external to individuals (4–5). According to Chambers (1984), a similar mercantile conversion has already occurred in the development of modern fiction: 'if literature no longer has a use value (by which I understand the sort of value an act of direct communication might have), it has entered into the system of exchange value, in which its significance, or worth, is a function of its interpretability as a complex sign for which other discursive signs can be substituted' (12–13). Lyotard does not discuss literary fiction; but his argument about the close link between telling stories and circulating knowledge has implications for our own inquiry.

Lyotard sees 'modern' thought as having been supported by certain kinds of myth or philosophical arch-narrative, which have now lost their claim to legitimacy. The main myth of modernity has had two versions, in his view: the political epic of making progress towards an emancipated society and the scientific epic of achieving an enlightened epistemological unity 'that links the sciences together as moments in the becoming of spirit' (33). Disbelief in both versions of this grand narrative is what defines, for Lyotard, our postmodern condition. No longer structured and sanctioned at any meta-level by such dogmatic stories (now that the refrain is *Oh dear, what can the meta be?*), social action and intellectual inquiry have recourse instead to fragmentary mininarratives. Science must legitimate itself on its own performative terms. Larger ethical imperatives are taken over by the state and the multinational corporation, and knowledge becomes a market-driven service industry, a commodified and instrumentalised technology of information. (There is, however, something of a 'grand narrative' about the shape of Lyotard's own account of these historical processes. Dispossessively it derives force from them, reaffirming in practice the continuing quasi-mythic force of a storypower whose decline it theorises. Indeed, one can argue that 'past' myths are never simply abolished or superseded; at least residually, they persist, for whenever one of them weakens it provides ingredients for another.)

How is a postmodern condition exemplified in contemporary fictions? In order to suggest the range of ways in which textual exchanges can carry the imprint of the developments that Lyotard describes, this chapter will look closely at two very different cases: *The Aunt's Story* (published 1948),[2] a novel by Nobel Prize winner Patrick White which has come to be recognised as one of the outstanding achievements of late modernism, and 'The Hind of the Further' (1980), a collage of verbal and graphic elements assembled by the avant-garde American writer Jaimy Gordon. (Gordon's text is reproduced as Appendix C.)

Each of these texts can be read as responding to a question about the scope that remains for narrative in a fragmented culture. What is there left to tell? Their answers are different. White's novel seems sceptical about the communicative potential of any stories, grand or little, in the modern world; but in place of that lost function it affirms the value of imagined stories as a private hermeneutic, internalising the quest which society cannot satisfy. 'Truth' is still envisaged as the goal, in keeping with the author's stated conviction that 'What to tell and what to leave out while conveying the truth remains the great question' (White 1983: 134). *The Aunt's Story* represents fragmentation in psychological and spiritual terms: as a plight to be faced individually. A cultural crisis is sketched, one that draws directly on the author's own 'fragmented memories' of the 1930s and 1940s (White 1983: 128), but the emphasis falls on the adequacy or inadequacy of one's inner resources when faced with suffering. Theodora Goodman, the aunt figure through whom nearly everything is focalised, is presented as an exemplary soul in search of transcendence through visionary self-knowledge. Accordingly the form in which her story is related combines features of modernist fiction (such as stylistic experimentation, stream of consciousness, social satire) with features of allegorical romance underpinned by religious structures (salient for example in the protagonist's name, in the tripartite *rite de passage* structure by which her journeying is intratextually framed, and in a number of other elements – noted by Mackenzie 1965).

'The Hind of the Further' poses (and implicitly answers) the question of tellability differently: by laying bare the basic constituents of any textual exchange, showing it to be fundamentally substitutive and dispossessive in such a way that when cohesive props are removed the yearning for story-shaped coherence remains. Fragmentation is textualised here. What one can know and narrate, Gordon's text implies, is no more or less than the substance of previous texts. To tell is to retell: to seize, divide and reassemble another's utterance. Thus Gordon's text incorporates the 'agonistic' aspect of language games (Lyotard 1984: 10) into its own formal substance.

II

Narration in *The Aunt's Story* is circumtextually framed by the title. Will it be told about this aunt, or by her, or both? Theodora Goodman turns out not to act as narrator, except in a special sense; indeed, she sees herself, at least initially, as one of those 'people who do not have many stories to tell' (136). Numerous references to storytelling in this novel are formulated in similar terms. The word 'tell' itself often recurs at important moments; but, curiously, it is almost always incorporated into a clause whose terms are negative ('There is nothing to tell . . .') or conditionally deferred ('I could tell you . . .'). Seldom in the first or last of its three Parts do characters in *The Aunt's Story* tell stories to one another. When they do it is usually represented as a bit of self-indulgent chatter. Frank Parrott, smug after his successful display of rabbit-shooting with Fanny and Theodora Goodman, 'told them about the time he swam the Barwon River in flood' (73) – but we are given no details; they are not necessary, because his is obviously a nugatory narration. So it is also when, finding Theodora on her doorstep, a woman in America's mid-west at once begins to silence her own surprise by recourse to habitual talk:

> She had a lot to tell. She would not ask much, but she would tell. And Theodora was glad of this, as she could not have answered. She did say that she had come by train. But the woman could not pause. She had to tell about her younger Frances, who was multiplying on the coast, and her elder daughter Myra, at Topeka, who had the hand for cheese cake.
> (271–2)

In contrast to such garrulity, Theodora herself almost invariably responds with a quiet deprecation when urged to tell a story, as

NARRATIVE EXCHANGES

she is time and again. Most of Part 1 is framed within her repeated denial (20, 136) that she has anything much to recount about Meroë, her rural Australian home; and yet the narrating voice fills the intervening space with what its chief character declines to divulge. Her boisterous nephews pester her for stories: 'Tell us something, Aunt Theo, they cried. Yes, yes, she said; but first I must find my breath. Where; they said; is it under the bunya-bunya tree? Because it was a joke' (13). Even when her especially beloved niece Lou, whose 'breath ... was almost her own' (136), makes a similar request in the same opening chapter, Theodora is reluctant to be drawn into a narratorial role:

> 'Tell me about something,' said Lou, the words warm in Theodora's shoulder. 'Tell me about Meroë.'
> 'Meroë?' said Theodora. 'But my darling, you have heard it, and there is very little to tell.'
>
> (19)

This becomes a refrain sounded in every chapter of Part 1 and often thereafter. Frank, on the verge of proposing to the vivacious Fanny, finds himself instead seeking out her 'unattractive' sister Theodora and, despite his uneasiness, pursuing a conversation in which he gropes for meanings beyond Fanny's ken:

> 'I could tell you,' Frank began.
> 'What could you tell?' she [Theodora] asked.
> 'Nothing,' he said.
>
> (85)

Earlier, the Man who was Given his Dinner had announced to Theodora, 'I could tell you a lot of things' (46), but when Fanny thrice importunes him he refuses to say any more. And years later, when Theodora meets Pearl Brawne, once the Goodmans' servant at Meroë and now a prostitute in Sydney, part of their conversation goes like this:

> 'Well, Theo, tell,' said Pearl, arranging her big white hands in front of her bust.
> 'There is nothing to tell,' said Theodora.
> 'Go on, Theo,' Pearl said, 'there is always everything to tell.'
> 'I am forty-five,' said Theodora, 'and very little has happened.'
>
> (131)

To be sure, despite the similar phrasing, these non-narrations do not have identical significance. In some cases, stories apparently cannot be told because the narrator is too self-enclosed; this is so not only of Frank's inability to articulate his feelings but also of Violet Adams's gushy letter to Theodora, 'telling nothing and all' (64), or of that American woman's recital of family trivia in Part 3. In other cases a story remains untold because the potential narrator deems the audience to be deficient in some quality, as when the Man who was Given his Dinner brushes off Fanny's demands that he tell them something. But the effect is still much the same: to underline the epigraph for Part 1, with its emphasis on 'the narrowness of the limits within which a human soul may speak and be understood' (9). Theodora's own disinclination to act as narrator seems to stem from a lack of faith in the possibililty of spanning with words the gaps between people, of communicating across 'the distances that separate, even in love' (137). This indeed is the concluding note of Part 1:

> 'Will you really go away, Aunt Theo?' asked Lou.
> 'Yes,' said Theodora. 'I shall go away.'
> 'Then there will soon be a lot of other stories to tell.'
> 'I expect not,' Theodora said.
> 'Why?' asked Lou.
> 'Because there are the people who do not have many stories to tell.'
>
> (136)

If in Theodora's world there is scant satisfaction to be had from the little narratives of ordinary experience, there is equally scant consolation in the grander narratives of progressive human enlightenment. Through the pervasive motif of 'waiting', *The Aunt's Story* represents itself intratextually as suspended between those two sorts of storytelling. Four times in the first three pages Theodora is said to be 'waiting'. Her mother's death, announced in the opening sentence, allows her own story to begin; but at this stage she insists, as we have seen, that she has 'little to tell'. Part 2 intensifies the theme of suspended animation. No less than five times in the first paragraph of this section (141) are we told that Theo is waiting. The scene has shifted to Europe, which itself is depicted only a few pages further on as 'waiting for the crash' (146) not only of markets but also of tradition and of modernity. Staying at the Hôtel du Midi in southern France with a miscellany of eccentrics from several countries, Theodora lacks any clear sense of direction; she is 'waiting to be told', she says (207). In this state of passivity she becomes a kind of imaginary participant in the fragmentary life-stories of those around her. But this role, that of a character rather than a narrator, is merely vicarious, and in Part 3 she learns instead to 'tell' herself by creating independent inner stories.

Part 1 had ended with her feeling that 'there is no lifeline to other lives' (137), and hence that there can be no worthwhile storyline. Yet it turns out that she is partly mistaken about this; the rest of the novel moves towards her discovery that, although distances and divisions and silences dominate, our lives are nevertheless story-shaped and may be more bearable if understood as such. It is a discovery in which landscape plays an important part, for in the relation that develops between Theodora and her physical environment the text offers a model for a reader's relation to itself.

Already in the opening chapters an analogy has been set up between alert perception of the landscape and alert perception of human beings. Images of colour signal this particularly. To an unsympathetic gaze Theodora is 'dry, and leathery, and yellow', but her eyes 'burned still, under the black hair' (12); her beloved niece Lou, with the 'thin, yellow face', seems to Theodora 'like some dark and secret place in one's own body' (13). Similarly there is more to the plain old Goodman homestead, Meroë, than its 'flat biscuit colour'; for surrounding it are 'black volcanic hills', which she can imagine 'split deeper open' to reveal 'a fiercer, Ethiopian intensity' (21). Such passages (there are several others) indicate a doubleness in the way people and places may be apprehended: as outward aspect or as profound interiority. This latter, the dimension of depth, acquires more substance through descriptions of Meroë and its counterpart in myth. Theodora's father tells her that the name of their house is taken from an ancient place 'in the black country of Ethiopia' (25). That 'legendary landscape' of which he speaks, near the waters of the Nile, thereafter underlies Theodora's relationship with her immediate material world.

As the text itself openly declares, elements from the tales of Homer and Herodotus provide figurative reference-points for Theodora's journeyings (cf. Herring 1970). They are mentioned together as part of George Goodman's reading just when he first prefigures in its very syntax an imminent collapse), the licensed arch-narrators are merely vestigial phantoms, with nothing to tell. And the shabby little Hôtel du Midi offers no real refuge, only a *jardin exotique*, 'completely static, rigid, the equation of a garden' (146) – which, however, does have the negative virtue of allowing Theodora's soul 'little to hide behind'. Thus exposed, she begins to project herself imaginatively into the fictive recesses of her fellow-lodgers' lives; that is, she discovers the potential of empathetic narration as a kind of autotherapy. Burrows (1970) explains precisely how this figure-like storying process in Part 2 works in relation to the people and places of Part 1. There is no need to echo here the details of his exact exegesis, but some of it might be summarily restated in terms of the previous discussion by saying that 'the ghosts of Homer and St Paul and Tolstoy' are given a new lease of life: disengaged alike from the commodification of values and from those myths of endings in which heroic action or social progress culminates, they are drawn instead now into fragmentary and surreal episodes through which Theodora creates – for herself and for others – lifelines that are endlessly narratable. Thus she enters, as a character in the improvised fiction she shares with Sokolnikov, a Russia that gives her more imaginative space than might be found in the historical panorama of *War and Peace* ; and in one dream she can blend motifs from the worlds of the *Odyssey* and the *Acts of the Apostles* (206–7). As with spectral lives, so too with the physical environment, for these become interfused:

> Soon the sea would merge with the houses, and the almost empty asphalt promenade, and the dissolving lavender hills behind the town. So that there was no break in the continuity of being. The landscape was a state of interminable being, hope and despair devouring and disgorging endlessly, and the faces, whether Katina Pavlou, or Sokolnikov, or Mrs Rapallo, or Wetherby, only slightly different aspects of the same state.
>
> (187)

Like Himmelfarb in White's later novel *Riders in the Chariot*, who emerges from the holocaust to declare that 'the intellect has failed us', Theodora survives the hotel blaze at the end of Part 2 with no confidence left in what her fellow-lodger Wetherby calls 'the logical conclusion' (242); from Theodora's mind, 'reason and motive were rinsed out' (252).

Already in Part 1 it had been apparent to her that contemporary 'history was telling a story' (94) – a story whose trajectory did not match the one assumed by optimists such as her cultured and reasonable suitor Huntly Clarkson (neatly described by Mackenzie (1965) as 'a secretly utopian ruler of a social sultanate'). Clarkson is at his most confident among the palpable, substantial surroundings of the Easter Agricultural Show – 'as if this were his world, the world of ... towers of corn' (123). That materially comfortable relation with the natural environment is one of the things that Theodora, having declined Clarkson's proposal of marriage, explicitly rejects in Part 3, which begins by amplifying the resonance of the corn motif:

> All through the middle of America there was a trumpeting of corn. Its full, yellow, tremendous notes pressed close to the swelling sky. There were whole acres of time in which the yellow corn blared as if for a judgement. It had taken up and swallowed all other themes.
>
> (265)

Theodora, withdrawn 'into her own distance', watches – or hears – this landscape from a train. A fellow passenger, 'who wished to tell about his home, his mother, his cocktail cabinet, the vacation he had taken in Bermuda, and how he had sold papers as a boy', feels diminished by the 'corn song', and his attempts to talk to Theodora seem to her like 'the desperate hum of telephone wires, that tell of mortgages, and pie, and phosphates, and love, and movie contracts, and indigestion, and real estate, and loneliness' (265–6). Theodora herself, though unencumbered by narrative compulsions, has no sense of harmony with orderly, cultivated nature or with any regulated movement through it: 'In the bland corn song, in the theme of days, Theodora Goodman was a discord' – and so she dismounts at a country siding while the train proceeds 'with all its magnificence of purpose' (270). Encountering later the rustic Johnson family, to whom she whimsically announces herself as 'Miss Pilkington', Theodora finds difficulty in responding to their kindly puzzlement. ' "Tell us something about your travels, Miss Pilkington," Eunice said, as if you could tell all things always in words ' (281).

Unable to oblige, Theodora leaves their hospitable home and wanders to a deserted shack in the wooded hills nearby. Beside this hermitage is a spring; splashing its water on her eyes, 'she could almost have read a writing on the bark of any given tree' (290). Here is her private Meroë, 'beyond the dry flags of corn' (284). Here she can commune with a composite character/interlocutor of her own fiction, Holstius, whose imaginary voice helps her prepare herself for what is imminent:

> 'They will come for you soon, with every sign of the greatest kindness,' Holstius said. 'They will give you warm drinks, simple, nourishing food, and encourage you to relax in a white room and tell your life. Of course you will not be taken in by any of this, do you hear? But you will submit. It is part of the deference one pays to those who prescribe the reasonable life. They are admirable people really, though limited.'
> (295)

Theodora can accept this with equanimity because she has learned how to 'tell her life' in an alternative sense, unrestrained by the limits of rationality. She has learned how to internalise the narration of her relationships in such a way that they form a kind of psychic landscape in which her life extends plurally:

> In the peace that Holstius spread throughout her body and the speckled shade of surrounding trees, there was no end to the lives of Theodora Goodman. These met and parted, met and parted, movingly. They entered into each other, so that the impulse for music in Katina Pavlou's hands, and the steamy exasperation of Sokolnikov, and Mrs. Rapallo's baroque and narcotised despair were the same and understandable. And in the same way that the created lives of Theodora Goodman were interchangeable, the lives into which she had entered, making them momentarily dependent for love or hate, owing her this portion of their fluctuating personalities, whether George or Julia Goodman, only apparently deceased, or Huntly Clarkson, or Moraitis, or Lou, or Zack, these were the lives of Theodora Goodman, these too.
> (295)

The infinity of her storied lives can be celebrated in this way because she has rejected narrowly commercial exchanges ('such a buying and selling') and has given over her character and itinerary to potentially limitless substitutions. In this way the gaps between people become metonymic; narration continues as figures 'meet and part, movingly'.

If in this inner triumph there is a bleakly Pyrrhic quality, that is what must suffice – the novel suggests – in a world governed externally by the criteria of reason, a world in which tellability is either corrupted by a vain 'desire to strain perpetually after truth' (294) instead of waiting quietly for its advent, or constrained by a fondness such as Fanny's for 'the comfortable narrative of wives and mothers' (268). In one of her imaginary dialogues in Part 2, Theodora had declared 'I cannot tell you any more. Because I am waiting to be told' (207); now she knows she must tell herself – that is, must create stories to inhabit in silence. The invention of Holstius to share these secret narrative transactions is a sign of the peace she has made with her father's ghost. For her final condition is not so very different from that which he had experienced when they used to walk together around their own Meroë. 'Father did not speak. He respected silence, and besides, whether it was summer or winter, the landscape was more communicative than people talking' (34).

At the Hôtel du Midi, Mrs Rapallo had urged Theodora to relax with a book – 'a book where things happen' (199). *The Aunt's Story* itself is not, primarily, that sort of book. In lieu of events, it offers a sequence of images that relate Theodora's several lives in a landscape of inner narration. And yet by finally setting out its options in those terms, by proposing a spiritualised microgeography of individual discovery as antidote to the rationalised macro-history of social progress, the novel perhaps allows the object of its critique (uniformity in the name of reason) to dictate and distort the terms of that critique itself, which has become locked within a simplified oppositional rhetoric. The state of separateness or fragmentation, highlighted by the epigraphs to each part of the novel, is abstracted and endowed with a seemingly transcendental permanence. It is represented as 'given' at some fundamental level, and as needing to be 'accepted' (288) in one's own soulful privacy. Therefore the text's involvement with the wider circulation of stories, stories that make up what gets generally perceived as 'social reality', subsides into a sort of quietistic resignation. And this closing-in towards an isolated fantasy world in which reality and illusion merge amounts to a forgetting or suppressing by the text of some of its own earlier intuitions about the way real divisions and unities are materially constructed, shaped by specific social pressures and sustained ideologically by a system of representation.

Two brief examples will serve to show this. First, the Jack Frost episode surely resists, in its social particularity, any redemptive spiritualising formula. This pastry-cook's murder of his family is situated precisely within a set of economic circumstances, and the divisions in this case are to a large extent divisions of class:

> He kept a shop in George Street to which people went, the people who had names and good addresses, but Jack Frost himself lived in a street in Clovelly which was just a street. They felt his cakes in their stomachs. They saw the dark hairs on his wrist as he handed back the change.
> (100–1)

The incident resists interpretation, and irony is sharp in 'Truth had a full account', for even the printing of Frost's own letter in that sensationalist tabloid newspaper tells little. But the context of commercial dealings – the buying of cakes, and the buying of Truth 'over the garden fence' – is no less significant for being so sketchily indicated.

Or consider the Pearl Brawne story, a servant-girl's seduction and subsequent career in prostitution: in a similar way this shows the importance of material limits imposed on personal freedom by social categories. Gender divisions, combined with those of class, give substance to Theodora's reflection about Pearl: 'Life is full of alternatives, but no choice' (132). And yet this is something that the text does not consistently recognise. Quite early in the piece comes this passage: 'Life was divided . . . into the kinder moments and the cruel, which on the whole are not conditioned by sex' (34). A telltale detail here, a linguistic pointer to ideological tendencies, is the switch to a present tense proposition. It implies the omniscient narrator's endorsement of a supposedly general truth about the human condition rather than something that varies according to gender and class. This form of what linguists call modality (cf. Fowler 1986: 131–2) risks sentimentalising the realities of social division.

III

If White's novel seems typically modernist in its gesture towards an inward dimension of truth untouchable by the contingent everyday social world, what then does a typical gesture of postmodernist art look like? How one answers that question depends on whether its relational terms are understood as pertaining to periods, styles or attitudes. Some theorists want them to mean all these things; thus, while Jean-François Lyotard often uses the term postmodern to indicate a period, he also proffers the paradox that it is somehow a catalyst within the modern – a radical, avant-garde impulse of renovation (Lyotard 1984: 79–82). But Fredric Jameson wants to insist on a firm historical separation of what those binary terms designate: they remain, he declares, 'utterly distinct in their meaning and social function owing to the very different positioning of postmodernism in the economic system of late capital' (Jameson 1984b: 57). Indeed, 'high modernism can be definitively certified as dead and as a thing of the past: its Utopian ambitions were unrealisable and its formal innovations exhausted', becoming 'the object of the postmodernist pastiche' within a 'new social formation' (Jameson 1984a: xvii-xviii).[7]

Wishing to extend Jameson's analysis into a more self-reflexive critique, David Bennett still appears to accept the basic premise that definitions of postmodernism should be grounded in 'an altered relation between cultural production and its socioeconomic context' (Bennett 1988: 20). Postmodernist art, as he sees it, has been sucked ineluctably into a system of consumerist exchange. His prime example is the seemingly oppositional work of Christo, who parodies the institutionalised and commercial status of an art-object by putting under gigantic wraps a variety of bridges, towers, galleries and so forth, but whose own packaging project quickly becomes appropriated by the system it appears to subvert: his spectacular avant-garde feats not only require (because of their location and scale) the co-operation of civic bureaucracies but also become commodified through massproduced postcards and other such consumable images. In this kind of complicity Bennett sees support for Jameson's view that contemporary aesthetic experimentation is market-driven. By the same token, he regards theoretical discourse about postmodernism as (in part) a response to the same consuming desire for novelty value – for new definitions, strategies, readings and repackagings. Further, he notes that recent reader-oriented theories in literary criticism oscillate between a consumerist emphasis, as in the express wish to 'restore stories to their rightful owners – you and me' (Holland 1980: 370), and conversely a quasi-modernist emphasis on resisting 'the reduction of art/literature to the status of an exchangeable commodity' (Bennett 1988: 29). Bennett recognises that his own usage of 'modernist' and 'postmodernist' is arbitrary, projecting as a narrative sequence what are really 'co-existent moments in any self-reflexive discourse' (29). And yet, shrewd though his observations are, they do not take into account the manner by which a literary text may partly resist being positioned within a particular system of production, distribution and exchange. To take a Christo hyper-package as typifying postmodern art in general is to exaggerate the determining power of the marketplace. To consider instead, as we shall soon do, the exemplary features of an experimental para-narrative text is to recognise that commodification may be pre-emptively transvalued by the text's own framing strategies.

There is a further problem about Jameson's argument that 'a new social formation' has made modernist culture 'a thing of the past': in thus ascribing to the economy of the West a virtually monopolistic force, it also homogenises historical processes in an indiscriminate way. Simon During (1989) argues that 'Western culture' should not be lumped together so readily, since the generality of the concept occludes differential political realities, particularly in those countries (such as New Zealand and Australia, Canada and South Africa) where specific urgencies of multicultural contestation can render insignificant the very notion of modernity, let alone postmodernity. Europe of half a century ago could plausibly be represented in White's novel as 'waiting for the crash'; yet that message is still hardly deliverable in some places, where the cultural condition, During suggests, may be like 'waiting for the post' – waiting, that is, for a non-modern 'postcultural' identity rather than for anything postmodern.

If on the one hand a Jamesonian postmodernism that sees itself as Western has tended to presume cultural uniformity where it ought to defer to differences, is there on the other hand a postmodernism that does not endorse 'the claim by the West to have the union ticket to history' (Spivak 1989: 25)? One textual means of dismantling that grand narrative is to reframe it critically through a pastiche of its annexation of 'Eastern' culture. Edward Said has shown the pervasiveness of 'a Western style for dominating, restructuring, and having authority over the Orient' (Said 1978: 3); with that in mind, let us turn now to a curious little text (as postmodern in its own way as any Christo-wrapped edifice), which was published just a couple of years after Said's study and which represents with telling allusiveness the themes of fragmentation, commodification and Orientalism.

Jaimy Gordon's 'The Hind of the Further' (see Appendix C) may seem at first no more than a collage, assembling inconsequential oddments without connective sense; and Toolan is categorical in stating that 'a pure collage of described events, given in sequence, doesn't count as a narrative' (1988: 7). But by etymology and common acceptation, a collage consists of parts that have been merely placed together to form an inert shape, whereas mobility is not lacking in this case. While one could hardly derive a plot from 'The Hind of the Further', things do happen as one frames its components intratextually. Rhetorical allure engages interpretation in a strong drive forwards, a momentum of desire.

Some of those mobile components are verbal, others are pictorial. But they come together here in mutually substitutive ways, bearing out Nelson Goodman's contention in *The Languages of Art* (1976) that the two sign systems are differentiated not by 'essential' qualities but by the modes of reading that we apply to them respectively. Visual imagery is read as 'syntactically and semantically dense' (Mitchell 1986: 67), whereas the signifying effect of letters, words and sentences depends on their being read as relatively discrete items. Faced with 'The Hind of the Further', one may at first try to keep the verbal items separate from the visual, interpreting the former as constituting a (somewhat elliptical) storyline. They cannot easily be dismissed as utterly nonsensical, despite frequent deviation from the grammatical norms. Formally cohesive syntax and logical entailment are deficient here, but one thing can nevertheless seem to lead to another tropingly if a semantic relation is posited between the particles of near-sense.[8] Consider for example the first page and a half: 'Where did he get so much? The captain of everything that passed without being seen. Leaving the silver, he turned to the gold, a wife who flew wide open!' Because the opening question is so abrupt, a reader is likely to reach for the next phrase as a semantic handrail; 'the captain' will tend to be read as appositional, glossing the 'he'. Yet so far one is little the wiser; what the captain commands is a noun clause of unusual abstractness, hardly able to elucidate that whatever-it-is of which he has 'got so much'. On the other hand the verb within that noun clause, 'passed', records a kind of propulsion (through time and/or space), and so heightens an expectation of narrative development, which is then supported by

'Leaving the silver, he turned to the gold', for this permits an inference that the apparently discrete sentences are being held together by the topic of the captain's possessions. Even the startling shift to 'wife' can be read, at a stretch, as figuratively linked with the gold, so that 'a wife who flew wide open' becomes an acquisition of the highest value. To preserve a thread of apparent continuity, 'flying wide open' must be construed non-literally, perhaps as a metaphor for ecstatic sexual response. And so on: sense, while uncertain, continues to seem available – largely through the process of figurative substitution.

Visual components, as well, can entice a reader into the search for story-shaped meanings and tease along the desire to fit all the parts together plausibly. Because the etched images follow one another through their arrangement on succeeding pages, there is a strong compulsion to try to see them as semantically sequential, too. One is likely to want, for instance, to link together the different soaring figures or the several severings of the various arches and porches and portals so that they form a telling sequence in which *this* visible figure bears a certain relation to *that* one, and place A to place B. The difficulties in making these sorts of connections need not quite thwart the impulse to make them.

Relations between phrasal and visual elements intensify intra-textually the quasi-narrative forward movement. These relations are of three different kinds. First, the printed words themselves are sometimes so arranged as to form part of an unstable, virtually mobile, pictorial pattern; thus the first page juxtaposes segments in relatively large lettering, dispersed and tilted, with a step-shaped block containing smaller and denser print, and does so in such a way as to hint at a link with the pictorial item at the top (Is that hand dropping a word . . . ?). Secondly, a drawn image may appear to reinforce some verbal information; thus the 'quartered body' corresponds both to the large cut-up 'I' above it and to the cut-up female body on the following page, just as those two elements are brought together substitutively by the request 'to dispose of it as your own'. Thirdly, a drawn image may on the contrary be markedly discrepant with the verbal information; thus there is no discernible linkage between, on the one hand, the rearing horse or the twining snakes and, on the other hand, the shockingly 'strange request' or the enclosure of those incongruous 'four parts' – and therefore one reads on in search of a linkage.

However, the attempt to frame these narrative viabilities and obstacles intratextually will not suffice. 'The Hind of the Further' raises a larger question: for its puzzling manner has less to do with various relations and gaps between part and part within the tangible text-on-the-page than with relations between (1) any or all of those parts and (2) the *intertextual* framing on which their collective interpretability depends. Moreover, these relations are provokingly compounded by the elusiveness of *circumtextual* markers.

Take for example the final page, which apparently signals conclusiveness because it is the only one on which a visual image entirely encloses the accompanying words, as if to bring to rest the previously agitated motions of the text. And more than that, it explicitly announces an end, or at least a discontinuation: 'so the story left off'. But there is a catch: logically, it cannot be referring to its own completion as a past event when it is still continuous with the narration. Whose 'story', then, has 'left off', and what relation does it have to that which surrounds it and utters it?

In effect, this is a question about the assignability or provenance of voices that constitute the text. Who or what speaks in 'The Hind of the Further'? And indeed what does that odd titular phrase signify in relation to the rest of the text? Two figures are given speech, the captain and his wife. What *he* has to say is somewhat riddling, and refers only to present and future. What *she* has to say is cast in the first person, and some of it recounts things that have happened ('When I was lost ...') – that is, she tells, albeit fragmentarily, more of a 'story' in the orthodox sense, though it is he whose speech more nearly precedes the statement that 'the story left off'. At any rate their acts of speech are both enclosed within that of an apparently omniscient narrator.

But where then does this narratorial voice come from? Is it not, itself, implicitly embedded within another utterance, just as it embeds those of the two characters? Is not everything in this text (except perhaps the title and the authorial attribution) *visibly quoted*? Certainly the illustrations, and the hewn blocks of smaller-size print, are excerpted directly from a prior text. Their source is readily identifiable: they come from Edward Lane's enormously popular nineteenth-century translation of *The Thousand and One Nights*, with engravings by several hands.[9] So a famous English version of a famous oriental text has been chopped up and partially reassembled to form 'The Hind of the Further'. What narrative exchange is constituted by this seemingly whimsical dismembering of a classic?

Quoting, like translating, is a form of repetition-with-difference; rather than simply producing the same thing again, a quotation reads it and recontextualises it. The accents shift diacritically and dialogically (cf. Volosinov 1973: 109–59). Indeed, what 'The Hind of the Further' does to Lane's version of *The Thousand and One Nights* is similar to what that version itself has already done to its prior text. Edward Said in *Orientalism* describes as follows Lane's way of handling his Arabian sources: they 'are disembowelled for exposition, so to speak, then put together admonishingly by Lane' (Said 1978: 164). Actually that reference is not to Lane's rendering of *The Thousand and One Nights*, of which Said makes only the briefest mention in passing: it is an 'uninspired' translation, he says, though one that nevertheless 'consolidated the system of knowledge inaugurated by [Lane's] *Modern Egyptians*' (164). This latter text is the one that interests Said, who sees it as a violent act of cultural appropriation. Similarly, though Said does not make the comparison, Lane's 'translation' of *The Thousand and One Nights* involves textual violence, a process of cutting and reconnecting: 'I have thought it right', says Lane's editorial preface, 'to omit such tales, anecdotes, etc., as are comparatively uninteresting or on any account objectionable' (xiii). Tellingly, images of excision and truncation, already prolific enough in the original stories, are given emphatic prominence in the illustrations to Lane's text. Many, for instance, show an executioner's sword being wielded. The language of 'The Hind of the Further' brings this kind of motif into salience with phrases like 'divide the body', 'find the quartered body'; and all the words that comprise it are themselves obviously cut from Lane's text.[10]

Or are they? Is the series of phrases in larger type taken from the same source? Being so fragmentary, they are hard to trace. But in so far as we assume or want them to have that origin, we show again how eager we are for framed coherence. And the text seems to prefigure this, both in the desire (associated with the captain figure) to possess something of high value that yet does not remain the same, and the desire (associated with the wife) to be opened and to give. We are prevented, however, from simply allegorising these longings – either of which is attributable to either party in a textual exchange; for from another angle we can see a contrast here between a strong will-to-unity, figured as marriage or as containment, and a powerful contrary force that rends asunder, or flies away. The centrifugal, fragmented imagery is at odds with the gestures towards a sustained and symmetrical consummation.

When perplexed by a text, readers will hope to be able to make it more meaningful by circumtextual framing. But in this case the title, too, seems hardly intelligible even in its very syntax. While 'hind' in a noun position would normally be taken to mean a female deer, its genitival linking here with 'further' tends to draw in also something of the adjectival sense – situated at the back, or following after. The phrase elusively suggests a substitutive legerdemain.

Perhaps this can be elucidated a little *further* if we return briefly to another figure by which a comprehension of the text is framed intratextually: the figure of theft. Filling some narrative gaps, a reader may well suppose that it is the thieves who are 'particular to divide the body', who decide that 'it inclosed four parts', who abduct the wife in darkness, and who eventually hold their peace. They form a contrast with the seemingly wealthy captain; whereas he is a figure of control, they stand for dispossession – and so for the role of a reader (or translator, or rewriter). Reading is an attempt to seize and plunder what the text signifies; but when one opens up this text one finds only a *further* text be-*hind* it. The stolen signifiers, being relocated, now signify their difference from themselves. In an essay on Artaud, Derrida (1981) comments on this phenomenon:

> The structure of theft already lodges (itself in) the relation of speech to language [i.e., of a text to its discursive system]. Speech is stolen: since it is stolen from language it is, thus, stolen from itself, that is, from the thief who has always already lost speech as property and initiative. Because its forethought cannot be predicted, the act of reading perforates the act of speaking or writing. . . . That speech and writing are always unavowably [sic] taken from a reading is a form of the original theft, the most archaic elusion, which simultaneously hides me and purloins my powers of inauguration.
>
> (178)

What Gordon's 'Hind of the Further' does, then, is to lay bare ('Thus was I exposed') the way its own narrative exchanges are based on the workings of substitution and dispossession. Terry

Eagleton says that technology, late capitalism and consumerism have 'scattered our bodies to the winds as so many bits and pieces of reified technique, appetite, mechanical operation and reflex desire' (Eagleton 1985: 71); however, what the medium of representation can do is to show how that process is textualised. In narrative fiction, at least, the body of a text always comprises scatterings, bits and pieces of desire. These are lures to exchange, but not necessarily in a consumerist structure. Gordon's avant-garde para-narrative collage virtually eludes commodification by disclosing that acts of quasi-mercantile exchange depend on illusory unities – so that if texts undo themselves *and* their partner-texts by foregrounding divisions, gaps, and seizures, then no secure basis for textualised property relations can persist. Rather than resembling commercial transaction, the way texts are dealt with in being read and rewritten may sometimes be more like theft, abduction or carnal intercourse.

But those enact adult desire. From what desire does the narrative impulse initally emerge in us? Do the stories told by children bear out the lines of argument developed in the present study? The final chapter will confront such questions.

9

'DOWN A STRANGE STREET':
EMERGENT EXCHANGES

> When a book begins, there is nothing. Then something begins to be, and then things are, and then things undo themselves, and again there is nothing any more.
> (Robbe-Grillet, in Ricardou 1976: 77)

I

It may be instructive to end by looking at beginnings: at how the storytelling impulse first takes shape. Although there is no principled justification for confining narratological analysis to what adults call literary texts, in practice it has usually kept aloof from stories produced by children in the course of their early language development. (Toolan (1988) is a pleasant exception.) As a result, several interesting issues have hardly yet been treated by those versed in current literary theory. How do people first learn to take part in narrative exchanges? What similarities are there between canonical literary fictions and tales invented by the very young? Is a child's concept of storytelling based simply on that putative 'succession of events' which so many theorists have regarded as axiomatically definitive, or does it involve more importantly those processes of framing, substitution and dispossession which the present study has emphasised? Does the acquisition of genres need to be formalised during one's infant education in reading and writing to ensure competence in using them? Such are the questions to be considered in this final chapter, which will also glance back very briefly at most of the texts already discussed as well as introducing one by a youthful storyteller.

Two influential schools of thought in the area of language

learning, those associated chiefly with Michael Halliday and with James Britton, are often thought to be in disagreement; but both tend towards unduly restricted notions about what constitutes narrative. Let us take them one at a time, beginning with a certain application of Hallidayan sociolinguistics and looking at its alignment with William Labov's work on oral stories.

In work praised by Toolan (1988: 202–9), two disciples of Halliday have attempted to trace the development from infancy to late teens of children's skills in using written genres, with particular reference to educational situations.[1] Joan Rothery and Jim Martin (1980) think that this area of language competence manifests itself first in an elementary 'observation' genre, which simply records an item or two of personal experience; and out of this both narrative and expository types of writing subsequently emerge. Within each type, according to Rothery and Martin, a progression is evident during the years from pre-school onwards: in the case of narrative it moves from a so-called 'recount', comprising a mere sequence of events, through stories of personal and then vicarious experience. These fully-fledged narratives (which start to develop, they say, by about the age of 9) are supposedly distinguished from the rudimentary 'recount' by displaying a schematic structure of Orientation/Complication/ Resolution identified by Labov (1972) in his study of first-person oral storytelling. In another paper, Martin, Christie and Rothery (1987) emphasise the view that this Labovian pattern needs to be formally and firmly inculcated in the early years of schooling so that it will be reproduced in children's own writing. They propose, for instance, that a teacher should guide a class in 'modelling a genre *explicitly* by naming its stages; e.g. identifying the stages Orientation, Complication and Resolution in *Little Red Riding Hood*' (68; cf. 74).

On four counts such a categorical approach is unsatisfactory. First, it misunderstands the relation between cognitive development and generic skills. Second, it essentialises and dehistoricises genre, failing to recognise how the shape of a narrative text (or any other kind) varies according to its placement within a particular discursive formation. Third, it overlooks the complex ways in which (to use Halliday's own terminology) the situational components of field, tenor and mode may legitimately shift in the course of a text's unfolding, so that the notion of a fixed order of 'stages' becomes inappropiate. Fourth, it ignores the paramount fact that written stories are markedly mediated by the intervention of a surrogate communicative relationship; for, whereas speaker and narrator are held to be practically identical in a normal oral narrative situation, an act of writing requires an author to delegate the narratorial role to a simulated 'voice' on the page.[2] Each of these points needs amplification before we proceed to other matters.

First, then, with regard to cognitive development: pre-literate children are usually competent in a range of genres, including oral narrative. To be sure, it takes time to transfer this competence into the different semiotic medium of inscription, which requires them to combine new motor dexterity with an ability to recall a new set of signs (the shape of written words); but a basic understanding of narrative is already there. Moreover the young child's changing conceptual capacities and interests establish certain generic priorities. Myra Barrs (1987) argues cogently that learning to write narrative or expository prose is not primarily a matter of increasing one's grasp of a normative set of rules. In so far as young children's texts differ from those of more mature writers, she remarks, this is 'not because of a lack of knowledge of written genres or of textual conventions, but because they express a certain stage of thinking' (14). In the light of L.S. Vygotsky's observations on cognitive development, to be mentioned shortly, Barrs points out that those who are still on the brink of literacy tend mainly to record what they know in terms of what they remember, 'and for this sort of recording the most straightforward and readily available form is that of the simple list' (14–15). (This is clearly illustrated in the text that we shall soon consider, dictated by a five-year-old; much of it comprises an inventory of assorted items.) Her conclusion provides a salutary corrective to the Martin and Rothery approach: 'To focus on what young children are *not* able to do in their writing, on how far they fall short of adult forms, is unhelpful. It is more interesting to look for what it is they *are* doing and to identify the genres they use most naturally at their different point of development' (15). Carol Fox (1989) complements these remarks by showing how protonarrative forms serve for the child as a means of recording emergent intellectual and affective transactions with their social and physical world. That is, their story-shaping is driven as much by their need to process various sorts of changing knowledge as by their conscious imitation of conventionalised forms.

Moving to the second criticism: any concept of genre that is inattentive to cultural variation must need refinement. Martin *et al.* give only token acknowledgement to the fact that 'genres do change' (76); their way of invoking *Little Red Riding Hood* (quoted above) reveals that they can hardly have grasped what generic change involves, for no single model can be properly elicited from the several narratives associated with that name. *Little Red Riding Hood* does not exist in one definitive, authentic or original form (plot or theme or *fabula rasa*); it does not comprise one pattern of orientation, complication and resolution. Every occasion of retelling has been an opportunity to situate the tale within a different discursive formation, mixing its generic affiliations in a new way. Zipes (1983), having collected and studied numerous versions from different cultures and periods, shows that each has its particular social ideology: in one of them a resourceful peasant heroine shrewdly thwarts the wolf without any need for male protectors to intervene; in another, an upper-class cautionary version by Perrault, the girl becomes self-defenceless, spoilt and gullible; the Grimm brothers' later version imposes a new kind of resolution as part of the nineteenth-century middle-class regulatory process which Foucault (1981: 104) calls the pedagogisation of children's sexuality; and variants in our own century, from James Thurber's to Roald Dahl's to Angela Carter's, indicate in their structural innovations a further range of changing attitudes and circumstances such as the gradual (if still partial) emergence of women and children from subordinated roles. There is nothing exceptional about the permutations undergone by *Little Red Riding Hood*; Smith (1980) discusses Cinderella in similar terms. Nor should the general point here be tied to those traditional story-types that we know as folktales or fairytales. The absolutist error of the Martin and Rothery line can be shown just as easily by reference to ethnographic fieldwork such as that of Brice-Heath (1983), who made a comparative study of language development in three neighbouring communities in the southeastern United States, markedly different from one another in racial composition, economic structure and cultural values, and found (among other things) that what counts as an appropriately shaped narrative is very different from one setting to another.

My third point concerns that dubious notion of 'stages' which confuses the attempt made by Martin and Rothery to incorporate Labov's remarks into a formula for children's narrative compositions. Its undue rigidity becomes obvious when we consider a text produced by a 5-year-old and look at it initially in terms of Halliday's checklist of situational variables, which we found of some preliminary use in an earlier chapter. Here, first, is a transcription of the verbal content of this text, 'My Book' by Toby. Numbers on the left refer to successive pages, and asterisks indicate those on which there is only handwritten material, without accompanying drawings.

[1] My Book [cover]
[2] One day Ian came to my house. Ian knows Toby.
[3] This is me in my X-wing fighter. No I'm in the movie chair watching the X-wing fighter.
[4] The star-wars monster is opening Darth Vader's present.
[5] Ian is looking at me.
[6] Meryl's sewing machine.
[7] The alphabet.
[8] This is my slippery-dip.
[9] That's a fish heart. Yuk, erk!
[10] My house.
[11] A kangaroo in the zoo.
[12] A motor-car with a carriage on the side.
[13] A fish with a motor-bike hat on.
[14] This is my kite.
[15]* I like dad's work because he has got a nice shop where you can get treats.
[16]* I like my school best. One day I made a tug boat at school.
[17]* I like it at home. It is good, and it is very warm in bed.
[18]* One day I thought I was going down a strange street.
[19]* I met a tiger. He yawned and then he went to sleep.
[20]* Then I saw a giant and I yawned and then he yawned and he went to sleep.
[21]* Then I saw a soldier who was guarding the house so no baddies could go in.
[22]* I yawned, then he yawned and then he went to sleep.
[23]* I saw a wizard and he tickled you and made me go to sleep.
[24] The wizard.
[25] This is the guard.
[26] Toby.

If we examine this text according to the Hallidayan method followed by Martin and Rothery themselves, we need to ask first about its 'register' (virtually synonymous with genre, as Martin and Rothery use the term), which is composed of three variables: field (the social and discursive activity within which the text occurs), tenor (the relationship between those taking part in the communicative exchange) and mode (the nature and function of the language that is being used, e.g. oral or written). All three tend to merge shiftily in the particular language situation that constitutes Toby's booklet.

What is going on here? What is the field that surrounds and pervades 'My Book'? The circumstances of its production should be explained at this point, though they can be inferred fairly well from the transcription above. Five-year-old Toby wishes to present to someone visiting his family as a house guest (myself, as it happens) a little gift through which he can introduce himself and a sample of his interests and accomplishments. With his mother's help he assembles and staples together some sheets of paper, draws some pictures on some of them and then dictates captions to his maternal scribe. When the drawings peter out, improvised dictation nevertheless continues; finally a few more captioned drawings are added to round it all off. The field, then, could be described as an exercise (pre-literate practice in naming and listing), or as an entertainment (ludic self-profile and display of creative virtuosity), or as an exchange (manufacture of gift for presentation to friendly visitor); it has elements of each. Correspondingly, the tenor could be described as child-performer to parent-facilitator (since Toby is speaking to his mother); it could also be child-learner to himself (since he seems to be processing for his own information not only formal knowledge structures such as the alphabet but also interpersonal data – 'Ian knows Toby' and 'Ian is looking at me'); or it could be child-of-host-family to visitor (since 'My Book' is being produced as a gift). Thus, bearing in mind Vygotsky's observations on language development, one might discern within Toby's text an oscillation between 'egocentric speech' (thinking aloud, talking to oneself) and 'communicative speech'. Vygotsky (1962: 14–20) rejects Piaget's view that egocentric speech is a primary phase which simply fades out as the child becomes more socialised; rather, according to Vygotsky, it is a transitional phase which follows the earliest social uses of language and turns (at about the beginning of schooling, i.e. Toby's stage) into the inner speech through which we all think for ourselves. Vygotsky also draws attention to complex changes that occur in the function of egocentric speech, whereby the latter at first marks the end result of an activity and later shifts towards the middle and then the beginning of it, thus directing behaviour more purposefully. He notes a parallel here to 'the well-known developmental sequence in the naming of drawings. A small child draws first, then decides what it is that he has drawn; at a slightly older age, he names his drawing when it is half done; and finally he decides beforehand what he will draw' (17). Again, Toby's text indicates something of this pattern in a transitional way: there is retrospective naming (for instance, he revises his caption for [3]), but also some evidence of planning (as in [7], where his mother was asked to supply the list of twenty-six letters in lieu of one of Toby's own graphics, since he decided beforehand that he wanted to include an alphabet) – and of course the pictureless sequence from [15] to [23] represents a further development beyond mere captioning.

By the same token the mode of Toby's text is interestingly complicated. It has been preserved in written form but only *on behalf* of its author, who has instigated the text by a combination of oral dictation and non-verbal graphics. Unlike some writing, it is still closely dependent on a proximal context of exchanges, for 'My Book' comes into being with family help and for friendly circulation. Especially significant, however, is the modulation from visual/verbal mixture to words alone, which occurs more than half way through the text – just at the point where the 'I like . . .' series supersedes the mere list of objects and the past tense becomes established after repetition of the cue 'One day . . .', thus allowing what some would regard as the *proper* narrative to begin. Clearly this is a pivotal moment in the sequence of pages, and it poses a taxonomic problem for the kind of analysis favoured by Martin and Rothery. Are we to say that different types of text – including a rudimentary 'observation', a list and a tenuous fairy tale or fantasy – have been incongruously stitched together? Are we to adjudge this text as malformed, exhibiting narrative incompetence? Certainly it lacks the orderly schematic structure that Martin and Rothery value so highly (cf. Toolan 1988: 205, 224), supposed to be borne out by Labov's work: a structure segmented into orientation, complication and resolution (sometimes followed by a coda). One difficulty about this view is that it converts Labov's descriptive set of general qualities into a mandatory linear sequence. The difference is not trivial. For instance Labov recognises that 'orientation' (comprising aspects of the narrative through which basic expository information is conveyed) may not come at the outset; indeed it is often more effective if delayed, and anyway does not consist of a stage or section. Toby's text has several orienting features, but does not group them all at the start, as the Rothery and Martin model of stages would require. The actors and the spatio-temporal settings of 'My Book' shift, and are identified in different ways at different stages.

There is another difficulty with the notion of a canonical narrative schema – a notion which, incidentally, is shared by some who approach children's reading and writing from a certain corner of cognitive psychology, and who can declare dogmatically that in stories for the young 'there must be a proper ending with nothing left unexplained' (Kintsch 1979: 130–3). This difficulty results from glossing over the profound difference between an oral mode of so-called 'natural' narrative as studied by Labov and the written modes with which we are primarily concerned here. It is a difference that has been underrated by several theorists, including Pratt (1977) and Toolan (1988), who both try to apply Labov's observations more widely than is warranted.[3] We can hardly be surprised that Martin and Rothery are led into the same mistake, despite their intended emphasis on children's *writing*, because systemic linguistics generally strays (as noted in the Introduction to this book) into an assumption that spoken language is the paradigm case. On the contrary, the special factors that supervene when narrative exchanges take place through fictional writing are highly significant. Orientation, for instance, and what Labov calls 'evaluation' (the means by which a story's point is made) will both tend to be much more intricate in written narrative than in oral, since substantially mediated narrators (as distinct from speaker-performers) bring in a whole set of refractive exchange relations. In writing, the 'I' of the enunciation can become markedly separate from the 'I' of the utterance. Being mixed or transitional in its mode, Toby's text makes part of this process visible: the actual speaker's portrait of himself and his familiar everyday environment becomes converted through the magic of print into an alter ego fantasy protagonist 'going down a strange street' [18].

Accordingly, the rhetorical processes that we have called substitution and dispossession become articulated in complex ways. To be sure, both processes may occur in 'natural' oral narrative, but only in simple ways: there, substitution ordinarily takes the form of scene-shifting or character-shuffling, but figurative troping will be minimal, and similarly dispossession will be largely confined to interrupting or forestalling, when the speaker is either challenged directly by a listener or manages to hold the floor by some dilatory strategy.

Toby's text effects a number of substitutions characteristic of written narrative, for instance with its revisionary movement in [3], 'This is me in my X-wing fighter' being swiftly overlaid by 'No I'm in the movie chair watching the X-wing fighter'. The slippage between different functions of 'One day' in [2], [16] and [18] is another example: when it first occurs, the phrase tries to switch an event that is actually present at the moment of enunciation into a narrative past; but this tense cannot be sustained, and the present returns on the same page to preside over the next fourteen pages, whereupon 'One day' introduces the mention of an actual past event, soon to be followed by a further 'One day' which now signifies a generic key-signature in the 'Once upon a time' manner. As for dispossession, it is thematised intratextually by the successive encounters with tiger, giant, soldier and wizard, whose power can be pre-emptively defused or deflected (by the hypnotic device of yawning or, in the case of the climactically powerful wizard, by soporific tickling).

These features suggest that one should not draw a hasty line between the kind of narrative produced by the very young and the kind that we have learned to call literary. And yet some of those who discuss the former seem oddly anxious to emphasise its difference from the latter. Indeed, certain systemic linguists are at pains to insist that it *should* be different. Rather than admit that deviations in junior apprentice tales from what they regard as an orthodox schema may be structurally akin to (and suitably anticipatory of) the elaborately experimental fictions written by some adults, Martin, Christie and Rothery (1987) present the issue in these hyperbolic terms:

> Year 2 students are not James Joyce. They are not the artist who moved slowly, over a period of a lifetime, through the relatively conventional *Dubliners* and *Portrait of an Artist as a Young Man*, to the intriguing *Ulysses* and finally to *Finnegans Wake*, a book that had evolved so far beyond the narrative genres of its time that it still takes years of specialised

training to be able to read it at all. Like all individuals who learned to make new meanings, Joyce learned familiar meanings first. It is these meanings that [we] genre theorists propose to begin with in initial literacy programs. Once established, only if established, do they afford the possibility of creativity or social change.

(76)

This statement not only assumes a highly questionable norm of creative development, but also implies the peculiar logic that any pleasures of experimenting with generic innovation should be suppressed in the young so that they can eventually flourish in the mature. Why not follow the opposite reasoning – that children's skill in the playful manipulation of narrative structure should be judiciously encouraged so that they can achieve even greater discursive control as adults? Examples are available to support the view that many children do possess inventive flair in composing generically mixed texts *before* they learn that anyone wants them to submit to the dull discipline of orientation, complication and resolution. For instance, a 6-year-old's witty blend of parodic weather forecast and performed poem is discussed by Fox (1983: 16), and a 10-year-old's compact merger of story conventions with those of poem and journal is discussed by Reid (1984: 68–9).

II

Whereas systemic linguistics, for all its potential utility as an analytical method, has tended to produce a disciplinarian view of generic competence, the approach to language learning associated with James Britton has been seen – not only by Martin *et al.* (1987: 62–3) but also by their critics (e.g. Sawyer and Watson 1987: 50, 54) – as involving a somewhat different understanding of the way in which children develop their sense of how to narrate.[4] His fullest account of this developmental process is in the article 'Writing and the Story World' (Britton 1983), which begins by briefly discussing the phenomenon known to anthropologists and primatologists as the 'play face', a somatic signalling of unserious behaviour. Britton first observed this, he says, in his granddaughter Laurie when she was a little over a year old: adopting a consciously quaint expression and gait as if to solicit impunity from normal sanctions by acting in a manifestly 'pretend' mode, she would proceed to transgress certain ordinary social rules (e.g. by pulling books out of the bookcase or fiddling with the TV knob). In Laurie's case this behaviour lasted only a few months, and Britton speculates that its disappearance was linked to an increasing interest at that stage in the picture storybooks that were being read to her:

> If the play face was a device for opting out of the actual social world in order to suspend its sanctions, then I believe she no longer needs it: the story world, once established, provides that refuge, enabling her, within limits, to make happen what she wants to happen.
>
> (4–5)

The general question that this raises for Britton is about the relationship that a child perceives between experienced (real) and narrated (partly imaginary) events; but before we pursue his thoughts in that direction, it is worthwhile to pause for a moment over the phenomenon he has initially described. One might infer from his anecdotal preamble, though he does not assert this, that he regards the development from play-face behaviour to an engagement with the story world as part of a typical pattern of development. But that this is actually so must be doubtful; certainly it is by no means an invariable pattern. Whereas Laurie's environment was evidently a highly literate one, which would have enhanced her capacity for dealing confidently with the invented and mediated material of story books, general observation suggests that some children (in particular those who suffer early social impairment or family trauma of one kind or another) persist for years with intermittent play-face behaviour and often find difficulty in recognising a distinction between reality and fiction; they may for instance be easily scared by stories. It seems that, in order to enjoy passing from one 'world' to another, children need to feel securely in control of the terms of that passage and happy about 'pretending' – which means at least that they need to be able to trust parents not to be capricious or alarmingly unpredictable.[5] Given these conditions, a make-believe story world opens up possibilities for experiencing the satisfactions of control to a degree seldom available to a child in ordinary dealings with people and things.[6]

Britton's article then moves on to consider the role of written language acquisition with regard to this story world. Here his argument goes astray, because it is based on an inadequate model of communication and of narrative in particular. Writing, he contends, is 'less context-dependent than an item of conversational exchange. The move is towards a *constancy* of meaning, towards an ability to handle relationships that are less and less "embedded" in particular situations' (14). One can see what Britton has in mind, but this reasoning is plainly erroneous. Far from tending to make meaning more constant, the written medium destabilises it, because relatively few constraints can be placed on the interpretive reframing, in new contexts, of what is written down. Although in one sense a literary fiction or a newspaper report is obviously less dependent on some particular interlocutory setting than is a conversation, its semantic content does nevertheless remain subject to a kind of negotiation – all the more intricate for being highly mediated. But Britton is committed to the view that fictional narratives, including those invented by children, belong to a special discursive category which stands apart from those processes of exchange. He asserts that when reading 'transactional or non-literary discourse' one experiences a piecemeal give and take between what one already knows and what the text offers, whereas when reading a story one encounters the 'unity' of an aesthetic object. Accordingly, for a writer the task (as Britton sees it) in composing any so-called transactional text is 'to enmesh with the reader's state of knowledge, opinions, interests, and ... anticipate and play his role in the "inner debate" with the reader', but 'in story telling this element in the writing is missing' (19). As we shall see, Britton's attempt to remove narrative fiction from the sphere of communicative exchanges does not fit the facts; much more cogent is Bakhtin's point that, in literary prose as much as in other types of text, 'every word is directed toward an *answer* and cannot escape the profound influence of the answering word that it anticipates' (Bakhtin 1981: 280).

Why do Britton and his associates want to separate storytelling (whether that of the young apprentice or of the accomplished literary artist) from what they call 'transactional discourse'? It is because they have embraced a model of language functions in which a fundamental distinction is posited between a 'spectator role' and a 'participant role'. This derives from publications by Harding (1937, 1962) on psychological processes in the reading of fiction, and can readily be matched up with the theories and terminology of some other British linguists and educators – including Halliday, who sees a child's language development (at the stage of transition to the adult system – normally between the ages of about 18 months and two years) as comprising basically the same two functions: one in which the child is 'an observer to the extent that the language is serving as the means whereby he encodes his own experience of the phenomena around him, while himself remaining apart' and another in which 'he is using language to participate, as a means of action' (Halliday 1975: 29–30). Britton regards what is written in the spectator role as operating on a continuum from the informally expressive to the poetic, and what is written in the participant role as moving between the informally expressive and the transactional (Britton 1970: 164–80). Attempts have been made by several researchers, mainly in the 1970s, to apply this model. Applebee (1978) thought he found confirmation of it in his study of *The Child's Concept of Story*. Its inadequacy, however, was demonstrated empirically by the failure of Britton and his colleagues, in their own large-scale research project on school writing (Britton and Burgess *et al.* 1975), to agree amongst themselves, in no less than 1428 out of 2122 cases, which function category a script should be assigned to. Nevertheless, as far as narrative fiction is concerned, Britton persists with his categories: 'What I want to stress here is that the story world I have taken as my topic lies wholly on one side of my dividing line: it is activity in the spectator role . . . [not] a means to ends outside or beyond itself' (1983: 27). Turning back now to Toby's text, one can see how unsatisfactory is this categorical view.

'My Book' combines the enunciative roles of spectator and participant, and requires a correspondingly double role from its reader. It is no less transactional than expressive or poetic; and it inscribes this range of roles and functions within its own utterance. With marvellous economy, on pages [2]–[5], the text manages to represent its narrator–protagonist as acting in a real-but-fictive world and then as contemplating it detachedly (in the X-wing fighter, watching from the movie chair); to represent the designated co-participant in this textual exchange (the visitor for whom the book is to be a gift) as, equally, a spectator ('Ian is looking at me'); and to cite a movie image of a dubious transaction ('The starwars monster is opening Darth Vader's present'). This series of items is not linked by either the 'centering' or 'chaining' that Applebee (1978) sees as the devices of organisation in stories told by children of that age. The linkage here is substitutive; and some intuitive awareness, also, of the dispossessive factor in narration seems implicit in that wily alignment of the star-wars scene with the relation between textual partners.

Rather than existing at a remove from the give and take of other uses of language, from their semantic struggles and fiduciary agreements, storytelling does in fact share with all human communication both conflictual and contractual structures, as Greimas and Courtés (1982: 205) have observed. Bakhtin emphasises this in expounding a theory of the inescapably interlocutory orientation of all discourse. An utterance, he remarks, since it takes shape

> at a particular historical moment in a socially specific environment, cannot fail to brush up against thousands of living dialogic threads, woven by socio-ideological consciousness around the given object of an utterance; it cannot fail to become an active participant in social dialogue.
>
> (1981: 276)

This is as true of literary fiction as of other forms, notwithstanding certain differences:

> The phenomenon of internal dialogization, as we have said, is present to a greater or lesser extent in all realms of the life of the word. But if in extra-artistic prose (everyday, rhetorical, scholarly) dialogization usually stands apart, crystallizes into a special kind of act of its own and runs its course in ordinary dialogue or in other, compositionally marked forms for mixing and polemicizing with the discourse of another – then in *artistic* prose, and especially in the novel, this dialogization penetrates from within the very way in which the word conceives its object and its means for expressing itself, reformulating the semantics and syntactical structure of discourse. Here dialogic inter-orientation becomes, as it were, an event of discourse itself, animating from within and dramatizing discourse in all its aspects.
>
> (284)

III

Mentioned above in passing, Applebee's (1978) study of stories told by young children (2–5 years) aligns itself explicitly with Britton's ideas. Applebee identifies two principles by which narrative events are related to each other: 'centering' (e.g., grouping of events around a single character) and 'chaining' (direct sequential links between events). He goes on to suggest that these principles will apply equally to the organisation in a literary work not only of events but also of 'images, ideas, or even sounds' (70). *King Lear* is cited as an example, with its richly interwoven patterning at every textual level. Because of these intricacies, says Applebee, 'the full response to a poetic form cannot be a transactional, analytic one but must be the complex, assimilative, personal formulation that comes only in the spectator role' (71–2). This notion of what constitutes narrative structure, and literary works generally, is fallacious because it unwittingly disengages certain generic features from sociohistorical situations and tries to invest them with a transcendent quality. In Applebee's terms, not only Toby's composition but many esteemed literary artefacts as well would have to be judged defective. Many children take delight in non-sequential stories ('chaining' is surely intermittent in *Alice in Wonderland*, for instance, and defied in highly popular texts by Edward Gorey and Tomi Ungerer), while many adults admire narratives as decentered as Marguerite Duras's *The Vice-Consul* or as discontinuous as Calvino's *If on a Winter's Night a Traveller*, Konrad Bayer's *The Head of Vitus Bering*, several novels by Alain Robbe-Grillet, and Jaimy Gordon's 'The Hind of the Further', along with innumerable other contemporary fictions. What these offer a reader is no mere antitype; they are not dismissible as 'exceptions that prove the rule'. Rather, they indicate entirely different cultural norms from those that permeate *King Lear*. (And indeed some readers today would not frame a Shakespearean play for contemplation as an integrally aesthetic object.) Strong discursive tendencies in our own time work against any desire for 'an overall centre or point' (Applebee 1978 71–2), and a literary narrative is often framed intratextually and intertextually in such a way (as noted in the previous chapter when discussing 'The Hind of the Further') that one can hardly avoid a 'transactional, analytic' response of the sort which Applebee wants to reserve for non-literary texts.

The story world of 'My Book' is manufactured partly from the ingredients of a real world very different from that which left its imprint on *King Lear*, so that Toby's protagonist must seek his place among movies and motorbikes, sewing machines and fighter planes. Yet although it does not conform to the Applebee/Britton criteria for narrative form, it can still be seen as laying bare something very basic about stories in general: the way in which they depend at least rudimentarily on framing structures in order to generate the effect of movement.

A frame, as noted before, is something perceived as enclosing an area within which meanings can take shape. It marks off inside from outside, though the demarcation often turns out to be less clearcut than it first seems. Without framing, signification would be impossible – and so would narrative. Self-evidently, a child's earliest discriminations between inside and outside may involve various objects, experiences and perceptual fields: one's own bed, playpen, room, window and so on. But of these several primary frames, the one most likely to attract the strongest emotional investment is the house-as-home: the family's personal territory, the intimately known and occupied place, the familiar shelter.[7] Inside it lie (usually) relative security and comfort; outside lie an infinity of things heard about, glimpsed occasionally, or vaguely apprehended – many of them puzzling, fearsome, fabulous.[8] It is hardly surprising, then, that young children's stories tend to concentrate on an elementary 'home versus away' contrast, *not* necessarily structured as an event-based trajectory in accordance with a supposedly orthodox narrative schema but rather devising some set of confrontations through which framings of the inner and outer spaces can be tentatively tested.

This pattern is plain enough in 'My Book': its initial datum is the arrival of an outsider in Toby's house – reassuringly, someone who 'knows' the narrator-protagonist; an intertextual referent is soon invoked (the *Star Wars* film) with the function of establishing that there is a monstrously alien world further afield; a drawing of the child's house is presented between images from the moderately strange domain of real creatures (fish heart, zoo animal); then a few oases of pleasant familiarity in the wider social world are listed (dad's work, school) and linked with the snugness of home – whereupon, once all these boundary checks have been made, fantasy can go for a walk down 'a strange street'. Even then the reliability of the basic frame needs to be reaffirmed: 'guarding the house so no baddies could get in'. The text concludes by juxtaposing the guard with the child/narrator/protagonist.

Remarkably, some version of this simple home-versus-away structure serves to generate momentum in most of the texts discussed in previous chapters. We have seen how Daudet's white goat leaves the safety of home and heads for the dangerous mountain; how the domestic sanctuary of DeLillo's Gladney family is menaced by a toxic environment; how Snorri's tale about Thor turns on the contrast between Asgard (home of the gods) and its alien counterpart Utgard (literally 'Outer Region'); how Achebe's Okonkwo comes to grief when the tight circle of tribal village custom is invaded by white culture; how all three of Flaubert's tales begin within a strictly enclosed dwelling, and in each case extrinsic forces impinge to set things in motion; how Duras's *The Vice Consul* opens with the beggar-girl having been cast out by her mother, propelling the story along as she walks into unknown areas; how the starting-point for Mansfield's 'Prelude' is the upheaval of a family's move from one home to a new one, and 'At the Bay' reveals a pervasive anxiety about where to draw the line between the tamed domestic space and its unruly natural surroundings; how the preamble to Wordsworth's autobiographical poem is preoccupied with his choice of a home, and proceeds to trace associated tensions between internal and external; how the story of White's Theodora deals with a problematic relation between the Meroë homestead where she has grown up and that 'other Meroë' which she seeks in the uncongenial wider world before finding an equivalent within her imagination; and how Gordon's 'The Hind of the Further' poses a conundrum about the relation between images of familiarity ('walk together along the same streets') and images of alienation ('lost ... carried in darkness') that mingle with ambiguous borderlines ('They decided it enclosed four parts').

Undoubtedly that structure is fundamental in all sorts of narratives, from *King Lear*, which Applebee wants to regard as the exemplary literary object, to innumerable other canonical texts (any of Dickens's novels, Hawthorne's 'Young Goodman Brown', Kafka's 'A Country Doctor') and so-called metafictions. As an instance of this last kind, consider how Alain Robbe-Grillet's *In the Labyrinth* commences: with a seemingly random description of an inside and an outside, which is toyed with until the arbitrary nature of its self-framing figures sets something in train (but hardly a 'succession of events'). Robbe-Grillet's own comment on this is instructive:

> When a book begins, there is nothing. Then something begins to be, and then things are, and then things undo themselves, and again there is nothing any more. This movement becomes distinctly clear through nearly all my novels. . . . For *In the Labyrinth*, there was at the outset a generative cell: 'I am alone here now, under shelter.' That truly constitutes a cell, which seems to me all the more generative because I wrote the phrase without having any plan as to what would come next from a diegetic point of view. This inside soon engendered an outside. . . . And, step by step, everything arranged itself in terms of that cellular starting-point.
> (Ricardou 1976: 77–8)

IV

Britton notes that in all cases known to him of children who learn to write before being given any instruction in the art, there is one common feature: 'they all wrote stories, and characteristically they wrote them in the form of story books, stitched or clipped together, with a picture on the cover, and maybe pictures inside as well' (1983:18). This interests him (and indeed he makes the same observation in another article: Britton 1982: 160); he wonders what it might signify, but has no very definite answer. In the light of our own analysis, a reasonable conjecture might run like this: that in childhood one's developing sense of written narrative structure, particularly its inclination towards substitutive and dispossessive devices, stems in large measure from a tension between circumtextual and intratextual framing in early experiences with picture books, and that by reproducing the format one is trying to exercise some control over the terms of a story-shaped exchange.[9] On the one hand there is the physical entity of the book-object, initially made legible as a whole through the powerful agency of a literate parent (or other senior family member, friend, teacher). To be read a story is to be given access to that circumtextually framed unit, that tangible totality. But on the other hand, the act of reading is visibly performed by someone's turning of a series of separate pages, which in the simplest way serve to accentuate the tale's intratextual divisions. On each of these pages there is usually some picture – a figure, let us say – with a caption; and one page succeeds another in a substitutive progression. Correspondingly, the person who reads aloud to the child from those pages, and who has the capacity to linger or hasten, to add comments or to skip some of the text, is strongly in charge; and so, as writing turns into speech and narrator merges with performer, interruption becomes the child's only counter-strategy. By breaking in with questions and comments, requiring the parent to interact (explain, defend), the child can attempt to usurp the intermediate control exercised over (or through) the story's 'voice' by that supremely authoritative personage.[10] This interaction at the enunciative level, whatever particular form it takes, enhances in turn for the child-reader (who at other times will become child-narrator) the interest of any situations within the story which enact a struggle or negotiate a balance of forces.

Here, then, at the heart, hearth, foyer or focus of one's earliest encounters with written stories, the primary constitutive element is not any represented chain of events but rather a storytelling exchange in which the magic of textual movement is bound up with the sleight of hand that we have called substitution and with the power-play that we have called dispossession.

APPENDIX A

Extract from *Edda*

Snorri Sturluson

Then spoke Gangleri...
'Has Thor never got into such a situation that he has come up against such great power or might that he has found it more than he could manage because of strength or magic?'

Then spoke High: 'I expect there are few people that can tell about that, though he has found many situations hard to deal with. But even if it has happened that something or other has been so powerful or strong that Thor has not managed to defeat it, yet there is no need to speak of it, for there is much evidence to show, and everyone is bound to believe, that Thor is mightiest.'

Then spoke Gangleri: 'It looks to me as though I must have asked you something that none of you is capable of telling me.'

Then spoke Just-as-high: 'We have heard tell of some events which it seems to us impossible to believe can be true, but I guess there is one sitting not far off who will be able to give a true account of it, and you can be confident that he will not lie now for the first time who never lied before.'

Then spoke Gangleri: 'Here I shall stand and listen whether anyone offers a solution to this matter, and if not I declare you are overcome if you are not able to tell what I ask.'

Then spoke Third: 'It is clear now that he is determined to know this story even though it does not seem to us nice to tell. But you are not to interrupt.

'The beginning of this business is that Oku-Thor set off with his goats and chariot and with him the As called Loki. In the evening they arrived at a peasant's house and were given a night's lodging there. During the evening Thor took his goats and slaughtered them both. After this they were skinned and put in the pot. When it was cooked Thor sat down to his evening meal, he and his

APPENDIX A

companion. Thor invited the peasant and his wife and their children to share the meal with him. The farmer's son was called Thialfi, his daughter Roskva. Then Thor placed the goatskins on the other side of the fire and instructed the peasant and his household to throw the bones on to the goatskins. Thialfi, the peasant's son, took hold of the goat's ham-bone and split it open with his knife and broke it to get at the marrow. Thor stayed the night there, and in the small hours before dawn he got up and dressed, took the hammer Miollnir and raised it and blessed the goatskins. Then the goats got up and one of them was lame in the hind leg. Thor noticed this and declared that the peasant or one of his people must have not treated the goat's bone with proper care. He realized that the ham-bone was broken. There is no need to make a long tale about it, everyone can imagine how terrified the peasant must have been when he saw Thor making his brows sink down over his eyes; as for what could be seen of the eyes themselves, he thought he would collapse at just the very sight. Thor clenched his hands on the shaft of the hammer so that the knuckles went white, and the peasant did as one might expect, and all his household, they cried out fervently, begged for grace, offered to atone with all their possessions. And when he saw their terror then his wrath left him and he calmed down and accepted from them in settlement their children Thialfi and Roskva, and they then became Thor's bondservants and they have attended him ever since. He left the goats behind there and started on his journey east to Giantland and all the way to the sea, and then he went out across the great deep sea. And when he reached land he went ashore and with him Loki and Thialfi and Roskva. When they had gone a little way they were faced by a huge forest. They walked all the day until dark. Thialfi was the fastest of runners. He carried Thor's knapsack, but there was not much in the way of lodgings to be found. When it had got dark they looked for somewhere to spend the night and came upon a certain very large building. There was an entrance at one end and it was the full width of the building. Here they sought night-quarters for themselves. But at midnight there was a great earthquake, the ground moved under them in shudders and the building shook. Then Thor got up and called to his companions and they searched around and found a side-chamber on the right hand side half-way down the building and went in. Thor positioned himself in the doorway and the others were further in behind him and they were fearful, but Thor clasped the shaft of his hammer and planned to defend himself. Then they heard a great rumbling and groaning. And when dawn came Thor went out and saw someone lying a little way from him in the forest, and he was no midget. He was asleep and snoring mightily. Then Thor realized what the cause of the noise in the night had been. He clasped on his girdle of might and his As-strength grew, but at that moment the person awoke and stood up quickly. And then they say that Thor for once was afraid to strike him with the hammer, and asked him his name. And he said his name was Skrymir.

'"But I do not need," he said, "to ask you your name. I can tell that you are Thor of the Æsir. But you have been making off with my glove?"

'Then Skrymir reached over and picked up his glove. Then Thor realized that this was what he had been using during the night as a building, and the side-chamber, that was the thumb of the glove. Skrymir asked if Thor would like to have his company, and Thor agreed. Then Skrymir went and undid his knapsack and got ready to eat breakfast, and so did Thor and his companions in a separate place. Then Skrymir tied up all the provisions in one bag and put it on his back. He went ahead during the day and took rather long strides. And then in the evening Skrymir found them a place to spend the night under a certain large oak, – "but you take the knapsack and get on with the supper."

'Then Skrymir went to sleep and snored hard, and Thor took the knapsack and was about to undo it, and the story goes, incredible though it must seem, that no knot could he get undone and no strap-end moved so as to make it less tight than it was already. And when he realized that this labour was going to get nowhere, he got angry, grasped the hammer Miollnir in both hands and stepped forward with one foot to where Skrymir was lying and struck at his head. Skrymir awoke and asked whether some leaf of foliage had fallen on his head, and whether they had finished eating and were ready for bed. Thor said they were just about to go to sleep. They then went under another oak. To tell you the truth, it was not possible to sleep without fear.

'But at midnight Thor heard that Skrymir was snoring and sleeping deeply so that the forest resounded. Then he stood up and went up to him, swung the hammer quickly and hard and struck down in the centre of his crown. He felt the face of the hammer sink deep into the head. And at that moment Skrymir woke and said:

'"What's the matter now? Did an acorn or something fall on my head? And what are you doing Thor?"

'But Thor backed away quickly and replied that he had just woken up, said that it was now midnight and still time to sleep. Then Thor resolved that if he got an opportunity to strike him a third blow, he would never open his eyes again; he now lay waiting to see if Skrymir fell fast asleep. And a little before dawn, then he could hear that Skrymir must have fall asleep, and he got up and ran at him, swung the hammer with all his might and struck at the temple that was facing upwards. Then the hammer sank in up to the handle, but Skrymir sat up and stroked his cheek and said:

'"Can there be some birds sitting in the tree above me? I am sure as I awoke that some rubbish from the branches fell on my head. Are you awake Thor? It must be time to get up and dress. And you do not now have very far to go on to the castle called Utgard. I have heard you whispering among yourselves that I am a person of no small build, but you will see bigger men there if you get into Utgard. Now I will give you some good advice: don't act big. Utgarda-Loki's men will not easily put up with cheekiness from babies like you. Otherwise turn back, and that I think will be the better course for you to take. But if you are determined to go on, then make for the east, but my road now lies to the north to these mountains that you should be able to see."

'Skrymir took the knapsack and threw it on his back and turned abruptly away from them into the forest, and there is no report that the Æsir expressed hope for a happy reunion.

'Thor continued his journey with his companions and went on until midday. Then they saw a castle standing on some open ground and had to bend their heads back to touch their spines before they could see up over. They approached the castle and there was a gate across the entrance and it was shut. Thor went to the gate and was unable to open it, but by struggling to get into the castle they squeezed between the bars and thus got in, and then saw a great hall and went up to it. The door was open. They went in and saw there many people on two benches, most them a fair size. Next they came before the king, Utgarda-Loki, and addressed him, but he was slow to turn to them and bared his teeth in a smile and said:

EXTRACT FROM *EDDA*

'"News travels slowly over long distances. But am I wrong in thinking that this little fellow is Oku-Thor? You must be bigger than you look to me. And what are the feats that your party thinks they can perform? No one is allowed to stay here with us who does not have some art or skill in which he is superior to most people."

'Then the one who was in the rear of the party, which was Loki, said:

'"I know a feat that I am quite prepared to have a go at, that there is no one inside here who can eat his food quicker than I."

'Then Utgarda-Loki replied: "That is a feat if you can perform it, and we must try out these feats," – called down the bench that some one called Logi was to come out on to the floor and compete with Loki. Then a trencher was fetched and brought in on to the floor of the hall and filled with meat. Loki sat down at one end and Logi at the other, and each ate as quickly as he could and they met in the middle of the trencher. Loki had then eaten all the meat off the bones, but Logi had also eaten all the meat and the bones too and also the trencher, and it seemed to everyone now that Loki had lost the contest.

'Then Utgarda-Loki asked what that young man there could perform, and Thialfi said that he would attempt to run a race of some kind with anyone Utgarda-Loki put forward. He said, Utgarda-Loki, that this was a good feat and declared he would indeed have to be good at running if he was to achieve this feat, and yet he said he would soon put it to the test. Then Utgarda-Loki got up and went out, and there was a good course there for running over level ground. Then Utgarda-Loki called to him a certain little fellow called Hugi and bade him run a race with Thialfi. Then they began the first race, and Hugi was so far ahead that he turned back to meet him at the end of the race. Then said Utgarda-Loki:

'"You will have to make a greater effort, Thialfi, if you are going to win the contest, and yet it is true that never before have people come here that have seemed to me able to run faster than that."

'Then they began again another race, and when Hugi got to the end of the course and turned back, Thialfi was still a good arrow-shot behind. Then said Utgarda-Loki:

'"Thialfi has I think run a good race, but I no longer have any confidence in him that he will win the contest. But we shall see now when they run the third race."

'Then they started another race. And when Hugi had got to the end of the course and turned back, then Thialfi had not reached half-way. Then everyone said that this contest was decided.

'Then Utgarda-Loki asked Thor which of his accomplishments it was that he would be willing to display before them, such great stories as people had made of his exploits. Then Thor said that he would most willingly undertake to compete at drinking with someone. Utgarda-Loki said that would be fine and went inside the hall and called for his butler, bade him get the forfeit-horn that the men of his court were accustomed to drink from. Next the butler came forward with the horn and handed it to Thor. Then said Utgarda-Loki:

'"From this horn it is considered to be well drunk if it is drained in one draught, but some people drain it in two draughts. But no one is such a poor drinker that it is not emptied in three."

'Thor looked at the horn, and it did not seem all that big, though it was rather long. But he was very thirsty, began to drink and took great gulps and intended that it should not be necessary to address the horn again for the time being. But when he ran out of breath and straightened up from the horn and saw how his drinking was progressing, it seemed to him as though there could be very little difference by which the level in the horn was now lower than before. Then Utgarda-Loki spoke:

'"That was a good drink, and not excessive. I would not have believed it if anyone had told me that Thor of the Æsir would not have drunk a greater draught, but still I know that you will be intending to drink it off in the second draught."

'Thor made no reply, put the horn to his mouth and was determined now that he was going to drink a bigger draught and struggled with the drink as long as his breath held out, and found still that the point of the horn would not go as far up as he wanted. And when he took the horn from his mouth and looked in, it now seemed to him as though it had gone down less than the previous time. The level was now far enough down for the horn to be carried easily without spilling. Then spoke Utgarda-Loki:

'"What's the matter now, Thor? Are you not keeping back for one drink more than you will find easy to manage? It seems to me that if you are going to drain the horn with the third draught, then this must be intended to be the biggest one. But here among us you will not be able to be reckoned as great a person as the Æsir you are, if you do not give a better account of yourself in other

EXTRACT FROM *EDDA*

contests than it seems to me you are going to do with this one."

Then Thor got angry, put the horn to his mouth and drank as hard as he could and struggled as long as possible with the drink. And when he looked into the horn, this time it had made most of all some difference. And then he handed back the horn and would drink no more. Then spoke Utgarda-Loki:

'"It is obvious now that your might is not as great as we thought. Do you want to have a try at more contests? It is clear that you are going to get nowhere with this one."

Thor replied: "I may as well have a try at yet more contests. But I would have been surprised when I was back home with the Æsir if such drinks had been reckoned so slight. And what game do you want to offer me now?"

Then spoke Utgarda-Loki: "What the young lads here do though it may not seem of great significance, is lift up my cat off the ground. But I would not know how to mention such a thing to Thor of Æsir if I had not previously seen that you are a much less impressive person than I thought."

'Next a kind of grey cat ran out on to the hall floor, and it was rather big. Thor went up and took hold with his hand down under the middle of its belly and lifted it up. And when Thor reached as high up as the furthest he could, then the cat raised just one paw and Thor was not able to perform this feat. Then spoke Utgarda-Loki:

'"This game went just as I expected: the cat is rather big, but Thor is short and small in comparison with the big fellows here with us."

Then spoke Thor: "Small as you say I am, just let someone come out and fight me! Now I am angry!"

Then Utgarda-Loki replied, looking round the benches, and said: "I do not see anyone in here who will not think it demeaning to fight you." And then he went on: "Let's see a moment. Call here to me the old woman, my nurse Elli, and let Thor fight her if he likes. She has brought down people who have seemed to me no less strong-looking than Thor is."

'Next there came into the hall an old crone. Then Utgarda-Loki said that she was to have a wrestling match with Thor of the Æsir. There is not a great deal to be told about it. What happened in this match was that the harder Thor strained in the wrestling, the firmer she stood. Then the old woman started to try tricks, and then Thor began to lose his footing, and there was some very hard

APPENDIX A

pulling, and it was not long before Thor fell on to the knee of one leg. Then Utgarda-Loki went up, told them to stop the wrestling, and said this, that there was no point in Thor challenging any more people in his hall to a fight. It was also now late into the night. Utgarda-Loki showed Thor and his companions to places and they spent the night there with hospitable treatment. And in the morning as soon as it dawned Thor got up and so did his companions, they got dressed and were about to be off. Then Utgarda-Loki appeared and had a table laid for them. There was no lack of good cheer, and food and drink. And when they had finished eating then they set off. Utgarda-Loki went out with them, and accompanied them on their road out of the castle. And as they parted, Utgarda-Loki spoke to Thor and asked how he thought his expedition had gone, and whether he had come up against any person more powerful than himself. Thor said that he could not claim that he had suffered great loss of face in their encounter.

'"And moreover I know that you will say that I am a person of little account, and it is that which irks me."

Then spoke Utgarda-Loki: "Now you shall be told the truth, now you have come outside the castle, which is that if I live and can have my way you shall never again come into it. And I swear by my faith that you never would have come into it if I had known before that you had such great strength in you, and that you were going to bring us so close to great disaster. But I have deceived you by appearances, so that the first time when I discovered you in the forest it was I that came and met you. And when you tried to undo the knapsack I had fastened it with trick wire, and you could not find where it had to be unfastened. And next you struck me three blows with your hammer, and the first was the smallest and yet it was so hard that it would have been enough to kill me if it had struck its mark. But where you saw near my hall a table-mountain, and down in it you saw three square valleys, one deepest of all, these were the marks of your hammer. I moved the table-mountain in front of your blows, but you did not notice. So it was too with the games in which you competed with my men. The first was the one the Loki engaged in. He was very hungry and ate fast, but the one who is called Logi (flame), that was wildfire, and it burned the trencher just as quickly as the meat. And when Thialfi competed at running with the one called Hugi (thought), that was my thought, and Thialfi was not likely to be able to compete with its speed. And when you were drinking from the horn and it seemed to you that it was going slowly – I swear by my faith that then there took place a miracle that I would not have believed possible: the other end of the horn was out in the sea, and you did not notice, but now when you come to the sea then you will see what a lowering of the level you have made in the sea by your drinking."

'This is now known as the tides. And he went on:

'"It did not seem to me any less impressive either when you lifted up the cat, and to tell you the truth everyone that was watching was terrified when you raised one of its front feet from the ground. For the cat was not what it appeared to you: it was the Midgard serpent which lies encircling all lands, and its length was hardly enough for both its head and its tail to touch the ground. And so far did you reach up that you were not far from the sky. And that also was a great miracle with the wrestling when you stood so long and fell no further than on to the knee of one leg when you were fighting Elli (old age), for there never has been anyone, and there never will be anyone, if they get so old that they experience old age, that old age will not bring them all down. And the truth I must tell you now is that we must part, and it will now be better on both sides that you do not come to see me again. I shall again next time defend my castle with similar tricks or with others so that you will not get any power over me."

'And when Thor heard this speech he snatched up his hammer and swung it in the air, but when he was about to bring it down then he found he could nowhere see Utgarda-Loki. And then he turned back to the castle intending to smash the castle. Then all he saw there was a wide and beautiful open landscape, but no castle. Then he turned back and went on his way until he got back to Thrudvangar. But the fact is that he had then made up his mind to seek an opportunity for a meeting to take place between him and the Midgard serpent, as later occurred. Now I think there is no one that can give you a truer account of this expeditions of Thor's.'

Translated by Anthony Faulkes, and reproduced by kind permission of Dent Publishers, London.

APPENDIX B

Extract from *The Prelude*

William Wordsworth

    Fair seed-time had my soul, and I grew up   305
Fostered alike by beauty and by fear,
Much favoured in my birthplace, and no less
In that beloved vale to which erelong
I was transplanted. Well I call to mind –
'Twas at an early age, ere I had seen   310
Nine summers – when upon the mountain slope
The frost and breath of frosty wind had snapped
The last autumnal crocus, 'twas my joy
To wander half the night among the cliffs
And the smooth hollows where the woodcocks ran   315
Along the open turf. In thought and wish
That time, my shoulder all with springes hung,
I was a fell destroyer. On the heights
Scudding away from snare to snare, I plied
My anxious visitation, hurrying on,   320
Still hurrying, hurrying onward. Moon and stars
Were shining o'er my head; I was alone,
And seemed to be a trouble to the peace
That was among them. Sometimes it befel
In these night-wanderings, that a strong desire   325
O'erpowered my better reason, and the bird
Which was the captive of another's toils
Became my prey; and when the deed was done
I heard among the solitary hills
Low breathings coming after me, and sounds   330
Of undistinguishable motion, steps
Almost as silent as the turf they trod.

EXTRACT FROM *THE PRELUDE*

Nor less in springtime, when on southern banks
The shining sun had from her knot of leaves
Decoyed the primrose flower, and when the vales   335
And woods were warm, was I a plunderer then
In the high places, on the lonesome peaks,
Where'er among the mountains and the winds
The mother-bird had built her lodge. Though mean
My object and inglorious, yet the end   340
Was not ignoble. Oh, when I have hung
Above the raven's nest, by knots of grass
And half-inch fissures in the slippery rock
But ill sustained, and almost, as it seemed,
Suspended by the blast which blew amain,   345
Shouldering the naked crag, oh, at that time
While on perilous ridge I hung alone,
With what strange utterance did the loud dry wind
Blow through my ears; the sky seemed not a sky
Of earth, and with what motion moved the clouds!   350

   The mind of man is framed even like the breath
And harmony of music. There is a dark
Invisible workmanship that reconciles
Discordant elements, and makes them move
In one society. Ah me, that all   355
The terrors, all the early miseries,
Regrets, vexations, lassitudes, that all
The thoughts and feelings which have been infused
Into my mind, should ever have made up
The calm existence that is mine when I   360
Am worthy of myself. Praise to the end,
Thanks likewise for the means! But I believe
That Nature, oftentimes, when she would frame
A favored being, from his earliest dawn
Of infancy doth open out the clouds   365
As at the touch of lightning, seeking him
With gentlest visitation; not the less,
Though haply aiming at the self-same end,
Does it delight her sometimes to employ
Severer interventions, ministry   370
More palpable – and so she dealt with me.

APPENDIX B

   One evening – surely I was led by her –
I went alone into a shepherd's boat,
A skiff that to a willow-tree was tied
Within a rocky cave, its usual home.   375
'Twas by the shores of Patterdale, a vale
Wherein I was a stranger, thither come
A schoolboy traveller at the holidays.
Forth rambled from the village inn alone,
No sooner had I sight of this small skiff,   380
Discovered thus by unexpected chance,
Than I unloosed her tether and embarked.
The moon was up, the lake was shining clear
Among the hoary mountains; from the shore
I pushed, and struck the oars, and struck again   385
In cadence, and my little boat moved on
Even like a man who moves with stately step
Though bent on speed. It was an act of stealth
And troubled pleasure. Nor without the voice
Of mountain-echoes did my boat move on,   390
Leaving behind her still on either side
Small circles glittering idly in the moon,
Until they melted all into one trace
Of sparkling light. A rocky steep uprose
Above the cavern of the willow-tree,   395
And now, as suited one who proudly rowed
With his best skill, I fixed a steady view
Upon the top of the same craggy ridge,
The bound of the horizon – for behind   400
Was nothing but the stars and the grey sky.
She was an elfin pinnace; lustily
I dipped my oars into the silent lake,
And as I rose upon the stroke my boat
Went heaving through the water like a swan –   405
When from behind that craggy steep, till then
The bound of the horizon, a huge cliff,
As if with voluntary power instinct,
Upreared its head. I struck, and struck again,
And growing still in stature, the huge cliff   410
Rose up between me and the stars, and still
With measured motion, like a living thing
Strode after me. With trembling hands I turned

EXTRACT FROM *THE PRELUDE*

And through the silent water stole my way
Back to the cavern of the willow-tree.
There, in her mooring-place, I left my bark   415
And through the meadows homeward went with grave
And serious thoughts; and after I had seen
That spectacle, for many days my brain
Worked with a dim and undetermined sense
Of unknown modes of being. In my thoughts   420
There was a darkness – call it solitude
Or blank desertion – no familiar shapes
Of hourly objects, images of trees,
Of sea or sky, no colours of green fields
But huge and mighty forms that do not live   425
Like living men moved slowly through my mind
By day, and were the trouble of my dreams.

   Wisdom and spirit of the universe,
Thou soul that art the eternity of thought,
That giv'st to forms and images a breath   430
And everlasting motion – not in vain,
By day or star-light, thus from my first dawn
Of childhood didst thou intertwine for me
The passions that build up our human soul,
Not with the mean and vulgar works of man   435
But with high objects, with enduring things,
With life and Nature, purifying thus
The elements of feeling and of thought,
And sanctifying by such discipline
Both pain and fear, until we recognise   440
A grandeur in the beatings of the heart.
Nor was this fellowship vouchsafed to me
With stinted kindness. In November days,
When vapours rolling down the valleys made
A lonely scene more lonesome, among woods   445
At noon, and 'mid the calm of summer nights
When by the margin of the trembling lake
Beneath the gloomy hills I homeward went
In solitude, such intercourse was mine –
'Twas mine among the fields both day and night,   450
And by the waters all the summer long.

APPENDIX B

And in the frosty season, when the sun
Was set, and visible for many a mile
The cottage windows through the twilight blazed,
I heeded not the summons; happy time   455
It was indeed for all of us, to me
It was a time of rapture. Clear and loud
The village clock tolled six; I wheeled about
Proud and exulting, like an untired horse
That cares not for its home. All shod with steel   460
We hissed along the polished ice in games
Confederate, imitative of the chace
And woodland pleasures, the resounding horn,
The pack loud bellowing, and the hunted hare.
So through the darkness and the cold we flew,   465
And not a voice was idle. With the din,
Meanwhile, the precipices rang aloud;
The leafless trees and every icy crag
Tinkled like iron; while the distant hills
Into the tumult sent an alien sound   470
Of melancholy, not unnoticed; while the stars,
Eastward, were sparkling clear, and in the west
The orange sky of evening died away.

   Not seldom from the uproar I retired
Into a silent bay, or sportively   475
Glanced sideway, leaving the tumultuous throng,
To cut across the image of a star
That gleamed upon the ice. And oftentimes
When we had given our bodies to the wind,
And all the shadowy banks on either side   480
Came sweeping through the darkness, spinning still
the rapid line of motion, then at once
Have I, reclining back upon my heels,
Stopped short – yet still the solitary cliffs
Wheeled by me, even as if the earth had rolled   485
With visible motion her diurnal round.
Behind me did they stretch in solemn train,
Feebler and feebler, and I stood and watched
Till all was tranquil as a dreamless sleep.

EXTRACT FROM *THE PRELUDE*

   Ye presences of Nature, in the sky 490
Or on the earth, ye visions of the hills
And souls of lonely places, can I think
A vulgar hope was yours when ye employed
Such ministry – when ye through many a year
Haunting me thus among my boyish sports, 495
On caves and trees, upon the woods and hills,
Impressed upon all forms the characters
Of danger or desire, and thus did make
The surface of the universal earth
With triumph, and delight, and hope, and fear, 500
Work like a sea?

Extract from Book 1 of *The Prelude* (1805 version).

APPENDIX C

Jaimy Gordon, 'The Hind of the Further', *Diana's Second Almanac* (1980)

Where did he get so much?

The captain

of

ered him as meat to their king. But as to the companions of the
hey ate the flesh of men without roasting or otherwise cooking it.
when I saw them do thus, I was in the utmost anguish on my own acc
..... on account of my companions. The latter, by reason of the exce
tupefaction of their minds, knew not what was done unto them, and
..ple committed them to a person who took them every day and
orth to pasture them on that island like cattle.
But as for myself, I became, through the violence of fear and hung
run and wasted in body, and my flesh dried upon my bones. So
..embered me, nor did I occur to their minds, until I contrived a s
..em one day, and, going forth from that place, walked along the islan
..istance. And I saw a herdsman sitting upon something elevated
..idst of the sea; and I certified myself of him, and lo, he was the t
..hom they had committed my companions that he might pasture t
..nd he had with him many like them. As soon, therefore, as that m
..ed me, he knew that I was in possession of my reason, and that t
... that which had afflicted my companions had aff....
sign to me from a distance, and
.ght hand, I turned back, as this r
..ordingly, I turned back, as this r
..ng by reason of fear, a
..ken rest. Thus I cont
..e man who direct
..n. The sun had d
... I sat to rest an
.. account of t
.. was midnigh
..one, an
..roceed

everything that passed without being seen.

Leaving the silver, he turned to the gold, a wife who flew wide open!

This went on from evening to evening.

This went on from day to day

the thieves
rising high in the air,

particular

to divide the body
he had loaded himself with,

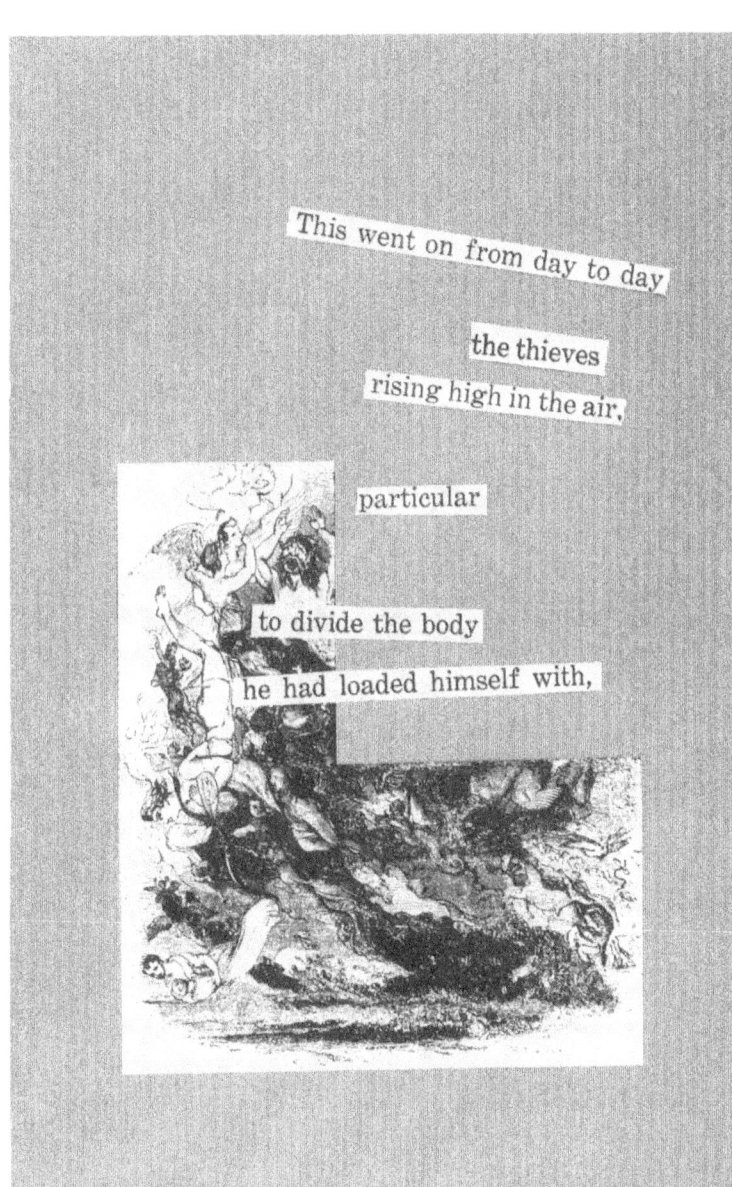

shocked at her strange request.

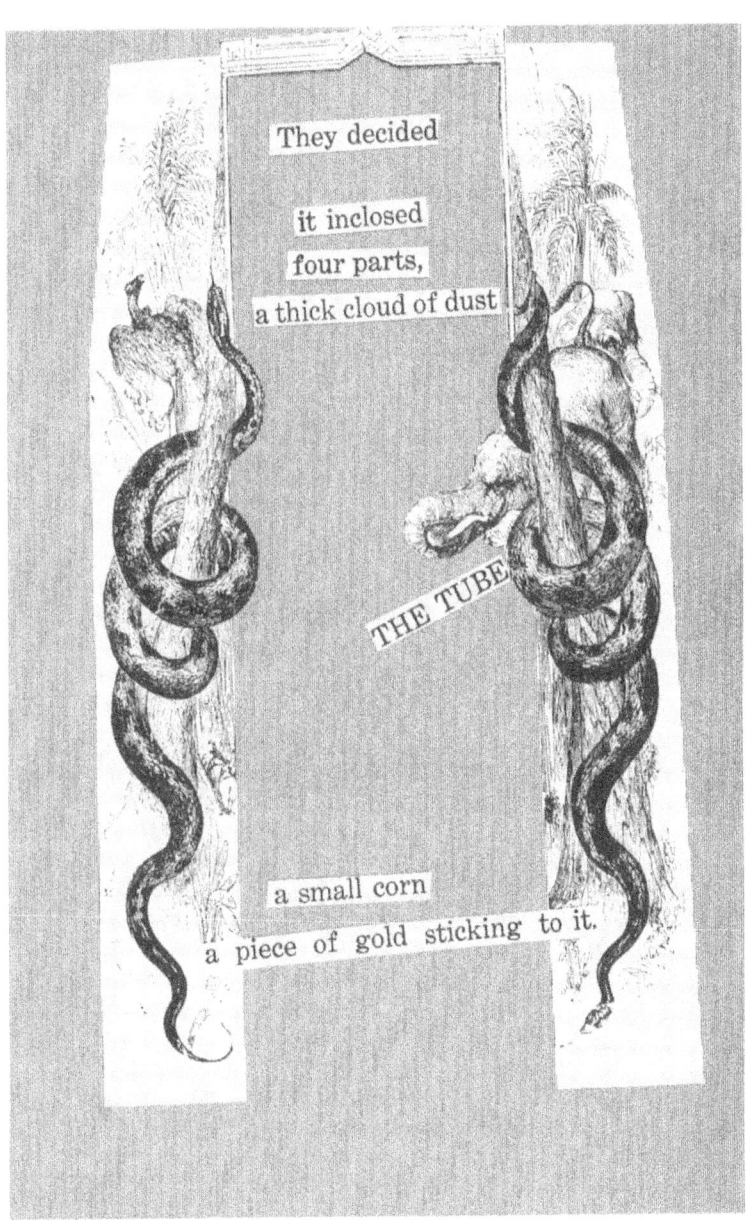

Here she swallowed and said:

I have to ask you to find the quartered body

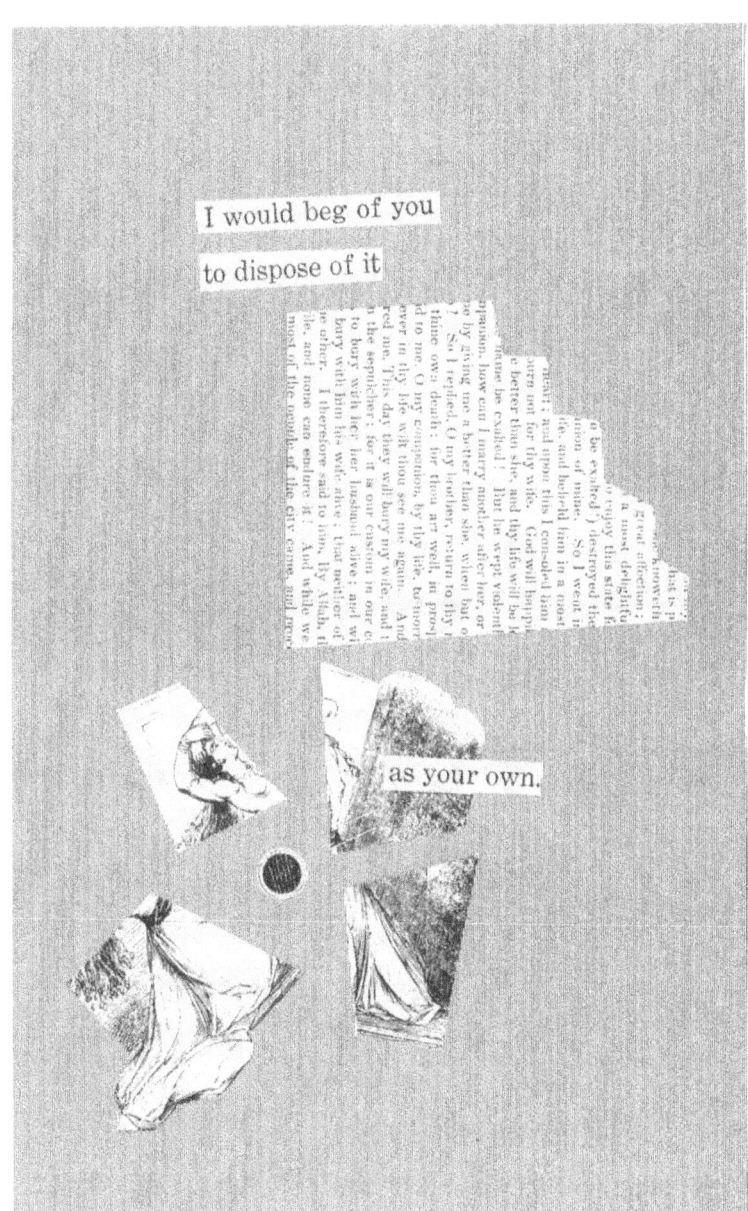

When

I was lost,

four little hills were the four islands

in the valley,

the secret of opening.

I was carried in darkness

with a hundred sequins,

I cannot tell how long

Thus was I exposed

I gave

excellent wine.

THIS hind

said the captain,

my wife,

myself and this hind:

At last

we will walk together

along

the same streets;

As long as I desire the same thing despair of saving my life.

Upon which
everyone held his peace,

the thieves

from the first to the last,

and for a long time

beheld something white

coming down,

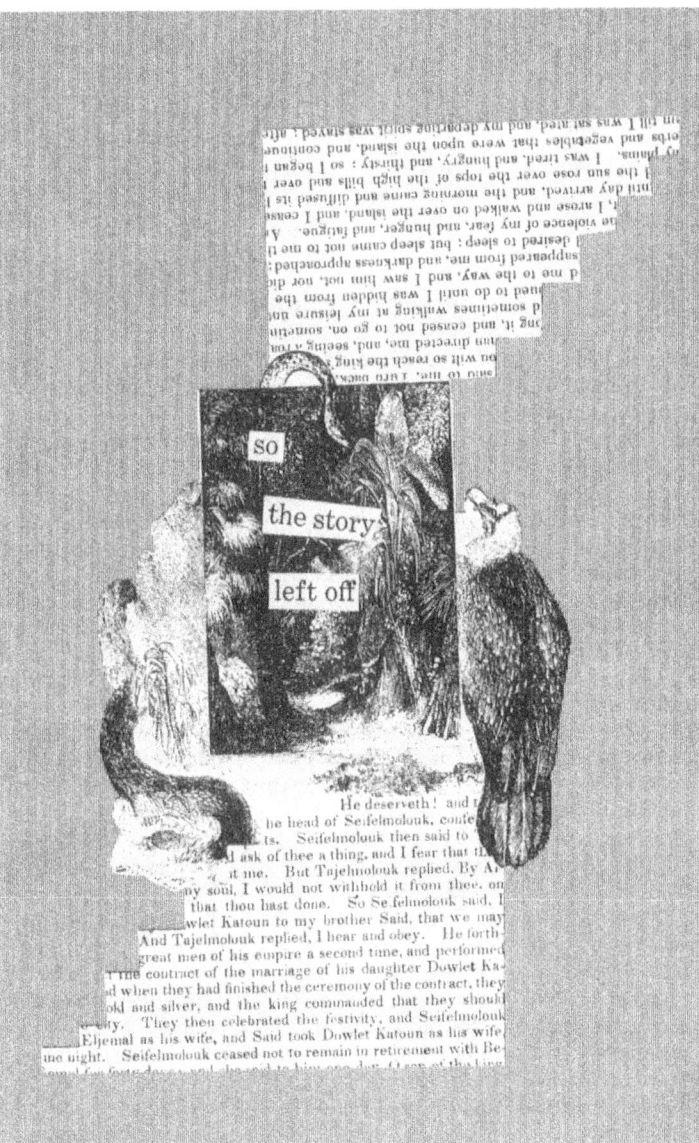

so

the story

left off

NOTES

INTRODUCTION

1 For use of the payoff model, see Gergen (1980: 99–101). The coinage 'homo reciprocus' comes from Becker (1956); for a critique of the reciprocal model, see Gergen, 215–37.
2 See Ekeh (1974). There is a useful synopsis of the issues in Gergen (1980: 189–96). Within sociology, one of the most influential developments beyond a restricted model of individual reward-seeking is Richard Emerson's conceptualising of a social relationship as a network structure of differential interdependencies; on Emerson's contribution, see Turner (1987: 223–38).
3 The kind of activity that is inconvenient for rationalist theory can be exemplified by one item from the earlier list of rhetorical questions about different exchanges: except in those few places where blood banks pay for blood, donors apparently receive nothing from anyone else in return. While it is possible to regard as transactional the actions of those who may be impelled by a sense of duty or general benevolence rather than an expectation of tangible reward, their action is still not one of exchange according to any strict criterion of rational choice. See Titmuss (1970).
4 One example is noted by Fish (1980: 80); for another, see Halliday and Hasan (1985: 13–14 (text 1.2)). There are brief critiques in Reid (1984: 57) and Hendricks (1988: 104–5).
5 This procedure is usual with other sociolinguists as well, who tend to assume in a matter-of-fact way that the so-called 'natural language' of conversation is the given primary field of inquiry. There is a further restriction in that such work is often carried out at a micro-level of discourse analysis, confining the term 'exchange' to a cluster of utterances, a minimal unit of interactive talk – most simply, a question/answer structure. See Stubbs (1983).
6 See for example Freund (1987: 141–51), on the differences between Wolfgang Iser's 'text-reader interaction' and Stanley Fish's more radically sceptical view; see also the comments on Louise Rosenblatt, Norman Holland and David Bleich (among others) in the useful introduction to Suleiman & Crosman (1980: 46–66).
7 See for example Apostolidès (1988); Dimock (1985); Trotter (1988);

Walker (1985). Of more general studies, noteworthy here are those of Smith (1978:79–154) Heinzelman (1980), and Rotman (1987) though none of these inquires into the particular forms of exchange that engage the present study. One or two semioticians (notably Greimas) offer interesting insights but these, mostly couched in abstract formulae, have not become well integrated with literary theory and criticism at large; see Greimas & Courtés (1982: 110).
8 Medievalists who have written incisively on exchange include Shoaf (1983, 1984) and Mann (1986). In the Renaissance field the most important discussions of this topic are by Greenblatt, who aims to trace the 'the circulation of social energy through Elizabethan dramatic texts' (1988: 1) as various discursive practices 'moved from one medium to another' (5) and 'from one culturally demarcated zone to another' (7).
9 But see Vernon (1984), and several items in *Diacritics* 18.2 (1988).

1 BEYOND NARRATOLOGY?

1 For a brief sample, see note 1 to ch. 6 below.
2 Chatman's *Story and Discourse* (1978) is less precise than Rimmon-Kenan on some matters, such as the concept of an implied author (see chap. 4 below); Prince's *Narratology* (1982) preserves the framework of his earlier book *A Grammar of Stories* (1973), and provides a basis for his useful *Dictionary of Narratology* (1987); Bal's *Narratology* (1985) makes many incisive remarks but is somewhat constricted by its adoption of a fabula/story/text classification.
3 See, for example, the remarks on William Faulkner's fiction in Ruthrof (1981) chap. 7; and on Christina Stead's novellas in Reid (1982).
4 The translation used is by Mark Musa and Peter E. Bondanella in the Norton Critical Edition of the *Decameron* (New York, Norton, 1977).
5 In general terms, this point has been discussed in the Introduction above, with reference to the observations of several social scientists and cultural theorists from Blau to Bourdieu and Baudrillard.
6 See *Poetics Today* 1.3 (1980), 107–118, and 2.1(b) (1980–1), 185–91.
7 The statement about this book's importance is quoted from Scholes (1974: 111); cf. also Hendricks (1973: 151) and Bremond (1973: 126). Propp's study (1968) continues to prove useful to theorists (e.g. Maclean 1988).
8 Page references are to Todorov (1969a), but I have translated the passages.
9 Todorov is not, of course, alone in his assumption. For an attempt to demonstrate experimentally that a schematic sense of mere plot can guide readers' comprehension of some *Decameron* tales, see Kintsch *et al.* (1977). It should hardly need to be emphasised, however, that the experimental reading situation in such cases is a very specialised kind of semantic exchange, and cannot provide a cogent basis for general conclusions about other experiences with texts.
10 See the discussion of this point in the Introduction above, and cf. also the critique by Thompson (1984: 125) of Fowler and Hodge *et al.* (1979) for their explicit assumption that meanings can be 'read off' from syntactic analysis.

2 FRAMING THE TEXT

1 This is my translation of a remark ('Il y a du cadre, mais le cadre n'existe pas') in Derrida's 'Parergon', part 2 of *La Vérité en peinture* ; the book has been rendered into English as *Truth in Painting* trans. G. Bennington and I. McLeod, University of Chicago Press, 1987.
2 Cf. Metzing (1980); van Dijk (1980); Eco (1984). Some would distinguish between 'frames' and 'scripts', though both terms refer to remembered data-patterns and hypotheses about textual organisation; cf. de Beaugrande and Dressler (1981). Among related usages from other disciplinary areas are those current in anthropology, e.g. Bateson (1972); in psychosociology, e.g. Goffman (1974); in philosophy, e.g. Morton (1980); and in the sociology of education, e.g. the chapter 'On the classification and framing of educational knowledge' in Bernstein (1971). Despite its title, Culler's *Framing the Sign* (1988) offers no sustained theoretical consideration of the concept, though he does summarise its importance in characteristically lucid and succinct terms (ix).
3 The discussion of certain composite texts in terms of an outer frame that encloses several stories has long been common in accounts of Chaucer's *Canterbury Tales*, Boccaccio's *Decameron*, and other such collections, but some recent studies of such texts use the term 'frame' with a fuller awareness of the complicated reading operations that can be involved; cf. Potter (1982). Additionally, within a given individual story, there may be a technique of embedded narration; cf. Moger (1985). This latter aspect of texts has of course been analysed also in a number of important studies that do not use the term 'frame'; cf. e.g. Chambers (1984).
4 Frow comments astutely on these matters (1986: 216–24); cf. Rosmarin (1985: 7–8 and 163–4), for a discussion of Blanchot and others on the relation between genre and book.
5 In Perry's usage, which is similar to that favoured by cognitive linguists (see note 1 above), the term designates conventional knowledge that prompts readers to ask questions about unspecified circumstances in a text and so to fill in the answers. Bal (1987: 17–20) has pointed out that Perry's concept of frames is too arbitrary to be consistently applicable.
6 As a matter of fact, they are unnumbered in the French edition (1954) that I use, which differs in other respects too; but we have complications enough without going into that set of comparisons as well. My thanks to Meredith Money for introducing me to Daudet by way of this edition, many years ago.
7 Caws (1985) remarks that inwardly mirrored images and passages of this sort 'often enable the intrusion of another genre into the narrative text' (xi). Caws makes many interesting observations about the kind of framing that I call 'intratextual'. She does not, however, attempt to theorise framing comprehensively; her attention is focused on the way 'certain passages stand out in relief' in selected nineteenth-century and modernist texts.

NOTES TO PAGES 52–64

8   For bibliographical details and further discussion of these writings, cf. Sachs (1965: 40–3).
9   There has been a lack of precision in 'frame studies' of this sort so far. As one critic remarks, 'Still unanswered questions are: how frames are activated, how they are acquired, to what extent they embody detailed "knowledge", etc. For these reasons it is unclear what it means to "understand" a text ... with the help of a frame' (Verdaasdonk 1982: 87–104).
10 Paris, Larousse, n.d., 47.
11 Cf. Zipes (1983). Such an approach gives ample scope for further versions and analogues to be considered, such as Charles Marelle's *Petit Chaperon d'or*, translated into English by Andrew Lang (1890: 215–19); this features a girl coincidentally (?) called Blanchette, alias Little Golden-Hood, whose dawdling in the forest is reminiscent of Seguin's goat on the mountainside ('picking Easter daisies, watching the little birds making their nests, and running after the butterflies') but whose magical hood saves her from the wolf – who, when he tries to escape from her Granny's cottage, runs straight into a waiting sack and is 'swallowed like a letter in the post'.
12 O'Sullivan and Scott (1987: 91). Mansfield's translation appeared in *The New Age* (new series), 21.19 (6 September 1917), 411–12. My thanks to Vincent O'Sullivan for drawing my attention to this piece.

3 CUTTING A LONG STORY SHORT

1   I am continuing here to use the term 'plot' in its usual sense, referring to a supposed chain of events – 'the global linking of sequences within a text', as defined in Ducrot and Todorov (1981: 298). Peter Brooks (1984) has attempted to enlarge its meaning substantially; but although I admire the force of his analyses and share his interest in 'the logic we use to shape and understand stories' (7) and in 'the interpretive activity' (13), it seems to me perverse to apply 'plot' to such reader-oriented concepts.
2   See Ducrot and Todorov (1981: 323–8); Todorov (1984: 41); Greimas and Courtés (1982: 103–5); Schleifer (1987: chap. 5).
3   For Bakhtin's critique of the Jakobsonian transmissive model, see Todorov (1984: 54–6).
4   Snorri Sturluson, *Edda*, trans. Anthony Faulkes (London and Melbourne, Dent, 1987), pp. 37–46. Faulkes has also produced the most recent scholarly edition of the *Edda* (Oxford, Clarendon Press, 1982).
5   Even Utgard has only a relational identity; lying somewhere beyond Asgard, in the 'outer regions', it is simply the 'other' of Asgard, with corresponding features.
6   On the propulsive, enigma-driven function of the so-called 'hermeneutic code' in narrative, see Barthes (1974: 18–21).
7   Michel Pêcheux (1982: 115–16) proposes a conception of meaning, or rather, 'the meaning effect', as 'a relationship of substitutability between elements (words, expressions, propositions) inside a given

discursive formation'. In his view, this relationship can take two basic forms: 'that of *equivalence* or symmetrical substitutability, such that the two substitutable elements a and b "have the same meaning" in the discursive formation considered, and that of *implication* or orientated substitutability, such that the relation of substitution $a \to b$ is not the same as the relation of substitution $b \to a$.' The second kind, implicated or orientated, which links substitutables in a concatenation, is obviously (though Pêcheux does not make this point) of special relevance to narrative discourse. The syncretic pattern in Snorri's text exemplifies what Pêcheux calls 'transverse-discourse' (116).

8 Angus Wilson, in the *Observer*, quoted on the cover of the 1976 paperback edition.

4 VOICE, SEQUENCE AND CONTROL

1 Cf. also Bakhtin's remark, quoted in Todorov (1984: 52), that 'the "image of the author", if the author-creator is meant by it, is a *contradictio in adjecto*; every image is something produced and not something producing'.
2 In a recent article, Chambers (1989a) does express dissatisfaction with Chatman's accommodation of the implied author within a unidirectional communicative model, and proposes instead a view of textual functions that resembles in some respects what is argued in the present chapter. Chambers further refines his account of 'narrative functions' and 'textual functions' within a triangular model in another recent article (Chambers 1989b).
3 That the postulate of an implied author is vacuous has been argued by Baker (1977), Juhl (1980) and Carroll (1982).
4 I adopt here the term used to translate the *parcours narratif* posited by Greimas and Courtés (1982: 207-8), but – for reasons that will become clear – without adopting their assumption that a 'logical chain' is the means by which components of a syntagmatic series are linked.
5 Jameson (1981: 60) remarks that 'interpretation proper ... always presupposes, if not a conception of the unconscious itself, then at least some mechanism of mystification or repression in terms of which it would make sense to seek a latent meaning behind the manifest one, or to rewrite the surface categories of a text in the stronger language of a more fundamental interpretive code'.
6 Chatman (1978: 148) remarks that 'unlike the narrator, the implied author can *tell* us nothing. He, or better, *it* has no voice, no direct means of communicating. It instructs us silently, through the design of the whole, with all the voices, by all the means it has chosen to let us learn.' However, this is not to say that an implied author can always keep 'all the voices' subordinated; they may take on a power of their own.
7 This feature of the text has been well described by Debray-Genette (1971: 43).

8 For remarks on the narratorial control that is being exercised over the representation of Herod's perceptions in this passage, see Banfield (1981: 75).
9 Willis (1987: 113) refers to this as 'the Vice-Consul's fantasy', overlooking the fact that it is first mentioned in connection with Rossett.
10 In chapter 15 of *Things Fall Apart* a bicycle whose murdered owner was the first white man to intrude on the local Ibo is secured to a sacred tree so that it will not run away and report his death. McEwan (1983: 20) comments that this scene symbolises the mismatch of 'a culture mostly ruled by the sacred with a culture mostly devoted to the mechanical'.
11 In saying that 'the Vinh-Long exchange proposes "a genealogical economy"', Marini (1977: 257) is quoting Irigaray (1974: 91). Willis (1987: 115–18) provides a careful critique of Marini's argument.
12 Bal (1974: 16) remarks that the word Battambang and the song identified with it are unilateral signs of the incapacity to communicate, though they do have a powerful effect on the white people.
13 Bal tries in various ways to recuperate the oddities of voice and sequence. Ignoring details that resist psychological analysis, she construes the Vice-Consul's disruptive howling as an expression of his pain and desperation, and Anne-Marie's tears as chagrin at having lost the chance of true love with the Vice-Consul. In the face of the text's denial of causative links (e.g. 146), Bal insists on finding a 'closed thematic network' in which emotional incapacity is seen as having 'as its cause and effect the lack of a relationship between mother and child' (1974: 15, 12, 18).
14 Some of these are illuminated by Borgomano (1981).

5 FICTIONS OF CHALLENGE AND RIPOSTE

1 The dedication to *The Phallic Forest* includes the words 'For those days' – a reminiscence of this statement by the narrator of 'The Nembutal Story': 'his account recalled to me those days'. Any reader who is thereby tempted to identify authors with narrators should note, however, that the narrator then says of those days: 'Dim though they are too.'
2 Gillard (1981) discusses some of these matters, mainly with reference to another pair of interrelated stories by Moorhouse and Wilding.
3 See note 4 of the Introduction for reference to examples.
4 This blend of the combative with the collusive, and of the spoken with the literary, recalls another linked story of that period. The topic of group compositions is discussed in 'Wesley's Brother at the Wake for Jack Kerouac' (Moorhouse 1973):

> Wesley's brother came over and said he and Milton were now 'working off each other' rather than working 'against each other'.
> He said it was communal literature.
> 'How does it operate?' I inquired...

'It operates this way', said Wesley's brother. 'Milton tells me over the telephone a key sentence from a story he is writing. I make a response to the key sentence while at the same time reacting creatively to his sentence there and then on the typewriter. I then telephone Carmel and tell her what I've written and she reacts to that and responds to it and then telephones Milton who writes some more and then telephones me again. Get it? We all write the same story processed communally but imprinted with our own individuality. Are you with me? ...'
(68)

5 This phrase is quoted from a letter to the editor in *Education*, September 11, 1974; but the same complaint recurs in many others printed in that number and in those of September 25 and October 9. For instance: 'I felt ashamed and disgusted when reading the article headed "A Piece of this Puzzle is Missing" by Amy Witting. To me it was just filthy reading and certainly not worthy of a place in our journal. It is a puzzle to me how such a piece of common low-down writing could pass through your hands.'

6 'ALWAYS A SACRIFICE': EXECUTING UNITIES

1 See Reid (1977), ch. 5, for a fuller discussion. Among the countless publications through which Poe's doctrine has become so widespread as to seem almost self-evidently valid, two are worth citing for their simplicity. As an example of the popular manual, take Forbes (1923), who declares unreservedly that a story 'must be formed of connected links, like a chain', that these links comprise 'a series of events', and that a neat sense of completion is requisite – thus a story 'must not present another story to the mind' (14–15). And as an example of the college textbook, take Boynton and Mack (1965): 'The word *story* implies a series of tied-together events; and *plot* is the technical term that is applied to these' (12). On other variants of holistic doctrine see Reid (1984), ch. 3.
2 Greimas and Courtés have resorted to the notion of 'pluri-isotopy' as a corrective to the unitary strictness of 'eliminating ambiguities'; but this seems tantamount to an admission that the isotopic grid is an inappropriate invention in the first place. Cf. Laden (1978: 157–88).
3 The edition consulted for both 'Prelude' and 'At the Bay' is that of Gordon (1974); but in order to facilitate reference to any other collection, section numbers rather than pages are cited.
4 See for example Coward and Ellis (1977: 50); Belsey (1980: 73, 90). For a critique of English 'screen theory' and the related work of the Tel Quel group in France, see Hall *et al*. (1980: 157ff., 163ff.).
5 Grigg (1985) makes an interesting attempt to revive the distinction. He argues that the semantic relation between signifiers in metonymy is always substitutive because it is genitive (e.g. glass for glass-of-wine); but that a metaphor, while it may be a genitive substitution (e.g. the hand of God), may alternatively be 'appositive' (e.g. a sea of

blood – a figure of identification) or 'extensive' (e.g. the mouth of a river). The problem here is that his terms seem somewhat narrowly defined, and arbitrarily distanced from one another. Why cannot apposition or extension be recognised as forms of substitution? It seems odd to disallow, for example, as Grigg does, 'A crowd flowed over London Bridge' as a substitutive figure.
6 In the original draft of this story, a longer version entitled 'The Aloe', there is an additonal specular motif of this kind. Doady Trout, sister of Beryl and Linda, mentally reshapes the material of her life in melodramatic terms: 'she made up perfect novels with herself for the heroine, all of them ending with some shocking catastrophe' (O'Sullivan 1982: 129).
7 According to Lacan's psychoanalytic outline of early childhood development, during which the 'specular *imago*' of the formative mirror stage supposedly becomes deflected into the 'social I', it is common for children between about two and five years old to imagine decapitation and other fragmentings of the body. See Lacan (1977: 11).
8 While this impression may be partly derivable from certain stylistic features (for instance the frequent use of an exclamatory 'Oh!'), it is also circumtextually framed: Lanser (1981) remarks that in general 'the presence of a female name on the title page signals a female narrative voice, in the absence of markings to the contrary' (167). Jonathan Culler (1988), while conceding that Lanser may be empirically correct in regarding this as a reading convention, argues that it is one to be challenged because it encourages the recuperative 'compulsion ... to explain textual details by relating them to qualities of persons' (206).

7 THE CHARACTERS OF DANGER AND DESIRE

1 All quotations are from the Norton critical edition of *The Prelude* : *1799, 1805, 1850* (Wordsworth, 1979), and are from the 1805 version unless otherwise indicated. An excerpt from Book 1 is printed as Appendix B.
2 Wordsworth's distaste for Adam Smith's doctrines is most vehemently expressed in his 'Essay, Supplementary to the Preface', where he describes Smith as 'the worst critic, David Hume not excepted, that Scotland, a soil to which this sort of weed seems natural, has produced' (Owen and Smyser 1974, vol. 3, 71).
3 Caudwell, writing in the 1930s about 'the bourgeios illusion' in English Romantic poetry, commented sternly that 'Wordsworth's "Nature" is of course a Nature freed ... by eons of human work. ... The division of labour involved in industrialism has made it possible ... to maintain a poet in austere idleness' (quoted in Gleckner and Enscoe (1962: 124). On the relation of Wordsworth's poetry to contemporary debates about the division of labour, see Simpson (1982: 142–54) and Spivak (1987: 70–6). Related but more general issues

are broached by Kiernan (1975).
4 This earlier allusion is noted by Bate (1985: 87).
5 'Advertisement' to *Lyrical Ballads* of 1798: Owen and Smyser (1974), vol. 1, 116. An example of a working-class regional locution being selfconsciously introduced into the poem occurs in Book 8, speaking of shepherds: 'long as the storm is "locked" / (So they do phrase it)' (8. 363–4).
6 This seems, by the way, another passing reminiscence of *The Tempest*: when Prospero, after the masque, says he is 'vexed' (4. i. 158) he implicitly links his state of mind with the stormy 'still-vexed' Bermuda islands of 1. ii. 229.
7 The words 'motion' and 'move' (or their inflections) occur eleven times within 155 lines. Helen Darbishire remarked sixty years ago on the importance to Wordsworth of physical movement in the natural world, and on the recurrence of the motif in *The Prelude*: her observations are reprinted in Harvey and Gravil (1972: 87).
8 My reading of the first three of these four passages is similar in some respects to that of Bahti (1984), who argues *inter alia* that the acts of theft in the trapping, climbing and rowing episodes indicate a more productive economy of exchange than the 'failed gift giving and countergiving' (92) of the opening passages of Book 1.
9 Heinzelman (1980) remarks that 'In Wordsworth's economy the *reader*, the nominal "consumer", must also be a productive labourer'.
10 A comparable view of the ideological dimension of Shakespeare's *The Tempest* is proposed by Hawkes (1986), ch. 1, who argues that Prospero's 'pastoral pageant . . . serves to support an established and work-dominated social order' (7).
11 Cf. Culler (1988), ch. 12, on the need to question the habit of recuperating a strange utterance by attributing a personality to the textual utterer and then interpreting in the light of that. What Barthes (1974) has to say about character and figure is also pertinent: on the one hand, 'to say *I* is inevitably to attribute signifieds to oneself; further, it gives one a biographical duration, it enables one to undergo, in one's imagination, an intelligible "evolution", to signify oneself as an object with a destiny, to give a meaning to time. On this level, *I* . . . is therefore a character. . . . As figure [on the other hand], the character can oscillate between two roles, without this oscillation having any meaning, for it occurs outside biographical time (outside chronology): the symbolic structure is completely reversible: it can be read in any direction. . . . As a symbolic ideality, the character . . . is nothing but a site for the passage (and return) of the figure' (68).

8 WAITING TO BE TOLD

1 As Morris (1988) remarks, Lyotard assigns inconsistent meanings to his key term, 'which variously refers to the state of culture after the scientific and artistic transformations of the end of the nineteenth century, or to the equivalent in culture of the "postindustrial" age that Lyotard dates in Europe from the end of the 1950s' (220–1).

NOTES TO PAGES 167–185

Indeed, he also uses it, as will emerge later in our discussion, to indicate a recurrent impulse within modernism, regardless of period.
2 Page references, which will be given parenthetically, are to the 1963 reprint listed in the References.
3 Not everyone does assume this. The case for regarding Samuel Johnson's *Rasselas* as a covert frame of reference is argued interestingly by Mackenzie (1965).
4 The intertextual structure is broadly similar to that which runs through a closely comparable Australian novel of that period, Christina Stead's *For Love Alone*, where a subtle critique of Nietzschean thought gives historical resonance to Teresa's personal story (cf. Reid 1979: 105–13).
5 To mention only a couple of examples: Louis Lavater's poem 'Meroë', subtitled 'From the prose of Winwood Reade', appeared in 1927 (details in the References); and Henry Handel Richardson records in her autobiography (1948: 123) that she lent her copy of *The Martyrdom of Man* to a student friend. A number of other Australian writers also refer to the book – but this is not the place for a general account of its influence. Parenthetical references are to the 1927 reprint listed in the References.
6 Spengler, mentioned in White's autobiography (1983: 74), certainly took a more pessimistic view than Reade of the prospects for modern culture, though he did see in Prussian Socialism a solution – 'above politics' – to the problems that he forecast. However, he shared Reade's idealist vision of great movements in the history of civilisation.
7 But if the modernist enterprise is itself seen as quintessentially capitalistic in its drive to 'make it new', then a useful corrective to Jameson's argument may be found in this remark by John Frow: 'Until our historical space is totally altered there can be no "beyond" of modernism which would not thereby be a moment of it' (Frow 1985: 111).
8 Cf. Brown and Yule (1983: 195): 'An important distinction needs to be drawn, which many students adopting Halliday and Hasan's approach have failed to draw, and which Halliday and Hasan themselves are ambivalent about.... This is the distinction between "meaning relations" which hold between items in a text and the explicit expression of those "meaning relations" within the text.' Brown and Yule go on to show that 'hearers and readers do not depend upon formal markers of cohesion in order to identify a text as a text' (198).
9 The edition used by Gordon is *The Thousand and One Nights*, trans. Edward William Lane, 'illustrated by many hundred engravings on wood, from original designs by William Harvey' and edited by E.S. Poole (London, John Murray, 1859).
10 The cultural specificity of this aspect of Lane's text should not obscure the fact that it is thematising something to be found generally in narrative: the act of omission underlying any substitutive element. Iser (1978: 191–2) refers to a sudden disjunction within a text as a 'cutting'.

9 'DOWN A STRANGE STREET': EMERGENT EXCHANGES

1 Cf. also Kress (1982), another systemic linguist who has advocated 'direct teaching of generic forms' (112). In more recent publications, Kress seems to modify that categorical position, though his emphasis is still on the need to place 'limits on the possibilities of creativity' (1987: 43).
2 This is not to ignore the mediated structure of *all* discourse; rather, it is to insist that written discourse, being more emphatically and elaborately mediated, is better taken as the paradigm case.
3 In seeking to abolish traditional distinctions between literary and ordinary ('natural') discourse, Pratt does not adequately consider the different though closely related distinction between oral and written forms of linguistic mediation. Indisputable though it is that 'literary narratives can be analysed in the same way as the short anecdotes scattered throughout our conversation' (Pratt 1977: 67), it does not follow by any means that 'they are utterances of the same type' (69). Written forms of storytelling are *markedly* mediated, incorporating a surrogate communicative relationship into the text; oral tales, though of course they can not be purely unmediated, can hardly incorporate in that way an intervening narrator/narratee level of exchange. Toolan (e.g. 1988:198) makes much of the findings of Peterson and McCabe (1983), which tend to vindicate the utility of a Labovian structure; but he appears to attach little importance to the fact that their study, interesting though it is, was based on stories elicited from casual conversation and cannot therefore be applied indiscriminately to written narration.
4 Britton's influence has been and continues to be strong internationally; see for example Applebee (1978) and Pradl (1989).
5 Cf. Yule (1979: 51–5), for a sample of stories told by disturbed children whose parents behave inconsistently towards them.
6 Kelly-Byrne (1989: 47, 68, 78) provides insights into the way adult-child power structures become fictively transformed in a young child's play. Smith (1978: 124–32) has some interesting remarks on children's early experiences with adult uses of fictive discourse, noting that 'Adults will allow the child to berate them as witches and revile them as monsters in terms and tones for which he would otherwise be scolded' (130).
7 Cf. Bachelard (1964) on the fundamental importance of the house as an archetypal image.
8 In a study of infants' oral narratives, Umiker-Sebeok (1979) found that nine-tenths of those produced by 3-year-olds dealt with the child's immediate environment, but among 5-year-old storytellers more than half dealt with 'remote' matters.
9 This view is supported by Cook-Gumperz and Green (1984), whose studies suggest that 'children's concepts about books and their structure may be part of the meaning of young children's stories', and that a crucial part of the acquisition and early development of

narrative is an 'emblematic phase' in which oral storytelling is influenced by written formats (211). Their conclusion is that in previous research there has been too much emphasis on 'only one type of narrative, the adult literate model of a well-formed story, and this approach may underestimate the actual knowledge of children' (217). For more general remarks on the theme that the book-form is prior to genre, see Blanchot as quoted by Rosmarin (1985: 7–8, 163–4).

10 Cf. Dombey (1983).

REFERENCES

Abrams, M.H. (1974), *Natural Supernaturalism*, London, Oxford University Press.
Achebe, Chinua (1976 (1958)), *Things Fall Apart*, London, Heinemann.
Apostolidès, Jean-Marie (1988), 'Molière and the Sociology of Exchange', *Critical Inquiry* 14.3, 477–92.
Applebee, Arthur N. (1978), *The Child's Concept of Story*, Chicago, University of Chicago Press.
Armstrong, Isobel (1982), *Language as Living Form in Nineteenth-Century Poetry*, Sussex, Harvester Press.
Auerbach, Erich (1953 (1946)), *Mimesis: The Representation of Reality in Western Literature*, trans. Willard R. Trask, Princeton, Princeton University Press.
Bachelard, Gaston (1964 (1958)), *The Poetics of Space*, trans. Maria Jolas, Boston, Beacon Press.
Bahti, Timothy (1984), 'Wordsworth's Rhetorical Theft', in *Romanticism and Language*, ed. Arden Reed, Ithaca, Cornell University Press, 86–124.
Baker, John Ross (1977), 'From Imitation to Rhetoric', in *Towards a Poetics of Fiction*, ed. Mark Spilka, Bloomington, Indiana University Press, 136–56.
Bakhtin, M.M. (1981), *The Dialogic Imagination: Four Essays*, ed. Michael Holquist, trans. Caryl Emerson and Michael Holquist, Austin, University of Texas Press.
Bal, Mieke (1974), 'Un roman dans le roman: encadrement ou enchassement? Quelques aspects du *Vice-Consul*', *Neophilologus* 58, 2–21.
——(1981), 'Notes on Narrative Embedding', Poetics Today 2.2, 41–59.
——(1985 (1980)), *Narratology: Introduction to the Theory of Narrative*, trans. Christine van Boheemen, Toronto, University of Toronto Press.
——(1986), 'Tell-tale Theories', Poetics Today 7.3, 555–64.
——(1987), *Lethal Love: Feminist Literary Readings of Biblical Love Stories*, Bloomington, Indiana University Press.
Banfield, Ann (1981), 'Reflective and Non-reflective Consciousness in the Language of Fiction', *Poetics Today* 2.2, 61–76.
Barrs, Myra (1987), 'Mapping a World', *English in Education* 21.1, 10–15.

REFERENCES

Barthes, Roland (1974 (1970)), *S/Z*, trans. Richard Miller, New York, Hill and Wang.
——(1975 (1973)), *The Pleasure of the Text*, trans. Richard Miller, New York, Hill and Wang.
Bate, Jonathan (1985), 'Wordsworth and Shakespeare', *The Wordsworth Circle* 16.2, 85–92.
Bateson, Gregory (1972), *Steps to an Ecology of Mind*, New York, Ballantine.
Baudrillard, Jean (1975 (1973)), *The Mirror of Production*, trans. Mark Poster, St Louis, Telos.
——(1988), *Selected Writings*, ed. Mark Poster, Cambridge, Polity Press.
Bayley, John (1976), *The Uses of Division: Unity and Disharmony in Literature*, London, Chatto and Windus.
Becker, H.P. (1956), *Man in Reciprocity*, New York, Praeger.
Belsey, Catherine (1980), *Critical Practice*, London, Methuen.
Benjamin, Walter (1969), *Illuminations*, ed. Hannah Arendt, New York, Schocken.
Bennett, David (1988), 'Wrapping up Postmodernism: the Subject of Consumption versus the Subject of Cognition', in *Postmodern Conditions*, ed. Andrew Milner, Philip Thomson and Chris Worth, Melbourne, Centre for General and Comparative Literature, Monash University, 15–36.
Berg, William, Grimaud, Michel and Moskos, George (1982), *Saint/ Oedipus: Psychocritical Approaches to Flaubert's Art*, Ithaca, Cornell University Press.
Bernstein, Basil (1971), *Class, Codes and Control*, vol. 1, London, Routledge and Kegan Paul.
Bialostosky, Don (1984), *Making Tales: The Poetics of Wordsworth's Narrative Experiments*, Chicago, University of Chicago Press.
Blau, Peter B. (1964), *Exchange and Power in Social Life*, New York, Wiley.
Boccaccio, Giovanni (1977 (1351)), *The Decameron*, trans. Mark Musa and Peter E. Bondanella, New York, Norton.
Booth, Wayne C. (1961), *The Rhetoric of Fiction*, Chicago, University of Chicago Press.
——(1979), *Critical Understanding*, Chicago, University of Chicago Press.
Borgomano, Madeleine (1981), 'L'histoire de la mendiante indienne: une cellule génératrice de l'œuvre de Marguerite Duras' *Poétique* 48, 479–93.
Bourdieu, Pierre (1977 (1972)), *Outline of a Theory of Practice*, trans. Richard Nice, Cambridge, Cambridge University Press.
Bowie, Malcolm (1979), 'Jacques Lacan', in *Structuralism and Since: From Lévi-Strauss to Derrida*, ed. John Sturrock, Oxford, Oxford University Press, 116–53.
Boynton, Robert W. and Mack, Maynard (1965), *Introduction to the Short Story*, New York, Hayden.
Bremond, Claude (1973), *Logique du récit*, Paris, Seuil.
Brice-Heath, Shirley (1983), *Ways with Words: Language, Life and Work in Communities and Classrooms*, Cambridge, Cambridge University Press.
Britton, James (1970), *Language and Learning*, Harmondsworth, Penguin.

REFERENCES

——(1982), 'Spectator Role and the Beginnings of Writing', in *What Writers Know: The Language, Process and Structure of Written Discourse*, ed. Martin Nystrand, New York, Academic Press, 149–69.

——(1983), 'Writing and the Story World', in *Explorations in the Development of Writing*, ed. Barry M. Kroll and Gordon Wells, Chichester, Wiley, 3–30.

Britton, James, Burgess, Tony, Martin, Nancy, McLeod, Alex and Rosen, Harold (1975), *The Development of Writing Abilities, 11–18*, London, Macmillan.

Brombert, Victor (1966), *The Novels of Flaubert: A Study of Themes and Techniques*, Princeton, Princeton University Press.

Brooks, Peter (1984), *Reading for the Plot: Design and Intention in Narrative*, Oxford, Clarendon Press.

Brown, Beverley (1983), 'Displacing the Difference', *M/f 8*, 79–89.

Brown, Gillian, and Yule, George (1983), *Discourse Analysis*, Cambridge University Press.

Burrows, J.F. (1970) '"Jardin Exotique": The Central Phase of *The Aunt's Story*', in *Ten Essays on Patrick White*, ed. G.A. Wilkes, Sydney, Angus and Robertson, 85–108.

Carroll, David, (1982), *The Subject in Question*, Chicago, University of Chicago Press.

Caws, Mary Ann (1985), *Reading Frames in Modern Fiction*, Princeton, Princeton University Press.

Chambers, Ross (1984), *Story and Situation: Narrative Seduction and the Power of Fiction*, Minneapolis, University of Minnesota Press.

——(1986), 'Gossip and the Novel: Knowing Narrative and Narrative Knowing in Balzac, Mme de Lafayette and Proust', *Australian Journal of French Studies* 23.2, 212–33.

——(1987), *Mélancolie et opposition: les débuts du modernisme en France*, Paris, Corti.

——(1989a), '"Narrative" and "Textual" Functions (with an example from La Fontaine)', in *Reading Narrative: Form, Ethics, Ideology*, ed. James Phelan, Columbus, Ohio State University Press, 27–39.

——(1989b), 'Narrative and Other Triangles', *The Journal of Narrative Technique* 19.1, 31–48.

Chase, Cynthia (1986), *Decomposing Figures: Rhetorical Readings in the Romantic Tradition*, Baltimore, Johns Hopkins University Press.

Chatman, Seymour (1975), 'The Structure of Narrative Transmission', in *Style and Structure in Literature*, ed. Roger Fowler, Oxford, Blackwell, 213–57.

——(1978), *Story and Discourse: Narrative Structure in Fiction and Film*, Ithaca, Cornell University Press.

Clarke, Colin (1962), *Romantic Paradox*, London, Routledge and Kegan Paul.

Cohan, Steven and Shires, Linda (1988), *Telling Stories: A Theoretical Analysis of Narrative Fiction*, New York, Routledge.

Cook-Gumperz, Jenny, and Green, Judith (1984), 'A Sense of Story: Influences on Children's Storytelling Ability', in *Coherence in Spoken and Written Discourse*, ed. Deborah Tannen, Norwood (N.J.), Ablex, 201–18.

REFERENCES

Coward, Rosalind and Ellis, John (1977), *Language and Materialism*, London, Routledge and Kegan Paul.
Crick, Malcolm (1982), 'Anthropology of Knowledge', *Annual Review of Anthropology* 11, 287–313.
Culler, Jonathan (1979), 'Jacques Derrida', in *Structuralism and Since: From Lévi-Strauss to Derrida*, ed. John Sturrock, Oxford, Oxford University Press, 154–80.
——(1981), *The Pursuit of Signs: Semiotics, Literature, Deconstruction*, London, Routledge and Kegan Paul.
——(1988), *Framing the Sign: Criticism and its Institutions*, Oxford, Blackwell.
Dällenbach, Lucien (1989 (1977)), *The Mirror in the Text*, trans. Jeremy Whitely and Emma Hughes, Cambridge, Polity Press.
Daniels, Douglas J. (1972), 'A Structural Analysis of Three Narrative Works of Gustave Flaubert', unpublished Ph.D. dissertation, University of Minnesota.
Danto, Arthur C. (1965), *Analytical Philosophy of History*, Cambridge, Cambridge University Press.
Darlington, Beth (ed.), (1977), *Home at Grasmere* (vol. 3 of The Cornell Wordsworth), Ithaca, Cornell University Press.
Daudet, Alphonse (1954 (1869)), *Lettres de mon moulin*, Paris, Flammarion.
——(1978 (1869)), *Letters from my Windmill*, trans. Frederick Davies, Harmondsworth, Penguin.
——(n.d.), Œuvres, vol. 5 (*Théatre*), Paris, Lemerre.
Debray-Genette, Raymonde (1970), 'Les figures du récit dans "Un Cœur Simple"' *Poétique* 3, 348–64.
——(1971), 'Du mode narratif dans les *Trois Contes*', *Littérature* 2, 39–62.
de Beaugrande, Robert-Alain, and Dressler, Wolfgang (1981), *Introduction to Text Linguistics*, New York, Longman.
de Man, Paul (1979), *Allegories of Reading: Figural Language in Rousseau, Nietzsche, Rilke and Proust*, New Haven, Yale University Press.
DeLillo, Don (1985), *White Noise*, New York, Viking.
Derrida, Jacques (1975), 'Le Facteur de la vérité', *Critique* 21, 96–147.
——(1976 (1967)), *Of Grammatology*, trans. Gayatri Chakravorty Spivak, Baltimore, Johns Hopkins University Press.
——(1978), *La Vérité en peinture,* trans. as *Truth in Painting*, by G. Bennington and I. McLeod, Chicago, University of Chicago Press, 1987.
——(1981 (1967)), *Writing and Difference*, trans. Alan Bass, London, Routledge and Kegan Paul.
de Saussure, Ferdinand (1983 (1916)), *Course in General Linguistics*, ed. Charles Bally, trans. Roy Harris, London, Duckworth.
Dimock, Wai-Chee (1985), 'Debasing Exchange: Edith Wharton's *The House of Mirth*', *PMLA* 100.1, 783–92.
Dombey, Henrietta (1983), 'Learning the Language of Books', in *Opening Moves: Work in Progress in the Study of Children's Language Development*, ed. Margaret Meek, Institute of Education, University of London, 26–43.
Dow, Louise (1987), 'Written Off', *Meanjin* 46.3, 219–22.
Ducrot, Oswald, and Todorov, Tzvetan (1981 (1972)), *Encyclopedic Dic-*

REFERENCES

tionary of the Sciences of Language, trans. Catherine Porter, Oxford, Blackwell.
Duras, Marguerite (1987 (1966)), *The Vice-Consul*, trans. Eileen Ellenbogen, New York, Pantheon.
During, Simon (1989), 'Waiting for the Post', *Ariel* 20.4.
Eagleton, Terry (1978), *Criticism and Ideology*, London, Verso.
——(1985), 'Capitalism, Modernism and Postmodernism', *New Left Review* 152, 60–73.
Eco, Umberto (1984), *Semiotics and the Philosophy of Language*, London, Macmillan.
Ekeh, Peter, (1974), *Social Exchange Theory: The Two Traditions*, Cambridge, Mass., Harvard University Press.
Felman, Shoshana (1978), *La folie et la chose littéraire*, Paris, Seuil.
Ferguson, Frances (1977), *Wordsworth: Language as Counter-Spirit*, New Haven, Yale University Press.
Fish, Stanley (1980), *Is There a Text in this Class? The Authority of Interpretive Communities*, Cambridge, Mass., Harvard University Press.
Flaubert, Gustave (1961 (1877)), *Three Tales*, trans. Robert Baldick, Harmondsworth, Penguin.
Forbes, Mildred P. (1923), *Good Citizenship through Storytelling: A Textbook for Teachers, Social Workers and Homemakers*, New York, Macmillan.
Foucault, Michel (1981 (1976)), *The History of Sexuality*, vol. 1, trans. Robert Hurley, Harmondsworth, Penguin.
Fowler, Roger (1977), *Linguistics and the Novel*, London, Methuen.
——(1981), *Literature as Social Discourse: The Practice of Linguistic Criticism*, Bloomington, Indiana University Press.
——(1986), *Linguistic Criticism*, Oxford, Oxford University Press.
Fowler, Roger, Hodge, Bob, Kress, Gunther and Trew, Tony (1979), *Language and Control*, London, Routledge and Kegan Paul.
Fox, Carol (1983), 'Talking Like a Book: Young Children's Oral Monologues', in *Opening Moves: Work in Progress in the Study of Children's Language Development*, ed. Margaret Meek, London, Institute of Education, University of London, 12–25.
——(1989), 'Children Thinking Through Story', *English in Education* 23.2, 25–36.
Freadman, Anne (1983), 'Sandpaper', *Southern Review* 16.1, 161–73.
——(1987), 'Anyone for Tennis?' in *The Place of Genre in Learning: Current Debates*, ed. Ian Reid, Geelong, Centre for Studies in Literary Education, Deakin University, 91–124.
Freund, Elizabeth (1987), *The Return of the Reader: Reader-Response Criticism*, London, Methuen.
Friedman, Michael (1979), *The Making of a Tory Humanist: William Wordsworth and the Idea of Community*, New York, Columbia University Press.
Frow, John (1985), untitled review of Lyotard (1984), in *Public/Private*, ed. Don Barry and Peter Botsman, Sydney, Local Consumption, 97–111.
——(1986), *Marxism and Literary History*, Oxford, Blackwell.
Genette, Gérard (1972) *Figures III*, Paris, Seuil, trans. as *Narrative*

REFERENCES

Discourse by Jane E. Lewin, Ithaca, Cornell University Press, 1980.
——(1987), *Seuils*, Paris, Seuil.
——(1988 (1983)), *Narrative Discourse Revisited*, ed. Jane E. Lewin, Ithaca, Cornell University Press.
Gergen, Kenneth J., Greenberg, Martin S. and Willis, Richard H. (eds) (1980), *Social Exchange: Advances in Theory and Research*, New York, Plenum Press.
Gillard, G.M. (1981), 'The New Writing: Whodunnit?', *Meanjin* 40.2, 167–74.
Gillison, Gillian (1980), 'Images of Nature in Gimi Thought', in *Nature, Culture and Gender*, ed. Carol MacCormack and Marilyn Strathern, Cambridge, Cambridge University Press, 143–73.
Gleckner, Robert F. and Enscoe, Gerald E. (eds) (1962), *Romanticism: Points of View*, Englewood Cliffs, N.J., Prentice-Hall.
Goffman, Erving (1974), *Frame Analysis*, New York, Harper and Row.
Goodman, Nelson (1976), *Languages of Art*, Indianapolis, Hackett.
Gordon, Ian (ed.) (1974), *Undiscovered Country: The New Zealand Stories of Katherine Mansfield*, London, Longman.
Gordon, Jaimy (1980), 'The Hind of the Further', *Diana's Second Almanac*, Providence, R.I., Diana's Bimonthly Press.
Goux, Jean-Joseph (1973), *Économie et symbolique*, Paris, Seuil.
——(1984), *Les monnayeurs du langage*, Paris, Galilée.
Greenblatt, Stephen (1988), *Shakespearean Negotiations: The Circulation of Social Energy in Renaissance England*, Oxford, Clarendon Press.
Greimas, A.J. (1985), 'The Love-Life of the Hippopotamus', in *On Signs: A Semiotic Reader*, ed. Marshall Blonsky, Oxford, Blackwell, 341–62.
Greimas, A.J. and Courtés, J. (1982 (1979)), *Semiotics and Language: An Analytical Dictionary*, trans. Larry Crist and Daniel Patte, Bloomington, Indiana University Press.
Grigg, Russell (1985), 'Jakobson et Lacan', *Ornicar* 35, 12–34.
Gubar, Susan (1983), 'The Birth of the Artist as Heroine: (Re)production, the Kunstlerroman Tradition, and the Fiction of Katherine Mansfield', in *The Representation of Women in Fiction*, ed. Carolyn G. Heilbrun and Margaret R. Higonnet, Baltimore, Johns Hopkins University Press, 19–59.
Hall, Stuart, Hobson, Dorothy, Lowe, Andrew and Willis, Paul (1980), *Culture, Media, Language: Working Papers in Cultural Studies*, 1972–79, London, Hutchinson/C.C.C.
Halliday, M.A.K. (1975), *Learning How to Mean: Explorations in the Development of Language*, London, Edward Arnold.
——(1978), *Language as Social Semiotic: The Social Interpretation of Language and Meaning*, London, Edward Arnold.
Halliday, M.A.K. and Hasan, Ruqaiya (1976), *Cohesion in English*, London, Longman.
——(1985), *Language, Context and Text: Aspects of Language in a Social-Semiotic Perspective*, Geelong, Deakin University Press.
Hankin, C.A. (1983), *Katherine Mansfield and her Confessional Stories*, London, Macmillan.

REFERENCES

Hanoulle, Marie-Julie (1972), 'Quelques manifestations du discours dans *Trois Contes*', *Poétique* 9, 41–9.

Harding, D.W. (1937), 'The Role of the Onlooker', *Scrutiny* 6, 247–58.

——(1962), 'Psychological Processes in the Reading of Fiction', *British Journal of Aesthetics* 2, 133–47.

Hartman, Geoffrey H. (1964), *Wordsworth's Poetry, 1787–1814*, New Haven, Yale University Press.

Harvey, W.J. and Gravil, Richard (eds), (1972), *Wordsworth's Prelude: A Casebook*, London, Macmillan.

Hasan, Ruqaiya (1980), 'The Identity of a Text', *Sophia Linguistica* 6, 75–91.

Hawkes, Terence (1977), *Structuralism and Semiotics*, London, Methuen.

——(1986) *That Shakespeherian Rag: Essays on a Critical Process*, London, Methuen.

Heath, Anthony (1976), *Rational Choice and Social Exchange*, Cambridge, Cambridge University Press.

Heinzelman, Kurt (1980), *The Economics of the Imagination*, Amherst, University of Massachusetts Press.

Hendricks, William O. (1973), *Essays on Semiolinguistics and Verbal Art*, The Hague, Mouton.

——(1980), 'The Semiolinguistic Theory of Narrative Structures', in *On Text and Context*, ed. E. Forastieri-Brascietal, Editorial Universitara, University of Puerto Rico, 35–54.

——(1988), 'Discourse Analysis as a Semiotic Endeavor', *Semiotica* 72, 97–124.

Hernadi, Paul (1972), *Beyond Genre*, Ithaca, Cornell University Press.

Herring, Thelma (1970), 'Odyssey of a Spinster: A Study of *The Aunt's Story*', in *Ten Essays on Patrick White*, ed. G.A. Wilkes, Sydney, Angus and Robertson, 3–20.

Hirsch, E.D. (1967), *Validity in Interpretation*, New Haven, Yale University Press.

Holland, Norman (1980), 'Recovering "The Purloined Letter": Reading as a Personal Transaction', in *The Reader in the Text: Essays on Audience and Interpretation*, ed. Susan Suleiman and Inga Crosman, Princeton, Princeton University Press, 350–70.

Holloway, John (1979), *Narrative and Structure: Exploratory Essays*, Cambridge, Cambridge University Press.

Homans, George (1961), *Social Behaviour: Its Elementary Forms*, New York, Harcourt Brace.

Hospital, Janette Turner (1989), 'A Writer Comes in from the Cold', *The Sydney Morning Herald*, October 14, 1989, 80.

Irigaray, Luce (1974), *Speculum de l'autre femme*, Paris, Éditions de minuit.

——(1985 (1977)), *This Sex Which Is Not One*, trans. Catherine Porter and Carolyn Burke, Ithaca, Cornell University Press.

Iser, Wolfgang (1978), *The Act of Reading: A Theory of Aesthetic Response*, Baltimore, Johns Hopkins University Press.

Jakobson, Roman (1956), 'Two Aspects of Language and Two Types of Linguistic Disturbances', in R. Jakobson and M. Halle, *Fundamentals of Language*, The Hague, Mouton.

Jameson, Fredric (1981), *The Political Unconscious: Narrative as a Socially*

REFERENCES

Symbolic Act, Ithaca, Cornell University Press.
——(1984a), 'Foreword' to Jean-François Lyotard, *The Postmodern Condition*, trans. Geoff Bennington and Brian Massumi, Minneapolis, University of Minnesota Press, vii-xxi.
——(1984b), 'Postmodernism, or the Cultural Logic of Late Capitalism', *New Left Review* 146, 53–93.
Johnson, Barbara (1980), *The Critical Difference*, Baltimore, Johns Hopkins University Press.
Juhl, P.D. (1980), *Interpretation: An Essay in the Philosophy of Literary Criticism*, Princeton, Princeton University Press.
Kelly-Byrne, Diana (1989), *A Child's Play Life: An Ethnographic Study*, New York, Teachers College Press.
Kiernan, V.G. (1975), 'Wordsworth and the People', in *Marxists on Literature*, ed. David Craig, Harmondsworth, Penguin, 161–206.
Kintsch, Eileen and Walter (1979), *Skilled Reading*, Geelong, Deakin University Press.
Kintsch, Walter, Mandel, Theodore S. and Kozminsky, Ely (1977), 'Summarising Scrambled Stories', *Memory and Cognition* 5.5, 547–52.
Krappe, A.H. (1925), '"La Chävre de Monsieur Seguin" de Daudet et l'Ecbasis Captivi', *Revue de Littérature Comparée* 5.2, 339–42.
Kress, Gunther (1982), *Learning to Write*, London, Routledge and Kegan Paul.
——(1987), 'Genre in a Social Theory of Language', in *The Place of Genre in Learning: Current Debates*, ed. Ian Reid, Geelong, Centre for Studies in Literary Education, Deakin University, 35-45.
Kristeva, Julia (1980), *Desire in Language: A Semiotic Approach to Literature and Art*, trans. Thomas Gora, Alice Jardine and Léon S. Roudiez, New York, Columbia University Press.
Labov, William (1972), *Language in the Inner City*, Philadelphia, University of Pennsylvania Press.
Lacan, Jacques (1972 (1970)), 'Seminar on "The Purloined Letter"', trans. Jeffrey Mehlman, *Yale French Studies* 48, 38–72.
——(1977 (1966)), *Écrits: A Selection*, trans. Alan Sheridan, London, Tavistock.
Laden, Richard A. (1978), 'Les relais du verbe', *Glyph* 4, 157–88.
Lane, Edward W. trans. (1859), *The Thousand and One Nights*, ed. E.S. Poole, London, John Murray.
Lang, Andrew (1890), *The Red Fairy Book*, London, Longmans.
Lanser, Susan Sniader (1981), *The Narrative Act: Point of View in Prose Fiction*, Princeton, Princeton University Press.
Lavater, Louis (1927), 'Meroë: from the Prose of Winwood Reade', in *The Spinner: An Australasian Magazine of Verse* 3.11, 166
Le Guin, Ursula (1980), 'It Was a Dark and Stormy Night; or, Why Are We Huddling Around the Campfire?', *Critical Inquiry* 7.1, 191–9.
Lévi-Strauss, Claude (1949), *Les structures élémentaires de la parenté*, Paris, Presses Universitaires de France.
Lintvelt, Jaap (1981), *Essai de typologie narrative*, Paris, Corti.
Lyotard, Jean-François (1984 (1979)), *The Postmodern Condition*, trans. Geoff Bennington and Brian Massumi, Minneapolis, University of

REFERENCES

Minnesota Press.

McEwan, Neil (1983), *Africa and the Novel*, Atlantic Highlands, N.J., Humanities Press.

Mackenzie, Manfred (1965), 'Patrick White's Later Novels: A Generic Reading', *Southern Review* 1.3, 5–18.

Maclean, Marie (1988), *Narrative as Performance: The Baudelairean Experiment*, London, Routledge.

MacNamara, Matthew (1972), 'Some Oral Narrative Forms in *Lettres de mon moulin*', *Modern Languages Review* 60.2, 291–9.

Mann, Jill (1986), 'Price and Value in *Sir Gawain and the Green Knight*', *Essays in Criticism* 36, 294–318.

Marini, Marcelle (1977), *Territoires du féminin avec Marguerite Duras*, Paris, Éditions de minuit.

Martin, J.R., Christie, Frances and Rothery, Joan (1987), 'Social Processes in Education', in *The Place of Genre in Learning: Current Debates*, ed. Ian Reid, Geelong, Centre for Studies in Literary Education, Deakin University, 58–82.

Martin, Wallace (1986), *Recent Theories of Narrative*, Ithaca, Cornell University Press.

Mauss, Marcel (1950 (1925)), 'Essai sur le don', in his *Sociologie et anthropologie*, Paris, Presses Universitaires de France.

Meek, Margaret (1982), *Learning to Read*, London, Bodley Head.

Metz, Christian (1982), *Psychoanalysis and Cinema: The Imaginary Signifier*, trans. Celia Britton, Anwyl Williams, Ben Brewster, and Alfred Guzzetti, London, Macmillan.

Metzing, Dieter (ed.), (1980), *Frame Conceptions and Text Understanding*, Berlin, de Gruyter.

Mitchell, W.J.T. (1986), *Iconology: Image, Text, Ideology*, Chicago, University of Chicago Press.

Moger, Angela S. (1985),'Narrative Structure in Maupassant: Frames of Desire', *PMLA* 100.3, 315–27.

Moorhouse, Frank (n.d.), *The Illegal Relatives*, n.p.

——(ed.) (1973), *Coast to Coast: Australian Stories 1973*, Sydney, Angus and Robertson.

——(1977 (1972)), 'The Oracular Story', *Tales of Mystery and Romance*, Sydney, Angus and Robertson, 107–15.

Moravia, Alberto (1976), 'Boccaccio', in *Critical Perspectives on The Decameron*, ed. Robert S. Dombroski, London, Hodder and Stoughton, 102–7.

Morris, Meaghan (1988), *The Pirate's Fiancée: Feminism, Reading, Postmodernism*, London, Verso.

Morton, Adam (1980), *Frames of Mind: Constraints on the Common-Sense Conception of the Mental*, Oxford, Clarendon Press.

Murphy, Carol J. (1982), *Alienation and Absence in the Novels of Marguerite Duras*, Lexington, Kentucky, French Forum.

Murry, John Middleton (ed.), (1983 (1927)), *The Journal of Katherine Mansfield*, New York, Ecco Press.

Nystrand, Martin (1986), *The Structure of Written Communication: Studies in Reciprocity between Writers and Readers*, Orlando, Fl., Academic Press.

REFERENCES

Ortner, Sherry B. (1974), 'Is Female to Male as Nature is to Culture?', in *Woman, Culture and Society*, ed. M.Z. Rosaldo and L. Lamphere, Stanford, Stanford University Press, 67–88.
O'Sullivan, Vincent (ed.) (1982), *'The Aloe' with 'Prelude' by Katherine Mansfield*, Wellington, Port Nicholson Press.
O'Sullivan, Vincent and Scott, Margaret (eds) (1987), *The Collected Letters of Katherine Mansfield*, vol. 2, Oxford, Clarendon Press.
Owen, W.J.B., and Smyser, Jane Worthington (eds), (1974), *The Prose Works of William Wordsworth*, Oxford, Clarendon Press.
Pêcheux, Michel (1982 (1975)), *Language, Semantics and Ideology: Stating the Obvious*, trans. Harbans Nagpal, London, Macmillan.
Perry, Menakhem (1979), 'Literary Dynamics: How the Order of a Text Creates its Meanings', *Poetics Today* 1, 35–64, 311–61.
Peterson, C., and McCabe, A. (1983), *Developmental Psycholinguistics: Three Ways of Looking at a Child's Narrative*, New York, Plenum Press.
Potter, Joy H. (1982), *Five Frames for the Decameron: Communication and Social Systems in the Cornice*, Princeton, Princeton University Press.
Pradl, Gordon M. (1989), 'Recovering the Claim of the Story', *Typereader* Centre for Studies in Literary Education, Deakin University, 3, 5–20.
Pratt, Mary Louise (1977), *Towards a Speech-Act Theory of Literary Discourse*, Bloomington, Indiana University Press.
Prince, Gerald (1973), *A Grammar of Stories*, The Hague, Mouton.
——(1982), *Narratology*, The Hague, Mouton.
——(1987), *Dictionary of Narratology*, Lincoln, University of Nebraska Press.
Propp, Vladimir (1968 (1928)), *Morphology of the Folktale*, 2nd edn, trans. L. Scott, Austin, University of Texas Press.
Reade, Winwood (1927 (1872)), *The Martyrdom of Man*, London, Jonathan Cape.
Reid, Ian (1976), '"A Naked Guidepost's Double Head": The Wordsworthian Sense of Direction', *ELH* 43, 538–50.
——(1977), *The Short Story*, London, Methuen.
——(1979), *Fiction and the Great Depression*, Melbourne, Edward Arnold.
——(1982), 'Form and Expectation in Christina Stead's Novellas', in *An Introduction to Australian Literature*, ed. C.D. Narasimhaih, Brisbane, Wiley.
——(1984), *The Making of Literature*, Adelaide, A.A.T.E.
——(ed.) (1987), *The Place of Genre in Learning: Current Debates*, Geelong, Centre for Studies in Literary Education, Deakin University.
——(1988), 'Genre and Framing: The Case of Epitaphs', *Poetics* 17, 25–35.
Reiss, Timothy J. (1981), 'Semiotics and Materialism', *Semiotica* 34.1, 177–87.
Ricardou, Jean (ed.) (1976), *Robbe-Grillet: Analyse, Théorie*, vol. 2, Paris, Union Générale d'Éditions (Colloque de Cérisy).
Richardson, Henry Handel (1948), *Myself when Young*, Melbourne, Heinemann.
Rimmon-Kenan, Shlomith (1983), *Narrative Fiction: Contemporary Poetics*, London, Methuen.

REFERENCES

Rosen, Harold (1984), *Stories and Meanings*, Sheffield, National Association for the Teaching of English.

Rosmarin, Adena (1985), *The Power of Genre*, Minneapolis, University of Minnesota Press.

Rothery, Joan, and Martin, J.R. (1980), *Writing Project, paper 1: Narrative: Vicarious Experience*, Sydney, Department of Linguistics, University of Sydney.

Rotman, Brian (1987), *Signifying Nothing: The Semiotics of Zero*, Houndmills, Macmillan.

Ruegg, Maria (l979), 'Metaphor and Metonymy: The Logic of Structuralist "Rhetoric"', *Glyph* 6, 141–57.

Ruthrof, Horst (1981), *The Reader's Construction of Narrative*, London, Routledge and Kegan Paul.

Sachs, Murray (1965), *The Career of Alphonse Daudet: A Critical Study*, New Haven, Harvard University Press.

Sahlins, Marshall (1972), *Stone Age Economics*, Chicago, Aldine-Atherton.

——(1976), *Culture and Practical Reason*, Chicago, University of Chicago Press.

Said, Edward (1978), *Orientalism*, New York, Pantheon.

——(1983), *The World, the Text, and the Critic*, Cambridge Mass., Harvard University Press.

Sawyer, Wayne and Watson, Ken (1987), 'Questions of Genre', in *The Place of Genre in Learning: Current Debates*, ed. Ian Reid, Geelong, Centre for Studies in Literary Education, Deakin University, 46–57.

Schleifer, Ronald (1987), *A.J. Greimas and the Nature of Meaning: Linguistics, Semiotics and Discourse Theory*, London, Croom Helm.

Scholes, Robert (1974), *Structuralism in Literature*, New Haven, Yale University Press.

Serres, Michel (1982 (1980)), *The Parasite*, trans. Lawrence Schehr, Baltimore, Johns Hopkins University Press.

Shell, Marc (1978), *The Economy of Literature*, Baltimore, Johns Hopkins University Press.

——(1982), *Money, Language and Thought*, Berkeley, University of California Press.

Sherzer, Dina (1974), 'Narrative Figures in "La légende de St Julien l'Hospitalier"', *Genre* 7.1, 54–70.

Shoaf, R.A. (1983), *Dante, Chaucer and the Currency of the Word: Money, Images and Reference in Late Medieval Poetry*, Norman, Oklahoma, Pilgrim.

——(1984), *The Poem as Green Girdle: 'Commercium' in Sir Gawain and the Green Knight*, Gainesville, University of Florida Press

Simmel, Georg (1978 (1900)), *The Philosophy of Money*, trans. Tom Bottomore and David Frisby, London, Routledge and Kegan Paul.

Simpson, David (1982), *Wordsworth and the Figurings of the Real*, Atlantic Highlands, N.J., Humanities Press.

Smith, Adam (1937 (1776)), *An Inquiry into the Causes of the Wealth of Nations*, ed. Edwin Cannan, New York, Modern Library.

Smith, Barbara Herrnstein (1978), *On the Margins of Discourse: The Relations of Literature to Language*, Chicago, University of Chicago Press.

REFERENCES

——(1980), 'Narrative Versions, Narrative Theories', *Critical Inquiry* 7.1, 213–36.
Spivak, Gayatri Chakravorty (1987), *In Other Worlds: Essays in Cultural Politics*, New York, Methuen.
——(1989), 'Colloquium on Narrative', *Typereader*, Centre for Studies in Literary Education, Deakin University, 3, 21–37.
Stein, Gertrude (1969 (1935)), *Narration: Four Lectures*, Chicago, University of Chicago Press.
Stubbs, Michael (1983), *Discourse Analysis: The Sociolinguistic Analysis of Natural Language*, Oxford, Blackwell.
Sturluson, Snorri (1987), *Edda*, trans. Anthony Faulkes, London, Dent.
Suleiman, Susan and Crosman, Inge (eds) (1980), *The Reader in the Text: Essays on Audience and Interpretation*, Princeton, Princeton University Press.
Thompson, John B. (1984), *Studies in the Theory of Ideology*, Cambridge, Polity Press.
Titmuss, Richard M. (1970), *The Gift Relationship: From Human Blood to Social Policy*, London, Allen and Unwin.
Todorov, Tzvetan (1969a), *Grammaire du Décaméron*, The Hague, Mouton.
——(1969b), 'The Structural Analysis of Narrative', *Novel* 13.1, 70–6.
——(1977), *The Poetics of Prose*, trans. Richard Howard, Ithaca, Cornell University Press.
——(1984), *Mikhail Bakhtin: The Dialogical Principle*, trans. Wlad Godzich, Minneapolis, University of Minnesota Press.
Toolan, Michael J. (1988), *Narrative: A Critical Linguistic Introduction*, London, Routledge.
Trotter, David (1988), *Circulation: Defoe, Dickens and the Economics of the Novel*, London, Macmillan.
Turner, Jonathan (1987), 'Social Exchange: Future Directions', in Karen S. Cook (ed.), *Social Exchange Theory*, Newbury Park, Ca., Sage, 223–38.
Umiker-Sebeok, J.D. (1979), 'Preschool Children's Intraconversational Narratives', *Journal of Child Language* 6, 91–110.
van Dijk, Teun A. (1980), *Macrostructures: An Interdisciplinary Study of Global Structures in Discourse, Interaction and Cognition*, Hillsdale, N.J., Lawrence Erlbaum.
Vaneigem, Raoul (1983), *The Revolution of Everyday Life*, trans. Donald Nicholson-Smith, Paris, Left Bank Books and Rebel Press.
Verdaasdonk, H. (1982), 'Conceptions of Literature as Frames' *Poetics* 11, 87–104.
Vernon, John (1984), *Money and Fiction: Literary Realism in the Nineteenth and Early Twentieth Centuries*, Ithaca, Cornell University Press.
Volosinov, Valentin (1973), *Marxism and the Philosophy of Language*, trans. L. Matejka and I. Titunik, New York, Seminar Press.
Vygotsky, Lev S. (1962 (1934)), *Thought and Language*, trans. E. Hanfmann and G. Vakar, Cambridge, Mass., M.I.T. Press.
Walker, Jeanne Murray (1985), 'Exchange Short-Circuited: The Isolated Scientist in H.G. Wells's *The Invisible Man*', *Journal of Narrative Technique* 15.2, 156–68.
White, Patrick (1963 (1948)), *The Aunt's Story*, Harmondsworth, Penguin.

REFERENCES

——(1983 (1981)), *Flaws in the Glass*, Harmondsworth, Penguin.
Wilden, Anthony (1972), *System and Structure*, London, Tavistock.
Wilding, Michael (1978a (1973)), 'The Nembutal Story', *The Phallic Forest*, Sydney, Wild and Woolley, 44–50.
——(ed.) (1978b), *The Tabloid Story Pocket Book*, Sydney, Wild & Woolley.
Williams, Raymond (1976), *Keywords: A Vocabulary of Culture and Society*, Glasgow, Fontana.
Williamson, Judith (1978), *Decoding Advertisements: Ideology and Meaning in Advertising*, London, Boyars.
Willis, Sharon (1987), *Marguerite Duras: Writing on the Body*, Urbana, University of Illinois Press.
Witting, Amy (1978 (1974)), 'A Piece of this Puzzle is Missing', in Wilding 1978b, 158–63.
Wordsworth, William (1979), *The Prelude : 1799, 1805, 1850*, ed. Jonathan Wordsworth, M.H. Abrams and Stephen Gill, New York, Norton.
Yacobi, Tamar (1981), 'Fictional Reliability as a Communicative Problem', *Poetics Today* 2.2, 113–26.
Yule, Valerie (ed.) (1979), *What Happens to Children: The Origins of Social Violence: A Collection of Stories Told by Children who Could Not Write Them*, Sydney, Angus and Robertson.
Zipes, Jack (1983), *The Trials and Tribulations of Little Red Riding Hood: Versions of the Tale in Socio-cultural Context*, South Hadley, Mass., Bergin and Harvey.

INDEX

Abrams, M.H. 144, 149
Achebe, Chinua 6, 18, 59, 69–75, 97, 204
actants, 63, 100
allegories of reading *see* framing, intratextual
Altdorfer, Albrecht 15
anthropology 1–6, 68–9, 73–4
Apostolidès, Jean-Marie 237
Applebee, Arthur N. 200–4, 246
Aristotelian view of represented action 13, 20, 23, 143
Armstrong, Isobel 158
Artaud, Antonin 186
Auerbach, Erich 25

Bachelard, Gaston 246
Bahti, Timothy 244
Baker, John Ross 240
Bakhtin, Mikhail 11, 80–1, 199, 201, 239, 240
Bal, Mieke 1, 20, 77–8, 102, 237, 238, 241
Balzac, Honoré de 31, 57, 78–9, 106
Barrs, Myra 190
Barthes, Roland 2, 31, 57–8, 79, 82, 102, 127, 239, 244
Bate, Jonathan 244
Bateson, Gregory 238
Baudrillard, Jean 4, 12, 237
Bayer, Konrad 202
Beaugrande, Robert-Alain de 238
Becker, H. P. 236
Belsey, Catherine 77, 242

Benjamin, Walter 30
Bennett, David 180–1
Berg, Willam 90
Bernstein, Basil 238
Bialostosky, Don 143
Bizet, Georges 53
Blanchot, Maurice 238, 247
Blau, Peter 4, 6, 237
Boccaccio, Giovanni 25–9, 34–9
Booth, Wayne 76–7, 79
Borgomano, Madelaine 99, 241
Bosch, Hieronymus 15
Bourdieu, Pierre 7, 103, 237
Bowie, Malcolm 129
Boynton, Robert 242
Bremond, Claude 22, 237
Brice-Heath, Shirley 191
Britton, James 189, 197–201, 202, 205, 246
Brombert, Victor 88
Brooks, Peter 239
Brown, Beverley 138
Brown, Gillian 107, 245
Bruce, Mary Grant 41
Burgess, Tony 200
Burrows, J.F. 175

Calvino, Italo 80, 202
Carroll, David 245
Carter, Angela 191
Caudwell, Christopher 243
Caws, Mary Ann 238
Céline 78
Cézanne, Paul 15

261

INDEX

Chambers, Ross 13, 20–1, 29–33, 78, 83, 106–7, 112–13, 119, 167, 240
character 16, 23–4, 63, 97, 142, 143, 148, 165
Chase, Cynthia 164
Chatman, Seymour 20, 22, 76, 77, 78, 143, 237, 240
children's stories *see* narrative, child's concept of
Christie, Frances 189, 196
circumtextuality *see* framing
Clough, Arthur Hugh 42
codes 57–8
Cohan, Steven 20
coherence 124–5, 127, 169, 185
cohesion 108, 124–5, 169, 182, 245
Conrad, Joseph 77, 78
Cook-Gumperz, Jenny 246
Courtés, J. 63, 76, 125, 128, 159, 201
Coward, Rosalind 127, 242
Crick, Malcolm 139
Culler, Jonathan 1, 20, 109, 243, 244

Dahl, Roald 191
Dali, Salvador 15
Dällenbach, Lucien 30, 127
Daniels, Douglas J. 89
Danto, Arthur C. 131
Darlington, Beth 150
Darwin, Charles 72
Daudet, Alphonse 18, 45–57, 67, 204, 238
Dèbray-Genette, Raymonde 85, 87
DeLillo, Don 18, 59–62, 204
De Man, Paul 31
Derrida, Jacques 31, 40, 45, 156, 186
desire 4–5, 12, 30, 112–13, 165, 182
dialogue as a model of discourse 9–11, 83, 178, 201
Dickens, Charles 45, 204
Diderot, Denis 80
Dimock, Wai-Chee 237
dispossession 13, 16, 17, 27–9, 44, 50, 58, 59–63, 66–8, 69–70, 74–5, 81, 84, 91, 93, 98–9, 104, 112, 117, 118, 148, 154, 159, 165, 167, 169, 186, 195–6, 205–6

Dombey, Henrietta 247
Dow, Lousie 18, 118, 122–3
Ducrot, Oswald 239
Duras, Marguerite 18, 80, 95–102, 202, 204
During, Simon 181

Eagleton, Terry 55, 186–7
Eco, Umberto 57, 238
Ekeh, Peter P. 236
embedding *see* framing, intratextual
Engels, Friedrich 79
énoncé and *énonciation*, *see* utterance and enunciation respectively
enunciation 17, 38–9, 62–3, 66, 74–5, 76, 79, 80–1, 87, 95, 96, 98, 100, 149, 155, 158, 195, 200, 205
Ernst, Max 15
Escher, M.C. 30, 117
exchange, as general model 1–3; different types 2; and narrative 3–4, 68, 99–102; and individual self-interest 4–5; and social structures 5–6, 73–4; in linguistic theory 7 ff., 104; not reciprocal in written narrative 10; in literary theory 11–13; as theme in *The Decameron* 37–9; and parasitic relations 67, 75, 102, 116, 121; analogy between sexual and narrative exchanges 112, 121 *see also* substitution, dispossession
extratextuality *see* framing
Eyck, Jan van 15

Faulkes, Anthony 68, 215, 239
Faulkner, William 49
Felman, Shoshana 87
Ferguson, Frances 154
Firth, J. R. 8
Fish, Stanley 9, 38, 236
Flaubert, Gustave 6, 18, 54, 76, 80, 81–95, 97, 204
focalisation 22, 49, 118, 127, 131, 132

262

INDEX

Forbes, Mildred 20, 242
Foucault, Michel 191
Fowler, Roger 77, 104, 108, 116, 179, 237
Fox Carol 190, 197
framing 9, 13–16, 29, 33, 37, 40–58, 63, 66, 75, 124–5, 144, 185, 202–5, 238–9; circumtextual, 10, 14–15, 17, 44–5, 47–8, 64, 66, 67, 68, 69, 120, 122, 169, 183–4, 185, 205; extratextual 15, 17, 46–7, 54–7; intertextual, 15, 17, 51–4, 68, 70–2, 80, 94, 102; intratextual 15, 17, 48–51, 66, 70, 72, 80, 102, 131, 134, 139, 153, 168, 171, 182–3, 205
Freadman, Anne 8, 53, 105;
Freud, Sigmund 80
Freund, Elizabeth 236
Friedman, Michael 163
Frow, John 238, 245

Genette, Gérard 20, 22–3, 48, 78–9
genre 17–18, 53–5, 58, 94, 125, 154–5, 189–91, 193, 202
Gergen Kenneth 2, 4, 236
Gide, André 30
gift 2, 5, 8, 68, 100, 103, 105, 117, 193
Gillard, G.M. 241
Gillison, Gillian 138
Goffman, Erving 238
Golding, William 9
Goodman, Nelson 182
Gordon, Ian 124
Gordon, Jaimy 18, 168–9, 182–7, 202, 204, 222–35
Gorey, Edward 202
Goux, Jean-Joseph 12
Greenblatt, Stephen 237
Greimas, A.J. 10, 63, 76, 125, 128, 159, 201, 237, 240, 242
Grigg, Russell 242
Grimm, Jakob and Wilhelm 191
Gubar, Susan 125–7, 129–31, 133, 139

Hall, Stuart 242
Halliday, M.A.K. 7–11, 38, 103–5, 108, 117, 189, 200, 245
Hankin, C.A. 125
Hanoulle, Marie-Julie 85
Harding, D.W. 199
Hartman, Geoffrey 163
Hasan, Ruqaiya 8, 9, 104, 108, 117
Hawkes, Terence 129, 244
Hawthorne, Nathaniel 204
Heath, Anthony 5
Heinzelman, Kurt 237
Hemingway, Ernest 77
Hendricks, W.O. 20, 237
Hernadi, Paul 77
Herodotus 172–3
Herring, Thelma 172
Hirsch, E. D. 144, 147
Hodge, Bob 104, 237
Hogg, James 41
Holland, Norman 180
Holloway, John 36
Homans, George 4, 6
Homer 41, 45, 172–3, 175
Hospital, Janette Turner 121
Hugo, Victor 47, 51

illocutionary acts 48
implied author 62–3, 74–5, 76–102, 104, 111, 126
implied reader 63, 74, 76, 163
intertextuality *see* framing
intratextuality *see* framing
Irigaray, Luce 5, 100, 121, 241
irony 50, 55–6, 75, 179
isotopy 125, 128, 135

Jakobson, Roman 128
James, Henry 31
Jameson, Fredric 1, 150, 180–1, 240
Johnson, Barbara 31
Johnson, Samuel 156, 245
Joyce, James 31
Juhl, P. D. 240

Kafka, Franz 30, 204
Kelly-Byrne, Diana 246
Kiernan, V.G. 244
kinship *see* exchange and social structures
Kintsch, Walter 195, 237

INDEX

Krappe, A.H. 54
Kress, Gunther 246
Kristeva, Julia 52

Labov, William 189, 191, 194–5
Lacan, Jacques 31, 51, 133, 243
La Fontaine, Jean de 52
Lane Edward 184–5, 245
Lawrence, D. H. 23
Lanser, Susan 78, 80
Lawson, Henry 45
Leavis, F. R. 12
Le Guin, Ursula 19
Lévi-Strauss, Claude 5, 7
linguistic analysis 7–11, 103–8, 188–201, 236
Lintvelt, Jaap 77
Lorrain, Claude 15
Lukács, Georg 79
Lyotard, Jean-François 103, 123, 166–7, 169, 174, 180, 244

McCahon, Colin 15
McEwan, Neil 74
Mackenzie, Manfred 168, 176, 245
Maclean, Marie 13, 48, 107, 237
MacNamara, Michael 53
Magritte, Réné 15
Malinowski, Bronislaw 8
Mansfield, Katherine 6, 18, 57, 124–42, 204
Marini, Marcelle 99–100, 241
Martin, Jim 189–96
Martin, Wallace 77
Maupassant, Guy de 30
Mauss, Marcel 5
metafiction 80
metonymy 81, 97, 107, 108, 138–9, 141, 147, 164, 177; and metaphor 16, 128–30, 242–3
Metz, Christian 51
Miller, J. Hillis 32
Milton, John 146
mise-en-abyme 30–1, 49, 66, 82–3, 95, 98, 116, 127, 131, 140
mode 105, 107, 110–11, 118, 123, 189, 194
modernism 168, 179
Moger, Angela S. 238

Montherlant, Henri de 78
Moore, Thomas 41
Moorhouse, Frank 18, 103, 111, 114, 115, 118, 120–1, 241–2
Moravia, Alberto 25
Morris, Meaghan 244
Murphy, Carol J. 99

narratee, 32, 49, 50, 63, 66, 76, 147, 163
narrative as cognitive resource 1, 139; as transaction 13, 30; as succession of events 19; and self-situation *see* Chambers; based on illusion of figurative movement 24; and postmodernity 166–8; child's concept of 188–206
narratology 1, 3, 13, 20, 39, 63
narrator 28–9, 32, 39, 50, 59, 63, 74, 76–84, 87, 90–1, 94, 95–6, 111–15, 116–17, 118, 126–7, 141, 164, 169–71, 184

O'Brien, Flann 30
Ortner, Sherry 138
O'Sullivan, Vincent 239, 243

Pêcheux, Michel 239–40
Perrault, Charles 52, 191
Perry, Menakehem 238
Piaget, Jean 193
Picasso, Pablo 15
plot 16, 19, 34–5, 59, 69–70, 109, 116, 182, 239
Poe, Edgar Allan 22, 31, 56, 125, 242
postmodernity 166–8, 179–81
Potter, Joy H. 238
Pratt, Mary Louise 195, 238
Prince, Gerald 24, 237
Propp, Vladimir 33, 35, 52, 63

Reade, Winwood 173–4, 245
register 105, 114, 149, 154, 192–3
Reid, Ian 55, 58, 146, 197, 236, 237, 242, 245
Reiss, Timothy J. 13
Richardson, Henry Handel 245

INDEX

Rimmon-Kenan, Sholmith 20–4, 30, 32, 39, 66, 77–8
Robbe-Grillet, Alain 188, 202, 204–5
Rosen, Harold 1
Rosmarin, Adena 238
Rothery, Joan 189–96
Rotman, Brian 237
Ruegg, Maria 129
Ruthrof, Horst 24, 237

Sachs, Murray 53, 54, 239
sacrifice 124
Sahlins, Marshall 6, 68–9, 73
Said, Edward 16, 181, 185
Saussure, Ferdinand de 8, 11
Sawyer, Wayne 197
semiosis 64
Serres, Michel 2, 67, 75
Shakespeare, William 152, 157–9, 161–2, 202, 244
Shell, Marc 12–13
Sherzer, Dina 89
Shires, Linda 20
Shoaf, R. A. 237
Simmel, Georg 4
Simpson, David 243
Smith, Adam 150, 243
Smith, Barbara Herrnstein 20, 62, 116, 191, 237, 246
Sollers, Phillipe 80
Spengler, Oswald 174, 245
Spivak, Gayatri 181, 244
Stein, Gertrude 166
Sterne, Laurence 49, 80
structuralist poetics *see* narratology
Sturluson, Snorri 18, 63–8, 74, 204, 207–15, 239
substitution 13, 16, 17, 27, 44, 50, 51, 58, 63–4, 68, 74–5, 81, 85, 89, 97, 101, 104, 107–9, 111, 116–17, 118, 128–9, 147, 148, 149, 159, 165, 169, 177, 182–3, 185, 186, 195–6, 205–6, 239–40
supplementarity 157

Tennyson, Alfred 71–2
tenor 6, 74, 105–7, 110–11, 189, 193
Thomson, James 151, 237
Thurber, James 10, 191
Todorov, Tzvetan 11, 21, 25–6, 33–9, 125
Toolan, Michael 118, 182, 188, 189, 194, 195, 246
Turner, J. M. W. 15, 236

Umiker-Sebeok J.D. 246
Ungerer, Tomi 202
unity, textual 34–7, 39, 55, 79, 81, 98, 102, 104, 116, 117, 123, 124, 147, 165, 199
utterance (*énoncé*) 17, 38, 62–3, 66, 75, 79, 80–1, 87, 96, 155, 159, 195, 200

Vaneigem, Raoul 124
Valasquez, 15
Verdaasdonk, H. 239
voice *see* narrator
Volosinov, Valentin 82, 185
Vygotsky, Lev S. 190, 193

Watson, Ken 197
White, Patrick 18, 168, 175, 179, 204
Wilden, Anthony 68
Wilding, Michael 18, 103, 114, 115, 117, 120–1, 241
Williams, Raymond 150
Williamson, Judith 30
Willis, Sharon 99, 102, 241
Witting, Amy 18, 118, 120
Wordsworth, William 18, 45, 143–65, 204, 216–21, 243

Yacobi, Yamar 77
Yeats, W. B. 70, 72
Yule, George 107
Yule, Valerie 245, 246

Zipes, Jack 191, 239

For Product Safety Concerns and Information please contact our EU representative GPSR@taylorandfrancis.com
Taylor & Francis Verlag GmbH, Kaufingerstraße 24, 80331 München, Germany

www.ingramcontent.com/pod-product-compliance
Lightning Source LLC
Chambersburg PA
CBHW050434240426
43661CB00055B/2381